PRAISE FOR

MW00438333

"*Dumbing Down the Courts* is a critical read for anyone who seeks to understand the judicial confirmation battles of recent decades. Lott's meticulous research demonstrates that these contentious battles result from a politicized process in which both activist judges and partisan senators are to blame. When activist judges abandoned their limited, constitutional role and usurped the functions of elected legislators, senators reacted by using political litmus tests in assessing judicial candidates. The surest fix to drawn-out confirmation battles is to ensure that judges adhere to their proper role: to apply the law as it is written."

—Edwin Meese, former U.S. Attorney General

"John Lott provides a powerful critique, amply supported by facts, of the rapid deterioration of the process for confirming federal judges. As courts have become more political and government has grown increasingly intrusive, battles over confirmations have grown more intense and partisan, with the result, Mr. Lott concludes, that the quality of the judiciary is endangered."

—Robert Bork, former U.S. Appeals Court judge and Supreme Court nominee

"This book is a serious effort to identify and grapple with the current problems in our judicial nominations process. Unlike the many partisan works on the subject, John Lott does not lay the blame of our current troubles on one party's doorstep but demonstrates that there is more than enough fault to go around. Even those who disagree with the author's conclusions will be well advised to read this excellent book."

—William P. Marshall, professor, University of North Carolina Law School, and former Deputy White House Counsel to President Clinton

"The judicial confirmation process has become increasingly politicized on both sides of the aisle. The result has been increasing difficulty and delay in confirming presidential nominees. In this important study, John Lott marshals the evidence on this issue, that the modern confirmation process has affected not only the quantity but also the quality of federal judges."

—**Alan Sykes**, professor, New York University School of Law

"Clear, thoughtful, and eminently readable, *Dumbing Down the Courts* describes and explains the politicization of the judicial confirmation process. John Lott is carefully non-partisan throughout: neither party comes off looking clean. Be prepared to be troubled, however— badly troubled. The book will leave thoughtful readers concerned— concerned not just about the degraded judicial confirmation process, but about the effect that the process has had on the quality of the courts."

—**J. Mark Ramseyer**, professor, Harvard Law School

At the Brink: Will Obama Push Us Over the Edge?

*Debacle: Obama's War on Jobs and Growth and What We
Can Do Now to Regain Our Future*
(with Grover G. Norquist)

*More Guns, Less Crime: Understanding Crime and Gun
Control Laws*

Straight Shooting: Firearms, Economics and Public Policy

*Freedomnomics: Why the Free Market Works and Other
Half-Baked Theories Don't*

*The Bias Against Guns: Why Almost Everything You've
Heard About Gun Control Is Wrong*

*Are Predatory Commitments Credible? Who Should the
Courts Believe?*

DUMBING DOWN THE COURTS

DUMBING DOWN THE COURTS

HOW POLITICS KEEPS THE SMARTEST JUDGES OFF THE BENCH

JOHN R. LOTT, JR.

Bascom Hill Publishing Group | Minneapolis, MN

To Frank Easterbrook, a brilliant man

BASCOM HILL
PUBLISHING GROUP

Bascom Hill Publishing Group
322 First Avenue N, 5th floor
Minneapolis, MN 55401
612.455.2293
www.bascomhillpublishing.com

ISBN-13: 978-1-62652-249-7
LCCN: 2013942834

Distributed by Itasca Books

Book Design by Jenni Wheeler

Printed in the United States of America

CONTENTS

ACKNOWLEDGMENTS

I must particularly thank Frank Easterbrook, Richard Epstein, Mitu Gulati, John McGinnis, Nelson Lund, William Marshall, Mark Ramseyer, Peter Wallison, and the participants in seminars at the University of Chicago Law School, University of Tokyo, William and Mary Law School, American Law and Economic Association Meetings, and George Mason Law School, all of whom furnished valuable comments. Brian Blasé, Roger Lott, Ryan Lott, Jill Mitchell, Jack Soltysik, and Soojin Kim provided valuable research assistance on the book in many different ways, including spending numerous months collecting the data. I must particularly thank Maxim Lott, Karina Rollins, and Gertrud Fremling, as they offered extremely helpful advice and edited parts of the book.

Chapters 3 and 4 draw heavily on research that I have published in the *Journal of Empirical Legal Studies*, vol. 2, no. 3 (November 2005): 407–47. Chapter 5 is drawn from the research that I have published in *Public Choice* (2011).

INTRODUCTION

Why the Senate Shuns the Smartest Judges

Judges will ultimately decide whether people of the same sex can marry each other, whether marriages can involve more than two people, whether unions can mandate that employees pay dues that go to political campaigns, and countless other issues that will impact your life in fundamental ways. Yet, the personal characteristics that make some judges less confirmable than others have received little study. Who are the nominees that make it through the confirmation process to become a federal judge? Are they the brightest people who have the most detailed and sophisticated knowledge of the law? Are the most successful lower court judges also the most likely to get promoted to serve on higher courts?

Surprisingly, the qualities that make someone a successful judge also make them less likely to be confirmed for the same reason that smart, persuasive people are rarely asked to be jurors. Take Greg Mankiw, a well-known Harvard economics professor who was recently called up for jury duty in the Boston area. After sitting around most of the day waiting to be considered, Mankiw noted: "I was called up and sat in the jury box, but that lasted for only about five minutes [before] one of the sets of lawyers used a peremptory challenge to kick me [off the jury]."[1] The whole experience caused him to wonder: "Why does being a professor of economics at Harvard make one an undesirable juror in such a case?"

The answer is actually pretty simple: a smart person who makes his living persuading others could end up swaying other jurors. If lawyers on either side of the case have even a hint that someone like Mankiw may work against their side, they will use one of their peremptory challenges to remove him from the juror pool. In their eyes, removing him from the jury is the equivalent of removing several other equally biased jurors.

Similarly, for judges on a circuit court or the Supreme Court, a smart, persuasive judge might convince other judges to change their votes on a case. Judges who can write powerful judicial decisions also tend to be cited more frequently and influence judicial decisions made by other judges.

Citations are only one measure of intelligence. Recent research finds that judges who went to elite law schools decide cases more quickly and produce more opinions.[2] And more published opinions increase the influence of the judge. Political opponents are OK with a president nominating an idiot to represent his side. But they panic if he nominates an intellectual heavyweight.

Why Have the Battles Escalated Over Time?

"The Supreme Court has made itself a
political institution."[3]
—Judge Robert H. Bork, 2005

Obviously when more is at stake, people fight harder to win. That general rule explains a lot, from how competitively people play sports to how hard they fight to win business contracts and elections. Two baseball teams playing in the seventh game of the World Series are going to play harder than two teams competing in August with no chance of making the playoffs.

For most of our nation's history, federal judges have only occasionally caught the public's eye, usually through some wildly unpopular ruling that polarized the country. The infamous 1857 *Dred Scott* decision held that no black person, whether slave or free, could become a citizen of the United States.[4] The 1905 *Lochner v. New York* decision, which struck down legislation that limited the number of hours that bakers could work, supported the right of Americans to create the types of contracts that they wanted to make.[5] The case was brought by a small, family-owned, non-unionized bakery that depended on flexible work schedules. Large corporate bakeries and unions wanted to put their small competitors out of business. The public debate was extremely heated. Progressives were upset that the decision would limit regulation. Free market advocates loved it.

Similarly, the Supreme Court generated controversy when it struck down some of the basic government-expanding legislation of the New Deal in the mid-1930s, such as the National Recovery Administration, which established minimum wages and rules for "fair competition." The 1954 *Brown v. Board of Education* case, which required the integration of public schools, angered much of the South.

Over the past fifty years, however, polarizing decisions have become more numerous. Complaints about judges taking the law into their own hands are frequent. And every year, decisions are challenged for interpreting the law beyond its previous reach. During this same time, judicial nominations have become the focus of intense battles. Over the last decade, the Supreme Court has decided cases involving issues such as the constitutionality of the death penalty for minors and for crimes other than murder, whether the government can take someone's property to give to another private party, whether the federal or state governments can ban guns, and whether the Ten Commandments can be posted on public property.[6]

The courts' growing policy role relies on invoking the Constitution (especially the First and Fourteenth Amendments) to make policy in sensitive areas. It is also related to the growth of the regulatory state; that is, of Congress effectively assigning the courts a much broader role. Can the government ban the sale or rental of violent video games to minors?[7] Can proving discrimination against a few female employees working for Walmart serve as proof that Walmart discriminated against 1.3 million female employees?[8] Does the Federal government have the power to determine who is a minister?[9] Are residents undergoing training at a hospital considered students or employees?[10] Is carbon dioxide, part of the very air that we breathe out, a pollutant that the EPA can regulate?[11]

Law enforcement and terrorism concerns have also greatly expanded the issues facing the court. Can someone who brutally rapes a child receive the death penalty?[12] Is the government able to use GPS devices to monitor every move citizens make without securing a court order?[13] Can American citizens be classified as enemy combatants and held indefinitely without trial by their government?[14] Can our government assassinate Americans?[15]

Even recent Supreme Court decisions that did not generate many headlines—so-called "minor cases"—involved everything from where cell phone towers can be placed to whether the Federal Communications Commission has authority to regulate the rates cable companies charge for cable modem services.[16]

If the judges apply clear legal rules, there remains little to fight over. But if the rules are unclear—or if judges do not follow them, preferring to impose their own interpretations—then the choice of a judge matters greatly. Just take the recent cases over the constitutionality of President Obama's health care mandate. With just a couple of exceptions, most notably Supreme Court Chief Justice John Roberts, Democratic appointees have maintained that the law is constitutional, while Republicans have ruled that it isn't.[17] Judges today are perceived as biased in applying the law, and politically active groups often view federal judges as legislators with life tenure. When nearly everything can be litigated, and judges are seen as making up the rules as they go, the confirmation of a judge becomes crucial. The growing role of the federal courts and the polarization of the Senate have exacerbated the process.

These same factors explain the growth in campaign expenditures. The more areas governments get involved in, the more voters will donate to help their candidates win.[18] For state and gubernatorial races, the growth in state government expenditures alone explains 65 to 80 percent of the growth in campaign expenditures, even after allowing for the separate effects from such factors as the closeness of races, the number of candidates, and the cost of campaigns. Likewise, the growth of the federal government explains about 80 to 90 percent of the growth in congressional campaign expenditures.[19]

Alas, courts have strayed further and further into decisions traditionally made by legislatures, often having the final word. So it should be no surprise that nomination battles have become more contested. As federal regulations have expanded and the federal courts have found more reasons to expand their jurisdiction, Americans naturally care more than they used to about the people who will have the power to affect the law so directly. The increased interest is reflected in the growing debates in the media over the more difficult confirmation process.

This debate didn't exist forty years ago.

The conversation quickly grows serious as soon as a Supreme Court justice announces retirement. Consider Justice Sandra Day O'Connor's retirement on July 1, 2005. Politicians returned to Washington from across the country to hold press conferences. Within ten minutes, People for the American Way described O'Connor's retirement using the following terms: "devastating," "historic," "ominous," "critical," "freedoms hang in the balance," "reinventing monarchy," and a "state of emergency."[20] Forty minutes after the announcement, the first television ads were announced.[21] Two hours and thirty minutes after the announcement, the conservative Committee for Justice responded: "We will be watching Senate Democrats and intend to link moderate and red states [*sic*] senators to their liberal Senate colleagues and outside groups."[22]

And O'Connor's replacement, Samuel Alito, was hardly the most controversial as Supreme Court appointments go. Some confirmations, such as those involving Robert Bork and Clarence Thomas, can become the center of national attention for weeks, completely dominating the evening news broadcasts and the front pages of newspapers.[23]

As a result of Anita Hill's sexual harassment allegations, Thomas's hearings were a major draw. On Friday, October 11, 1991, Thomas's response to Hill's charges was viewed by about 30 percent of American homes with television, which didn't include those who might have watched the hearings from their office.[24] As *The New York Times* reported: "The ratings for the hearing so reduced the number for CBS's coverage of the Minnesota-Toronto playoff game, which ran against the hearing coverage on the two other major networks, that the game apparently attracted the smallest audience of any post-season baseball game ever."[25] While Bork's testimony didn't garner such lofty ratings, ABC, CBS, and NBC covered his testimony live in addition to the wall-to-wall coverage of his hearings provided by CNN, public television, and C-SPAN.[26] By contrast, only cable news channels and public television covered Alito's hearings.[27]

Again, the battle over judgeships goes beyond the federal courts. While it is outside the scope of this book, it should be mentioned that new research, published in 2011, argues that state judicial elections have also become more competitive and politicized, likely due to higher stakes regarding tort law and other issues handled primarily on the state level.[28]

The Courts as Legislative Bodies

> "It is not a cliché to make a distinction
> between a judge interpreting and a
> judge legislating. For example, Justice
> [William] Brennan has said that he
> finds the death penalty unconstitutional
> despite the fact that the Constitution itself
> about four times explicitly recognizes the
> validity of the death penalty."[29]
> —Judge Robert H. Bork, 1990

"[The Constitution's] framers placed in that document words so vague and amorphous that it did allow for modern twenty-first century thinking to interpret issues in light of the needs of the time. In my opinion, that is not a negative; that is not a pejorative. In my opinion, that is a part of what the framers had in mind in the creation of what is the life and breath of this country."[30]

—Congresswoman Barbara Jordan, 1990

The politicization of the courts should not necessitate that judges are interpreters of law; yet, like politicians, they are routinely classified as "conservative," "liberal," or "moderate."

Federal judges are supposed to implement legal rules written by *others*, not come up with their own rules. This seems straightforward and simple in principle, but in real life, executing this philosophy can be very hard. If laws were never ambiguous, never confusing, there wouldn't be a whole industry built around the interpretation of it. So it is up to judges to find the truest meaning of a particular law, and to explain what that means to the rest of us. By definition, this gives them a certain amount of power, which means they must consistently demonstrate the highest degree of personal disinterest. Today's controversy stems from the ever-growing number of cases where it is obvious that a judge is not disinterested and is using the law to create a whole new one, in line with his personal view.

Sure, judges have generated heated controversy in the past. In 1803, Chief Justice John Marshall determined in *Marbury v. Madison* that federal judges have the authority to declare acts of Congress (and, by implication, those of the president) unconstitutional.[31] Infamous decisions such as those mentioned earlier—*Dred Scott* in 1857 and *Lochner* in 1905—outraged many.[32, 33] Legal rulings rejecting New Deal legislation incensed President Franklin Roosevelt and his supporters. Segregationists were distraught by *Brown v. Board of Education*, which declared that education segregated by race is unconstitutional.[34]

No doubt groups opposed to these various legal rulings accused the judges of advancing personal agendas. These were all famous cases, but they were also rare. In the vast majority of cases, it was taken for granted that judges kept their personal views out of their rulings. Today, we have the opposite situation. Any decision on a controversial issue is immediately greeted with skepticism about the judge's neutrality. What are the rights of criminal suspects during an arrest? Under what circumstances can police conduct a search without a warrant? Does the Constitution permit or forbid prayer at school football games and graduation ceremonies? Are pornography and nude dance clubs constitutionally protected under the First Amendment? Judges deciding such issues must be prepared for accusations of advancing their personal beliefs.

After the 2000 presidential election fiasco, hundreds of law professors signed a letter accusing the Supreme Court justices who ruled in George W. Bush's favor in *Bush v. Gore* of doing so because of the Justices' personal political views.[35] Of course, many of these liberal law professors could hardly be viewed as dispassionate interpreters of the law.

But few battles have been more bitter than those concerning the right to privacy. (Read: abortion.) Though the 1973 *Roe* decision is the most famous, the abortion wars started in 1965 with *Griswold v. Connecticut*, when the Supreme Court declared Connecticut's ban on contraceptives unconstitutional on the grounds that the law violated the right to "marital privacy."[36]

It was Justice William Douglas who wrote the opinion in *Griswold*. He could not find an explicit justification for the decision, but maintained that not finding this right in the Constitution or the Bill of Rights did *not* mean it was not protected under the Constitution. Douglas essentially created a new right by extending clearly defined and explicit rights, like the protection from warrantless house searches, to married couples' right to use birth control. *Griswold* laid the groundwork for *Roe*, the decision that eight years later declared a Texas law that criminalized abortion unconstitutional.[37]

Critics of *Roe* are generally dismissed as abortion opponents. But that ignores one of their central concerns: the court's failure to find support in the Constitution. In *Roe*, the authority to decide the legality of abortion was shifted from fifty individual state governments to a handful of judges. Prior to *Roe*, all states allowed abortions, though there was a wide range in terms of how easy it was to obtain them.[38] Federalizing this decision made an already contentious issue all the more politically difficult since many states were forced to abide by rules that differed dramatically from what they would have otherwise adopted.

The case, of course, is not closed. The abortion wars have raged for the past four decades. Myriad suits have been filed by critics in attempts to place limits on *Roe*. The best-known suits have focused on the late-term "partial-birth" abortions and on whether minors need to obtain parental consent before having an abortion. There have been many judges and judicial nominees who have questioned the soundness of *Roe*, and who therefore also question how closely judges must abide by that ruling. Clearly, the selection of judges to the Supreme Court could play an important role in the future of abortion rights.

Another hot-button issue is gay marriage; specifically, whether same-sex couples have a right to the same legally recognized union as those of the opposite sex. This particular battle has been playing out before courts and in newspaper headlines across the country for years. Other aspects of the gay rights debate have garnered national attention, too. In 2003, the Supreme Court decided in *Lawrence v. Texas* that no "rational" reason exists for criminalizing sodomy.[39] That same year, the highest court in Massachusetts similarly ruled in *Goodridge v. Department of Public Health* that no rational reason exists for preventing two men or two women from getting married.[40]

There are many similar cases before federal courts today to determine whether polygamy, adoption by homosexual couples, and openly gay military service are rights guaranteed by the Constitution.[41] Justice Antonin Scalia pointed out in his dissent from *Lawrence* that "[S]tate laws against bigamy, same-sex marriage, adult incest, prostitution, masturbation, adultery, fornication, bestiality, and obscenity . . . [are] all called into question."[42] Until 2003, all such questions were addressed by individual state legislatures. Today, a single legal ruling can determine the law for the entire country.

So far-reaching is this shift in judicial authority that even those who support the outcome of the rulings (mostly liberals) are sometimes troubled by this newly created power. The pro-gay-marriage *Washington Post* complained about the "judicial arrogance" of the Massachusetts Supreme Court.[43] The *Post* explained: "Now the same majority has stretched still further, finding that the state constitution not only grants to same-sex couples a substantive right to marry but also dictates the nomenclature of the unions."[44]

In 2005, the Supreme Court ruled in *Roper v. Simmons* that the death penalty for juveniles violates the Constitution.[45] In a near scandal, the court based its decision partly on the laws and court decisions of other countries. In this situation, where the judges relied on sources other than the U.S. Constitution and domestic precedent, it seems impossible that they could maintain complete neutrality and not rely on those particulars in international law that coincide with their personal preferences.

This is what Justice Scalia, in agreement with Chief Justice Rehnquist and Justice Thomas, had to say:

> Worse still, the Court says in so many words that what our people's laws say about the issue does not, in the last analysis, matter: "[I]n the end our own judgment will be brought to bear on the question of the acceptability of the death penalty under the Eighth Amendment." . . . The Court thus proclaims itself sole arbiter of our Nation's moral standards—and in the course of discharging that awesome responsibility purports to take guidance from the views of foreign courts and legislatures. Because I do not believe that the meaning of our Eighth Amendment, any more than the meaning of other provisions of our Constitution, should be determined by the subjective views of five members of this Court and like-minded foreigners, I dissent.[46]

Naturally, liberals on the Supreme Court similarly accuse conservatives such as Scalia and Thomas of being the ones who base law on personal opinion. For example, in the two recent Supreme Court decisions that struck down the D.C. and Chicago handgun bans, Justice Stephen Breyer accused the majority of ignoring past precedent and making up a "fundamental" right to self-defense.[47] Conservatives would respond by saying that liberals find rights where nothing is written in the Constitution and deny rights when the Constitution explicitly asserts them. But what is at issue here is not the debate over who is right about particular cases, but rather that opposing interest groups, who otherwise can't agree on anything, often share the same complaint about the lack of judicial constraint. They recognize—and rightly fear—the growing power in the hands of federal courts. They believe that wide-ranging rights are created or denied based on the beliefs of a handful of judges.

Consensus as the Norm

As Judge Frank Easterbrook once pointed out, only a tiny fraction of circuit court decisions produce any disagreement.[48] He noted that the "vast bulk" of opinions are unpublished and unanimous. "Even in published opinions . . . most are unanimous." In nearly all instances, judges across the country decide similar cases *the same way*.[49] That alone implies that the vast majority of judges in this country still apply the law disinterestedly in most cases. And when differences in interpretation arise between judges, it is not immediately obvious that those differences can be ascribed to the political leanings of the president who appointed those judges.

It is a simple empirical observation, but not everyone is convinced. In September 2002, Charles Schumer, a Democratic senator from New York, held hearings on the alleged political imbalance among judges on the Circuit Court of the District of Columbia.[50] He argued that political bias affected the outcome of so many cases that the Senate needed to keep a special eye on the personal ideologies of judicial nominees.[51] Schumer claimed, "Perhaps more than any other court, aside from the Supreme Court, the D.C. Circuit vote break[s] down on ideological grounds with amazing frequency."

Although differences in judicial nominees' political backgrounds are important enough for even a few cases to drive many nomination fights, Schumer's characterization of ideology affecting an "amazing" number of cases is a bit extreme. The real surprise is how rarely disagreements arise among D.C. Circuit Court judges. In 2004, for example, when the three-judge circuit court panels decided 258 published opinions, there were only eight published dissents—3.1 percent of total cases. Nor was there anything unusual about that year. From 2000 to 2003, there were forty-one dissents in 773 published rulings—5.3 percent.[52]

Typically, court cases that do not get a published opinion are those in which the judges agree that there are not enough novelties or interesting aspects of the case to warrant publication. Fifty-eight percent of the D.C. Circuit Court's opinions and 80 percent of all circuit court opinions are unpublished.[53]

Even if the judges generally agree on most cases that come before the courts, it is possible that the disagreements that do exist reflect differences in political views on sensitive cases. That, at least, is the argument pushed by many law professors. The way professors commonly assess political differences is by reference to the political party of the president who appointed each judge; they assume that judges appointed by Republican presidents will necessarily come to different conclusions than judges appointed by Democrats.

Cass Sunstein, David Schkade, and Lisa Ellman of the University of Chicago Law School examined 4,488 published circuit court panel decisions from 1982 to 2002 on the most ideologically controversial issues: abortion, capital punishment, affirmative action, the Americans with Disabilities Act, campaign finance laws, criminal procedure, federalism, race and sex discrimination, and takings (the rules under which the government can seize private property).[54] By limiting themselves to published opinions and those involving politically polarized disputes, they focused on a fairly small set of cases, where disagreements were most likely to be seen. For those cases, Republican judges voted "liberally" 38 percent of the time; Democrats, 51 percent of the time. Given what a small percentage of all cases met the researchers' criteria, and that such cases are the ones in which people are likely to conflict with each other, a thirteen-percentage-point difference in how any individual judge voted does not seem large.

In some cases, the differences are larger and more statistically significant: affirmative action cases produced the largest difference between Republican and Democratic appointees (twenty-six percentage points) followed by capital punishment (twenty-two percentage points) and abortion (twenty-one percentage points). Sunstein, Schkade, and Ellman concluded that for these three categories, how judges vote "can be predicted by the party of the appointing president."

That a judge would be twenty or twenty-six percentage points more likely to vote in one's favor could be an important factor for some constituencies. For example, suppose that each of the three circuit court judges on a panel was only 38 percent likely to vote in one's favor. One's chances of getting at least two of the judges on one's side is only 32 percent. Increasing the probability by nineteen percentage points (the difference between Republicans and Democrats across all controversial cases) raises one's probability of getting the support of at least two judges to 51 percent. Depending on what is at stake in the case, such a change in probabilities could be worth a lot.

The estimate of Sunstein and his colleagues of a twenty-six-percentage-point difference for affirmative action cases (in which Republicans vote liberally 48 percent of the time, and Democrats vote liberally 74 percent of the time) implies a huge difference in the likelihood of how the case will be decided. Three Republicans on a circuit court panel have a 47 percent chance of voting for affirmative action, whereas three Democrats have an 83 percent chance. A thirty-five-percentage-point increase in the likelihood of a win for the affirmative action side represents a significant advantage.

Enough evidence supports this conclusion that in most courts in this country, especially the U.S. Court of Appeals, judges usually make rulings on the basis of neutral interpretation of law, not personal opinion. Since 1953, about 40 percent of Supreme Court cases were decided unanimously—quite a feat when you have to get nine different people to agree on a decision.[55] During the 1990s, the unanimity rate reached its height, ranging between 38 and 50 percent.[56] Another 27 percent of cases were determined by either eight-to-one or seven-to-two votes.[57]

But judges do disagree on a small number of highly controversial issues that people intensely care about, such as those noted by Sunstein and his coauthors. The disagreements often occur in cases with the fewest clear guidelines from legal authorities, and in some of those cases, personal views may help shape judgments. There are a few exceptions to this rule. For reasons of national unity and respect for the court's own authority, the Supreme Court has delayed judgment to ensure that the court rule unanimously, such as with civil rights cases including *Brown v. Board of Education*.[58] The same has been true for major battles between the branches; an obvious example is when the Supreme Court forced Richard Nixon to turn over his tapes.

One simple fact implies that differences in opinion will be smaller among circuit court judges than among Supreme Court justices: circuit court judges tend to tread cautiously to avoid the embarrassing reversals that can occur when the Supreme Court reviews their decisions. Reversals are especially damaging when they occur as a result of mistakes or incompetence.

No one oversees Supreme Court decisions.[59] Yet my analysis of the ten non-unanimous Supreme Court decisions on abortion since 1990 suggests that the difference among Supreme Court justices was smaller than among circuit court judges.[60] Republican appointees voted for the liberal position 41 percent of the time, whereas Democratic appointees voted that way 53 percent of the time. (Byron White, a Kennedy nominee, was consistently conservative in his votes on the issue.)

Even this twelve-percentage-point difference produces a potentially big impact when you consider groups of judges. Indeed, having all justices nominated by Republicans results in only a 29 percent chance that five or more justices would vote for a liberal stance on abortion. By contrast, the probability would be 57 percent if all justices had been nominated by Democrats: a twenty-eight-percentage-point difference in the outcome of the court. For death penalty cases, however, the margin between the party nominees on the Supreme Court is even greater than it is among judges on the circuit court.

Robert Bork has suggested that in cases where judges cannot resolve a dispute by relying exclusively on neutral legal authority, they should let the status quo stay rather than risk creating a law by relying to any degree on personal opinion.[61] Declining to rule on a case, of course, can just as easily result in charges of political decision making. In *Bush v. Gore*, after the close 2000 election,[62] the U.S. Supreme Court washed its hands of the matter after the Florida Supreme Court's revision of the state election law, a non-move that was inevitably regarded as politically motivated.

Think, too, of the Watergate scandal surrounding President Nixon; it would have been virtually impossible to credibly deny political motivation had the federal courts ignored Nixon's refusal to turn over the recordings.

Out of millions of rulings, only a relatively small percentage is clearly influenced by personal ideology. But those few cases are so important that politicians and interest groups will spend much time and money attempting to influence the judicial confirmation process. The battles we watch every time a Supreme Court justice retires are just a small part of a much larger war to control the direction of the country.

The Ever-Growing Role of the Federal Courts

Most criminal, divorce, and traffic cases—everyday legal disputes—are heard in state courts. The rulings of these courts apply only to individual states. Federal courts deal with cases of national importance that determine constitutionality or assess the proper authority of the federal government. As the role of the federal government has expanded, federal courts have had a growing effect on the lives of average Americans.

The change has not been uniform over time. The rise in criminal and civil cases during Prohibition caused the number of district court cases to briefly soar from 1920 to 1933. The more permanent and far-reaching explosion in court cases, however, has happened during the past fifty years.

The increase in the number of federal cases has greatly outstripped America's population growth. Since the 1960s, the number of circuit court cases has increased from 21 per million Americans to 223 per million—eleven times faster than the population growth. District court cases over the same period have grown from 448 to 1,252 per million Americans (Figures 1 and 2).

Figure 1: Growth in Federal District Court Cases

*To view a larger version of each graph, please refer to Supplement: Full-Page Graphs.

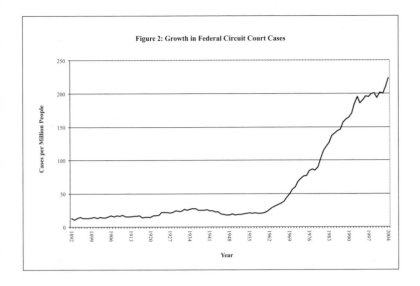

Figure 2: Growth in Federal Circuit Court Cases

To understand the trends, we must look at changes in the types of laws overseen by federal courts. As it turns out, entire branches of law only came into existence within the past fifty years. These new bodies of law revolve around several recently created government agencies. In the 1960s, the Equal Employment and Opportunity Commission (EEOC) and the National Transportation Safety Board (NTSB) were created. In the 1970s, new regulatory bodies sprang up all over the place, including the Environmental Protection Agency (EPA), the Consumer Product Safety Commission (CPSC), the Federal Election Commission (FEC), the Occupational Safety and Health Administration (OSHA), the Nuclear Regulatory Commission (NRC), and the U.S. Commodity Futures Trading Commission (CFTC). Each of these organizations created a host of new, often controversial regulations that fall under the jurisdiction of federal courts. Existing agencies have also been given new regulatory authority. The number of lawsuits generated by regulatory agencies increased as the agencies took advantage of their growing regulatory authority and issued new regulations.

Created in 1970, the EPA administers the Clean Air Act, the Clean Water Act, the Safe Drinking Water Act, the Water Pollution Control Act, the National Environmental Policy Act, the Superfund Act, and the Toxic Substances Control Act.[63] The EPA's annual budget is about $8 billion, and the agency has about 18,000 employees.[64] With every law that it oversees, the EPA generates litigation for the federal courts, and neither the agency nor its major laws existed before 1970. The EPA not only brings suits, but suits are frequently brought against the agency itself. For example, in 2005, eight states sued the EPA, charging that the EPA's "air quality rules for power plants ... do not protect the public from mercury pollution."[65]

The EEOC, originally created when President John Kennedy signed an executive order, can bring suits on behalf of alleged victims of discrimination. The agency enforces the Equal Pay Act of 1963, the Age Discrimination in Employment Act of 1967, the Rehabilitation Act of 1973, the Americans with Disabilities Act of 1990, and the Civil Rights Act of 1991.[66] None of these cases were brought before the federal courts prior to the early 1960s.

In addition, plenty of new antidiscrimination laws have been created that are not under the supervision of an agency. The Voting Rights Act (1965), the Fair Housing

Act (1968), and Title IX of the Education Act (1972) all contribute to the increase in federal legislation.

Title IX was part of the Education Amendments of 1972 and prohibited institutions of higher education from discriminating on the basis of gender.[67] It was later expanded to include any U.S. educational institution. Although many government agencies can oversee compliance, enforcement responsibilities primarily rest with the U.S. Department of Education. But countless unanticipated questions have arisen, and federal judges have had to answer them, as in the case of a high school coach who sued his school district under Title IX, arguing that he was fired for speaking out about the inequality of the sports teams.

Of course, new areas of law are created all the time. In 2002, as a result of the public reaction to the corporate scandals involving Enron, Tyco, and WorldCom, Congress felt they had to do something,[68] even though these cases involved only a tiny fraction of the over 10,000 publicly traded companies in the United States. As a result, Congress passed the Sarbanes-Oxley Act, which burdens corporations with complex regulations, an accounting oversight board, and additional disclosure rules.[69] It's no wonder the area of law surrounding corporate fraud has become one of the fastest growing fields in the business.

The greater the costs that laws impose on people, the harder potential litigants will look for loopholes. It doesn't help that many regulations are vague. Lawsuits often occur when both parties to the suit have different expectations of what the courts are likely to decide.

Modern technologies also create new issues for the federal courts. In 2005, the Supreme Court decided a case in which an owner of a cell phone tower in a wealthy Los Angeles suburb engaged in an expensive, long-running legal fight with the town over his right to use the tower. In *Rancho Palos Verdes v. Abrams*, the Supreme Court awarded the tower owner money damages and ruled that he had a right to leave the tower where it was.[70]

Dramatic changes have occurred in criminal law as well. The number of federal criminal trials has doubled over the past four decades. Trials have also become more complicated and take longer, in part because many actions that are crimes today were not previously considered an offense. People are thrown in jail for not wearing a seat belt, a twelve-year-old girl was handcuffed and arrested for eating french fries inside a Washington, D.C., subway station,[71] a pregnant woman was arrested for talking loudly on a cell phone at another Washington, D.C., subway station,[72] and three Americans were sentenced to eight-year prison terms for importing lobster tails from Honduras in plastic bags instead of cardboard boxes.[73] This last case went all the way up to the Supreme Court, but the court declined to intervene.[74] In another case, a former corporate officer was charged with criminal violations under the Clean Water Act for actions that occurred after he had left the company.[75] He was sentenced to forty-six months in prison.

At just the federal level, the growth in the number of criminal offenses has been astounding. In 1790, the first criminal statute in the United States contained thirty different crimes. That grew to 165 by 1900; 561 by 1930; 1,980 by 1970; and around 4,500 by 2008.[76] The complexity of what constitutes a crime has increased as well. While the U.S. population has increased by 36 percent over the last thirty years, the number of people sentenced to federal prison has increased almost threefold to 83,000 annually.[77]

The scope of the law and its vagueness produces a lot of cases that do not end in conviction. In the area of terrorism, the federal government has tried many novel ways to bring criminal charges. When a woman suffered a fatal heart attack from natural causes in 2004, paramedics and police detectives discovered a home laboratory with petri dishes.[78] The husband had been working on an exhibit that looked at genetically modified organisms contained in store-bought foods for the Massachusetts Museum of Contemporary Art. The FBI determined that his work presented no public health risk, but he was charged with a federal crime because some items bought from a private vendor were used in ways not allowed by that private contract. A judge eventually dismissed the case and ruled that the indictment did not spell out any specific crime.

Even the way in which the courts apply the rules has become more complicated. I worked for the U.S. Sentencing Commission as its chief economist during the late 1980s. The Sentencing Commission sets the guidelines that judges must follow in determining federal criminal penalties. The rules were rigid. For example, even if you don't make a single dollar from insider trading, if convicted, you will go to jail for two to eight months; if you make $250, you face four to ten months. When the Sentencing Commission released the guidelines in 1998, the document was 342 pages long.[79] By 2004, shortly before the Supreme Court declared that making the guidelines mandatory was unconstitutional, the guidelines had grown to 1,738 pages.[80]

Stricter laws for corporations, new laws to confront the post-9/11 terror threat, and even international treaties are further sources of new obligations and litigation.

*

Using by far the largest data set of its kind, *Dumbing Down the Courts* analyzes how the judicial confirmation process for circuit and district court judgeships has changed over the past thirty-four years. Data are studied for 345 circuit and 1,215 district court nominees, from the beginning of the Carter administration through George W. Bush's first full term in office. More limited data extend this evidence to examine the confirmation process through President Obama's first two years in office.

This book is much more comprehensive than previous studies and examines many more questions. In the two largest previous studies, Professor Jim Lindgren at Northwestern looked at forty-nine circuit court nominees and I examined one hundred and fourteen. Both studies covered just the Clinton and George H. W. Bush administrations, accounted for relatively few factors in explaining the confirmation process, and examined the narrower issue of how the American Bar Association rates nominees.[81] Examining only two administrations makes it pretty difficult to infer whether Republicans and Democrats behave differently.

Naturally, political partisans offer contradictory assessments of these changes, and each side trumpets detailed lists of the other's transgressions while claiming their own innocence. Republicans allege that their candidates have received worse treatment by supposedly nonpartisan groups than have the Democrats' candidates. Democrats, of course, disagree. *Dumbing Down the Courts* supplies the data to determine who is right. I will attempt to put the arguments in perspective and, using some extensive data, try to objectively explore which assertions are accurate.

As we shall see, both sides are right when they complain that their nominees are delayed longer and more often than in previous years. They are also right in that their most qualified candidates often are the most ferociously attacked. *Dumbing Down the Courts* will show that the judicial confirmation battle not only is a fight over which party gets "their" candidate, but is a battle that affects the quality of the judges as well.

The very brightest nominees will not end up on the bench. Courts face many difficult and technical issues, and getting those decisions right is important, not only for the parties involved, but also for others who will make decisions based on those verdicts. With courts being used to obtain policy goals, opposing the other political party's smartest picks for judges is perfectly rational. But the downside should be obvious: dismissing the smartest nominees means more mistakes will be made.

1: THE BATTLES ARE GETTING WORSE

Most of us know the basic mechanics of judicial confirmations. Federal judges are appointed by the president of the United States. The appointments are made with the "advice and consent" of the Senate: the president nominates a judge, and the Senate either confirms or rejects the nomination. The president must take this process into account when deciding whom to nominate. Strong Senate opposition to certain types of nominees will prevent these judges from being nominated in the first place.

It used to be a fairly simple procedure for a judge to get confirmed. From the first Supreme Court nomination in 1789 until 1950, eighty-seven justices were nominated; the time from nomination to confirmation averaged just over eleven days. But this changed dramatically over the next half century. From 1951 through 1976, the average confirmation process increased to more than fifty days, and from 1976 to the present, it has averaged seventy-two days. As of this writing in 2012, the president and a majority of senators are all Democrats; however, it is still possible for the Republican minority to slow or, in a rare case, stop the confirmation process.

While there has been the occasional tussle about nominees in the past, nothing prepared the country for the all-consuming wars that have taken place over the last twenty-five years. The Supreme Court nominations of Robert Bork in 1987 and Clarence Thomas in 1991 caused the most uproar—and still are frequently mentioned in the media even when there are no pending Supreme Court nominations.[82] Yet vicious, drawn-out, interest-group-based nomination fights in federal courts around the country have become the norm.

Republicans and Democrats alike have complained about the increasingly time-consuming nomination process. And both sides have switched their positions on how long a nominee can be grilled when it suits their political goals. During the Clinton administration, Attorney General Janet Reno accused the Republican-controlled Senate of an "unprecedented slowdown" in confirming new federal judges. During George W. Bush's first term in office, Republicans complained of "inexcusable" delays.[83]

In 2000, with Bill Clinton in the White House, Democrat Senator Charles Schumer of New York was anxious to confirm some Clinton nominees before the November election. Schumer argued for a quick majority vote: "I also plead with my colleagues to move judges with alacrity— vote them up or down. But this delay makes a mockery of the Constitution, makes a mockery of the fact that we are here working, and makes a mockery of the lives of very sincere people who have put themselves forward to be judges and then they hang out there in limbo."[84] By 2005, with a Republican president nominating judges, Schumer's solicitude for judicial nominees in limbo had vanished. Not only did he no longer think judges should automatically get a floor vote, Schumer no longer believed certain nominees should be confirmed even if a majority of senators supported the candidate: "There's nothing in the Constitution that says that there has to be fifty-one votes for that judge."[85] Yet, by April 2010, with another Democrat in office as president for just over a year, Schumer switched back to his earlier stance and criticized the delays facing Obama's nominees as "unpardonable."[86] Once again he was upset that Republicans were not "let[ting] more nominees through.... We're going to stay in as long as it takes, even if it means nights, weekends to get these nominees through."[87]

The late Senator Edward Kennedy of Massachusetts, also a Democrat, similarly flip-flopped. In 1995, Kennedy, a former chairman of the Judiciary Committee, declared: "Senators who believe in fairness will not let a minority of the Senate deny [a judicial nominee] his vote by the entire Senate."[88] In 1998, Kennedy, along with eighteen other Democrats, sought to completely abolish the filibuster for any use, not just for judicial confirmations, where a minority of at least forty-one senators can prevent a vote from taking place.[89] Yet, less than a decade later, under a Republican administration and with Democrats in control of the Senate, he consistently filibustered judicial nominations, voting time after time to deny Bush's judicial nominees a vote.

Of course, such reversals over filibusters have not been limited to Democrats. Republicans were outraged over the filibusters against judicial nominees under George W. Bush, particularly those against his circuit court nominees such as Miguel Estrada and Priscilla Owen, who were both first nominated in 2001. C. Boyden Gray, a Republican who oversaw judicial nominations during the George H. W. Bush administration, warned: "The Senate Democrats are engaged in an unprecedented filibuster. They have changed rules and broken Senate tradition. Never in our history has the filibuster defeated a judicial nominee."[90] Nevertheless, Republicans changed their tune, and under President Obama in May 2011, forty-two of the forty-seven Senate Republicans successfully voted to filibuster the Democrats' first judicial appointment, circuit court nominee Goodwin Liu.[91, 92] Thus, it was now the Democrats' turn to claim that Republicans had broken precedent. *The Hill* reported: "Democrats . . . said that the standard for filibustering judicial nominees has been lowered significantly as a result of Liu's defeat."[93]

The rhetoric over the delays can be nasty. Bill Clinton maintained that delays over his minority and female nominees exposed not mere political resistance, but racism and sexism on the part of the hesitating senators.[94] President Clinton said that "politics and paybacks" meant that minorities were "twice as likely to be rejected as whites."[95] Further, Democrats charged that during the last two years of the Clinton administration, the "delay of judicial nominations" was "unprecedented" and wholly "political."[96]

The process slowed still further during George W. Bush's administration, especially when the Democrats took control of the Senate. Under Clinton, the average confirmation process for circuit court nominees lasted a brutal 230 days. During George W. Bush's administration, the process was even more brutal, averaging 362 days. President Barack Obama didn't face as many problems during his first two years in office given the eighteen- to twenty-seat Democratic majority, but the 255 days to confirmation were still longer than the battles Clinton faced.

Brazenly, over the last decade, Democratic senators have not even tried to hide their plans to preemptively oppose virtually all Republican nominees because their ideology is not in line with that of the Democrats. As New York's Charles Schumer put it, "We believe we're protecting America from extremists."[97] As clarification, he pointed to George W. Bush's nominees: "They are almost all pro-life, they are almost all extremely conservative."[98]

Anger against Republicans has continued during the Obama administration, with Patrick Leahy (D-VT) accusing Republicans of "reflexive partisanship, not principled argument."[99] Nan Aron, president of the liberal Alliance for Justice, has complained that nominations have become "more bitter and more partisan than the Clinton years. It is obstructionism across the board."[100]

Perhaps with all these accusations being hurled around, it isn't too surprising that a 2005 Gallup survey found that a majority of adults described both Democratic and Republican Senate leaders as acting like "spoiled children" in their debates over federal judges.[101]

How times have changed. Senators used to recognize that it is a president's prerogative to pick judges who share his philosophy; they would oppose nominees solely based

on a lack of competence, integrity, or judicial temperament. Up through the 1970s, Supreme Court confirmation battles rarely lasted over a month. The current era
of one long confirmation battle after another didn't start
until the mid-1980s, with William Rehnquist's elevation
to chief justice and Antonin Scalia's nomination to be an
associate justice. But the battles over ideology really only
began with Robert Bork's failed nomination in 1987.

While this book examines the data on federal judgeships, the battle over judges isn't limited to the federal
courts. Michael S. Kang and Joanna Shepherd point out
in a recent issue of the *New York University Law Review*
that state judicial elections have become increasingly
contentious over the last couple of decades.[102] In 2000,
incumbent state judges were defeated twice as often in
either nonpartisan or partisan elections as two decades
earlier. That year the reelection rate was 92 percent for
nonpartisan judges and 50 percent for partisan judges.
By contrast, the reelection rate for members of the U.S.
House of Representatives was 98 percent.

Waiting to Be Judges: The Personal Costs

> "Well, what [Deputy White House
> Chief of Staff Karl Rove] told me is that
> some of those [potential nominees for
> the U.S. Supreme Court] took them-
> selves off that list and they would not

allow their names to be considered, because the process has become so vicious and so vitriolic and so bitter that they didn't want to subject themselves or the members of their families to it."[103]
—Dr. James Dobson, founder and chairman emeritus of Focus on the Family, 2005

Neal Conan (Host of NPR's *Talk of the Nation*): As somebody who actually went through this [confirmation] process that we're talking about this afternoon, we were hoping you could put a bit of a human face on it. What's it like?

Lillian BeVier (Professor, University of Virginia): It's awful. I don't think I'd wish it even on my worst enemy. From the beginning to the end, I was sort of in the process for about two years. I was identified as a candidate and told I was going to be nominated . . . toward the very end of 1990; I was finally nominated in October of 1991, and then sort of held in limbo with lots of stuff going on in the background for a year without having a hearing.

Conan: Now, I assume that the day you're nominated for a seat on the federal bench—I mean, this has got to be one of the great days of your life.

BeVier: Well, you'd think it would be. . . . I suppose it would be if you end up getting confirmed and you believe that you can make a contribution on the bench. If you're nominated—at least my experience was you're nominated and you go through what is a long period of uncertainty and scrutiny and quite a bit of behind-the-scenes politicking in which you, as a person, actually are not so much the focus, but you become sort of a pawn in somebody else's political game. And then when it turns out you don't even get a hearing, you don't have a chance to defend yourself against, you know, the sort of whispered complaints or the kinds of things that perhaps the interest groups have been telling the senators about you. You don't have a chance to make your case in public. You never do have a chance to make your case in public if you don't have a hearing. It turns out to have been sort of awful because you can't really have a clear-your-name day.

Jeffrey Rosen (Professor, George Washington University): I'm so glad we heard from Professor Lillian BeVier because she's a really good example of a respected academic, conservative certainly, but so intelligent and careful in her scholarship that any system that really took seriously excellence would have confirmed her eagerly. And I was almost going to ask her—instead, I'll just raise my fear that as a result of this process, excellent nominees may be deterred from going up.[104]

—*Talk of the Nation*, September 9, 2002

Nominees who get caught up in the turmoil pay a price, especially if they fail to get confirmed. Their reputations are damaged, their families are hurt, and their careers are put in jeopardy. The damage isn't just limited to those nominated for the Supreme Court; even those nominated for lower-level positions have had their reputations damaged. Charles W. Pickering, Sr., whom President George W. Bush nominated to a circuit judgeship, cited the turmoil suffered by his family even after he withdrew himself from further consideration. He had been called a racist on the basis of an inference drawn from a single case.[105] "The bitter fight over judicial confirmations threatens the quality and the independence of the judiciary," he said. "[It] reduces the pool of nominees willing to offer themselves for service on the bench."[106]

Pickering explained: "I did not enjoy what I went through. Had I known in advance what was going to happen, I doubt if I would have gone far with it. But once the fight started, I could not step down or withdraw. To do so would have given some credibility to the charge."[107] Eventually, however, a Democratic filibuster made it clear that Pickering would not be confirmed, and he had no option but to withdraw his nomination.

Pickering's withdrawal is hardly unusual. The current problems facing circuit court nominees started during the last two years of Ronald Reagan's last term as president, when the Democrats regained control of the Senate. Take the experience of Bernard Siegan, one of the first nominees to encounter these drawn-out, bitter, personally destructive confirmation battles. Siegan was a Reagan nominee to the Ninth Circuit Court of Appeals. Few people outside of academia knew of him before his nomination. Siegan, a professor at the University of San Diego Law School, had authored several nationally recognized academic books on property and zoning laws, and his 1980 book *Economic Liberties and the Constitution* received much praise.[108] Siegan had an impressive record: graduate of the University of Chicago Law School, associate editor of the *University of Chicago Law Review*, recipient of an extremely competitive law and economics fellowship at the University of Chicago, successful private practice attorney for twenty-nine years, and legal consultant for the Department of Housing and Urban Development.

Yet, despite those qualifications, Siegan is one of the

few circuit court nominees who failed to reach the Senate floor because of a negative vote in the Judiciary Committee.[109] Most failed nominations either make it out of committee to languish as they wait for a Senate vote or never even make it to a Judiciary Committee hearing. Siegan related to me that he found the process, which spanned almost two years, quite "unpleasant."[110] He went on: "I did not suffer professionally. But you don't want to waste that much time. . . . There were so many critical stories and so much interest. I wanted the chance to talk about the attacks. I was being attacked but I wasn't able to talk about it. Even years later, every now and then you meet someone who [will] ask, 'What kind of a terrible person are you?' You meet someone who would have been persuaded by all the horrible things that they had read about. Sometimes it made no difference what I said [to them]."

According to Siegan, attackers would remark, "How could Reagan have appointed such a stupid guy?" He complains that it was "unpleasant to be before the committee and be badgered." Even his sixteen-year-old son ran into problems: "Some of his friends would say that they knew about what a bad guy his dad was."

Siegan was not alone in his experience. When discussing his 114-day confirmation battle, former Supreme Court nominee Robert Bork told me: "The main effect [of Bork's confirmation process on his kids] was that they got disgusted with Washington."[111] He also spoke of how it has affected him personally: "I'm viewed as much more controversial than previously. Some institutions, I don't want to name them, that would invite me to give a commencement address, and many did, would be afraid of the reaction from some people there. You have to understand how different academia is." He noted that "[Although] you can never be sure what people would do when they actually get a nomination, some [potential nominees] say offhand that they wouldn't want to go through the process that I went through." Even though Bork had much more of a platform from which he could respond to attacks than did other nominees, he was also concerned that "as a sitting federal judge, [he] could not publicly respond [to the] public campaign of miseducation" that was being directed against him.[112]

Bork mentioned to me that opposition to judicial nominees can arise specifically because of their strengths over other contenders. This can be seen for non-judicial nominations as well. Bork pointed to John Bolton's battle in April and May of 2005 to be confirmed as ambassador to the United Nations. "Bolton is a victim of that, [the] fear that he would be too effective, that he simply would do too good of a job." Of course, the notion of personal destruction holds true here, too. Bolton was accused of everything from abusing employees to altering intelligence to fit his personal biases. As part of the Senate's negotiation to end the judicial filibuster, Senator Joseph Biden (D-DE) attempted to allow the vote on Bolton in exchange for denying votes on a few Republican circuit court nominees. One Democratic Senate staffer was quoted as saying, "But nothing came of it, and that's a good thing. There are quite a few people here who want to see Bolton squirm."[113]

Merely the threat of having to endure a battle deters some candidates from accepting a nomination in the first place. After Siegan eventually withdrew, he said, "I don't know if I would want to do it again."[114] Even Justice David Souter, who underwent a relatively mild confirmation process to the Supreme Court before being confirmed, and whose nomination was the seventh fastest of the nine nominations since 1986, told Senator Warren Rudman (R-NH), his friend and sponsor, "If I had known how vicious this process is, I wouldn't have let you propose my nomination."[115]

Potential nominees have heard the same stories. Two Republican law school professors who were friends and colleagues of mine told me privately that they had been approached early on in the George W. Bush presidency to be judges, but turned down nominations to circuit courts because they had seen how vicious the battles had been for others.

Drawing out the confirmation process leaves judgeships vacant, and this in turn adds to the workload of other judges and often results in piles of undecided cases.[116] And the longer the confirmation process, the more likely a nominee will withdraw his candidacy. While waiting to be confirmed, judicial nominees must put their law practice and any other business commitments on hold. As described in detail earlier in Chapter 1, nominees are also often attacked personally, yet they are expected to keep their responses muted. This expectation works in favor of the opponents, as no matter how unfounded a rumor, if it is circulated long enough, at least some people will believe it.

While we may not be able to objectively measure these personal costs, they are no doubt very important. And the greater the personal costs, the more likely it is that a greater fraction of the potential nominees will simply refuse being nominated in the first place. Unfortunately, there are no publicly available records on those who have been queried by an administration as to whether they are willing to accept a nomination. Any measure of confirmation rates thus underestimates the difficulty that the president has in getting his nominees confirmed. The nominees whom I interviewed complained that the personal costs had been significant, and many would not go through the process again if they had the chance. Given how public these confirmation battles are, there is no hiding this process from other potential nominees.

Well-known anecdotes illustrate the pain of confirmations. Take the case of Supreme Court Justice Samuel Alito's wife, Martha-Ann, who broke down in tears and left the hearing room as Democratic charges that Alito was a bigot were recounted.[117] To try to fill in the details on personal costs, I called a dozen exceptionally bright circuit court nominees who were not confirmed from the past four administrations: seven Republican and five Democratic nominees. Only seven nominees would talk to me in depth, and only four—Bernie Siegan, Robert Raymar, Lillian BeVier, and Charles Pickering—were willing to go on the record.[118] I also tried talking to current judges who had gone through difficult confirmations, but they were reticent to publicly discuss their confirmations, preferring instead to concentrate on what they were able to accomplish since being on the court. Yet there is one rather public exception to this rule: Supreme Court Justice Clarence Thomas, who discussed his confirmation hearing in his memoir, *My Grandfather's Son*.

Virtually all seven nominees were concerned about being drawn into the political debate over the confirmation process, though I made it clear that I was not interested in settling old partisan scores, nor did I believe that the data showed that either political party had completely clean hands. I simply wanted to understand the personal costs the nominees and their families experienced as a result of the nomination process.

Consider the case of Robert Raymar. In June 1998, President Clinton nominated Raymar, a successful lawyer, to the U.S. Court of Appeals for the Third Circuit. For the next eighteen months—the remainder of that Congress—the Senate essentially ignored Raymar's nomination. Raymar never received a hearing, let alone confirmation. He was not even interviewed by the Senate Judiciary Committee.[119]

At Yale Law School he had been an editor of the *Yale Law Journal*, and he had an impressive résumé that is associated with only the brightest nominees. He had clerked for Judge Leonard Garth on the Third Circuit and had worked as the deputy attorney general for New Jersey.

At the same time, he noted: "I went to law school with Bill and Hillary Clinton. There was no mystery that I was a friend of the Clintons."[120]

Though his life was in limbo for eighteen months, Raymar believes that he was fortunate compared with other nominees who he recognized had to live with much deeper scars from the personal attacks; his nomination was stalled from the beginning solely due to the Senate's opposition to Clinton in the aftermath of the Monica Lewinsky scandal. Although he does not think that he would have been subject to personal attacks, he said, "If [one] is not going to be confirmed, it is better not to have a negative hearing. At least if someone is going to do a Google search on your name they aren't going to come up with 4,000 negative hits."[121]

Lillian BeVier told a similar story. George H. W. Bush nominated her to the Fourth Circuit in 1991. She had graduated from Stanford at the top of her class, worked as an editor for the *Stanford Law Review*, and received multiple distinguished awards. Despite assurances from Senator Joseph Biden and others, she also never received a hearing.

BeVier told me that she was "surprised at how exercised [she] can get about it after twelve years" and lamented that she "really felt sandbagged by the process."[122] Her complaints were echoed in my conversations with others. Among the problems I heard were: "You can't answer objections and concerns that are raised" and "[It] just puts your life on hold, you don't know what to work on, and you don't have a sense of what your future will be." I also heard complaints about the "very extensive" forms that had to be filled out, including financial disclosure forms, from the American Bar Association (ABA) and the Federal Bureau of Investigation (FBI).[123]

The most difficult problems arose from how the attacks affected what others thought about the nominee. According to BeVier, "People normally don't tell you what they are thinking, but in one case [someone] raised [his] concerns [based on charges made during the confirmation process]. I found the comments so insulting, just stunned by what [that person] thought was happening."[124]

Charles Pickering's experience is worth exploring further. Nominated to the U.S. Court of Appeals for the Fifth Circuit early in Bush's first term in 2001, a decision on his nomination was delayed for more than three years. Pickering had graduated first in his class at the University of Mississippi Law School and served on the law review. He was elected to the Mississippi State Senate and was appointed to the U.S. District Court for Mississippi by George H. W. Bush. He was still serving as a district court judge when George W. Bush nominated him to a higher court.

Pickering spent much of his life working for racial equality. For example, in 1967, unlike many other Southern county prosecutors who "looked the other way," Pickering testified against an "imperial wizard" of the KKK, in a case where the Klan leader had been accused of firebombing the home of a civil rights worker.[125] Despite his record, he was subjected to an endless barrage of attacks from Democrats accusing him of racism. The prime "proof" of racism involved a case where Judge Pickering supposedly gave a white man convicted of a cross burning an inappropriately short two-year prison sentence. Senator Charles Schumer accused Pickering of "help[ing] a man who burnt a cross." But Pickering's explanation, broadcast on CBS's *60 Minutes*, proved that the issue was much more complicated: "Pickering said this was the worst case of disproportionate sentencing he'd ever seen, especially since the real ringleader (who didn't go to prison) had attacked the same house before."[126] Pickering felt that the prosecution had made a plea bargain with the wrong defendant, leaving the most-guilty defendant, indeed the "ring leader," with a misdemeanor and no jail time.[127]

Such attacks, according to Pickering, are difficult because "you have to depend upon someone else to defend you. It is difficult enough for you to remember events about your own life ten to fifteen years ago, but you can't really depend upon someone else to know everything that they would have to know to properly respond in every instance. Senators are just too busy to find out everything that they have to know."[128]

Pickering says that the attacks have real consequences for most nominees: "With some, you can't get back your reputation. Their minds are closed. Who wants to hear your story after so long? It is old news after the confirmation process is over. Speaking out also takes a lot of time. Just traveling around and talking to people takes a lot out of you."[129] The hardest part, said Pickering, is how much the attacks hurt and disrupt the families of the nominees.

In addition to the toll on their loved ones, Raymar, BeVier, and Pickering all complained about the paperwork and information requests. Pickering told me, "You have to produce so many documents. It just depletes you and drains you."[130] Senators who opposed Pickering just kept coming back with more and more demands for papers, and he lamented that fulfilling those requests just made it so that he could not get anything else done. Raymar also objected to the amount of paperwork: "The paperwork was a pain, and someone could provide a real service fixing this. The White House wants paperwork. The [attorney general] wants paperwork. The Senate wants paperwork. They would all ask the same questions in different ways so that you couldn't use the answers for one form for another. There was also a lack of clarity in the paperwork."[131]

The paperwork burden is greatest for the nominees with the most accomplishments. As Raymar pointed out: "People who have done more, written more, spoken more, have a much more difficult time. You have more things to explain, more possible misstatements. Sensibilities have changed over time. . . . I had questions from the White House about a footnote in a paper from law school. I can't even remember some recent events, let alone relatively minor events from law school."[132]

Clarence Thomas's autobiography reveals how even in victory the battle to get on the Supreme Court left scars still felt sixteen years later.[133] During his confirmation, Thomas made a searing charge about the message his hearings sent to other blacks: "A high-tech lynching for uppity blacks who in any way deign to think for themselves. . . . You will be lynched, destroyed, caricatured by a committee of the U.S. Senate rather than hung from a tree."[134] Thomas's book illustrates the pain he felt during his five days of testimony and throughout the rest of the hearings by referencing one of the most powerful books on racism towards blacks in American literature:[135]

> Somewhere in the back of my mind, I must have been thinking of *To Kill a Mockingbird*, in which Atticus Finch, a small-town southern lawyer, defends Tom Robinson, a black man on trial for the rape of a white woman. He was lucky to have had a trial at all—Atticus had already helped him escape a lynch mob's rope. The evidence presented at the trial shows that Tom's accuser had lured him into her house, then kissed him, after which he fled. The case against him is laughably flimsy, but in the Deep South you didn't need a strong case to send a black man to the gallows, and it is already clear that Tom will be convicted when Atticus goes before the jury to make his closing argument.

Thomas went from having a "spotless" reputation with no accusations of personal impropriety to facing charges of sexual harassment that will dog him through history.[136] He describes how his mother lost more than thirty pounds as a result of the stress and worry, and a reporter would go on to claim that his mother wasn't being honest about the number of children that she had.[137] Years later Thomas is still bothered by people who he says directly lied to his face during the process, such as a smiling and seemingly friendly then-Senator Joe Biden promising to ask one type of question so as to lower his guard and then instead asking something completely different involving a quote that was falsely attributed to Thomas.[138]

One liberal critically reviewing *My Grandfather's Son* reacted to Thomas's discussion of his confirmation this way: "And far from being dispassionate and detached, he is filled with burning rage against the Democrats who—in his mind—did him wrong, and [he is] determined to use any opportunity that comes his way to strike against them without mercy."[139] Apparently, a position on the Supreme Court is so important that no accusation seems out of bounds.

Does the judicial confirmation process accomplish anything positive besides bruising the reputations of nominees? Are the battles over judges necessary to prevent unqualified nominees—or nominees with truly extremist positions—from getting on the courts? Or, do these battles deter high-quality potential nominees from daring to go through the confirmation process? The answers to these questions will be explored in the chapters to come.

2: SUPREME BATTLES

"Justice Rehnquist might have made a brilliant 19th-century chief justice, but brilliance of judicial intellect in the service of racism and injustice is no virtue in our times."[140]
—Senator Edward Kennedy, 1986

"Nowadays a certain minimum competence is demanded (and [John] Roberts did receive some grudging respect for his outstanding credentials), but above that, contenders get little credit for being abler legal analysts than their competitors, and sometimes negative credit: the fate of Robert Bork, whose intellectual distinction was held against him as making him more dangerous."[141]
—Judge Richard Posner, 2005

"But being brilliant and accomplished is not the number one criteria for elevation to the Supreme Court. There are many who would use their considerable talents and legal acumen to set America back."[142]
—Senator Charles Schumer, 2005

"[Michael] Luttig, 51, is described as 'brilliant.' But the same trait that might get him nominated [to the Supreme Court] could also prevent his confirmation."[143]

—Brit Hume, Fox News, 2005

"A conservative lawyer who has worked with [Goodwin] Liu [an Obama nominee for the Ninth Circuit Court of Appeals being groomed to eventually be on the Supreme Court] confessed to me that he is 'scared' of Liu because he is 'more brilliant than [Antonin] Scalia without being nasty.'"[144]

—Marc Ambinder, *The Atlantic*, 2010

How did the judicial confirmation process become so nasty? Democrats say Republicans started it, Republicans say Democrats did—and that is how politicians and pundits justify current partisan assaults on judicial nominees.

This chapter focuses on the Supreme Court, even though those confirmations play only a limited, if highly visible, role in the judicial confirmation nightmare. The highest court in the land cannot easily be compared with others, and its relatively few nominations make it difficult to conduct statistical tests that account for other factors. Still, Supreme Court judicial battles can be a useful barometer of how the judicial confirmation process has changed in general. Naturally, the more important the court, the more contentious the battles.

How Nominations Have Changed

In the past, most nominees to the Supreme Court were confirmed quite quickly. The change over the last hundred years has been dramatic. From the time Theodore Roosevelt took office in 1901, through Gerald Ford, who left the presidency in 1977, fifty-one nominations to the Supreme Court were made. Thirty-nine of those nominees were confirmed in one month or less. Twenty of those thirty-nine were confirmed in ten days or less, and nine of those nominees were confirmed within just three days. John Paul Stevens, President Ford's sole nominee, was confirmed in just nineteen days even though Ford was a Republican and the Democrats controlled the Senate.[145] Only eight confirmations took longer than a month.

Four people during that time period were nominated but not confirmed,[146] and they faced the most contentious nominations: eighty days elapsed between the initial nomination and the final decision. When counting the four unconfirmed nominees along with the nominees who were successfully confirmed during this time, the duration of the average nomination process increases from twenty-three days to twenty-seven and a half days.

This pattern started to change sharply during Ronald Reagan's presidency. In the twelve confirmations from the Reagan administration through the Obama administration, not one nominee was confirmed in less than a month. The two shortest confirmation procedures were for Sandra Day O'Connor and Ruth Bader Ginsburg, thirty-three and forty-two days, respectively. That theirs were the shortest isn't particularly surprising as they were both confirmed when the same political party controlled the presidency and the Senate; they were also the first two women nominated. The average confirmation time in the Senate for all twelve of the justices confirmed between 1981 and 2010 (including O'Connor and Ginsburg) was seventy-three days. That is almost the same length as the confirmation time for the nominees who were *rejected* earlier in the century and roughly 3.2 times the average for justices nominated between 1900 and 1977.

Prior to the Reagan administration, the rare instances of protracted confirmation processes almost invariably involved race, religion, or serious questions about the competence of the nominee; however, even back then, concerns that the nominee was too smart could stall the confirmation, as in the case of Louis D. Brandeis.

Back in 1916, Woodrow Wilson nominated Brandeis for the Supreme Court. Brandeis survived an extremely bitter, 125-day confirmation battle to become the first Jewish member of the court.[147] Brandeis was likely the first nominee to be opposed for his intelligence. He graduated from Harvard Law School with the most outstanding record of any student in its history and had become an extremely successful lawyer in Boston. It was not uncommon to find the words "dangerous" and "brilliance" linked together in descriptions of Brandeis.[148]

Of course, "brilliance" was not the official reason for the opposition. The American Bar Association asserted that he did not fall within the mainstream of legal practice and did not have the necessary temperament to be a judge. Opposition focused on him being "sympathetic to the trade union movement" and on his belief that big businesses "were bilking their workers."[149] But it was his "brilliance" that made the opposition to his nomination so intense.[150] He was confirmed by a largely party-line vote with Democrats holding firm control of the Senate. Those opposed to his nomination were probably right to be concerned given that Brandeis became one of the most influential justices to ever serve on the court.

Race almost derailed the confirmation of Potter Stewart in 1958. Stewart was nominated by Dwight Eisenhower at age thirty-nine, and his confirmation was delayed in the Senate by a group of Southern Democrats,[151] who were outraged by the Supreme Court's 1954 decision in *Brown v. Board of Education*.[152] Immediately after Justice Harold Burton's retirement, Stewart received a temporary recess appointment from Eisenhower to the Supreme Court, but it was still necessary for the Senate to confirm him for a lifetime appointment. The Southern

Democrats wanted Supreme Court justices who would review and overturn *Brown*, but Stewart refused to provide them with that assurance. These Democrats were able to delay the Senate Judiciary Committee's confirmation vote by several months, resulting in a confirmation battle that took 108 days.[153]

The next Supreme Court nominee to run into a long delay was Thurgood Marshall, a black judge on the Court of Appeals for the Second Circuit and one of the architects behind the legal strategy that had resulted in *Brown v. Board*. Marshall, who was nominated by President Johnson in 1967, became the first black justice on the court, but only after a seventy-eight-day delay instigated by Democratic senators from the South.[154] Senator Robert Byrd (D-WV) went so far as to ask FBI director J. Edgar Hoover to investigate Marshall's links to the Communist Party.[155]

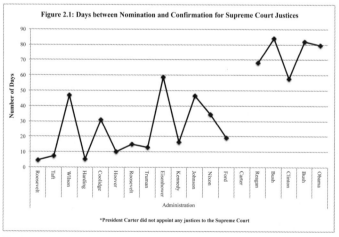

Figure 2.1: Days between Nomination and Confirmation for Supreme Court Justices

*President Carter did not appoint any justices to the Supreme Court

*To view a larger version of each graph, please refer to Supplement: Full-Page Graphs.

Figure 2.1 illustrates the lengthening of the confirmation process. The only real exception to the upward trend since the Reagan administration is the Clinton administration, when confirmation took an average of fifty-seven and a half days, about one and a half days less than it took under Eisenhower. Still, the confirmation time from the Eisenhower to Ford administrations averaged slightly less than half the time it took for nominees from Presidents Reagan through Obama. John Roberts's and Samuel Alito's confirmations under Bush II averaged eighty-two days, second only to the eighty-four-day average under Bush's father's administration. Even with the extremely large Senate majorities held by the Democrats during Obama's administration, nominees still had to wait an average of 79.5 days.

The 114-day war over Robert Bork notwithstanding, the average confirmation proceedings for the nominees in the past few administrations have not compared to Louis Brandeis' 125 days or Potter Stewart's 108 days. But for justices who were confirmed, nine of the next ten longest confirmation proceedings in the past 110 years occurred between 1986 and 2010, during the Reagan, Bush, Clinton, and Obama presidencies: Clarence Thomas, ninety-nine days; Samuel Alito, ninety-two days; Elena Kagan, eighty-seven days; Antonin Scalia, eighty-five days; William Rehnquist, eighty-two days for elevation to chief justice; Stephen Breyer, seventy-three days; John Roberts and Sonia Sotomayor, seventy-two days; and David Souter, sixty-nine days.

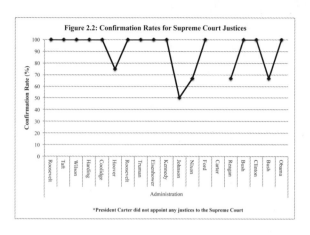

Figure 2.2: Confirmation Rates for Supreme Court Justices

*President Carter did not appoint any justices to the Supreme Court

Confirmation rates, or the proportion of nominees who are actually confirmed (Figure 2.2), provide another measure of how contentious the battles have become.

With greater frequency than ever before, a president's judicial picks are rejected. This tendency began even before the confirmation battles became so protracted. It used to be very rare for a nominee to be rejected. Between the presidencies of Theodore Roosevelt and John F. Kennedy, only one of forty-one Supreme Court nominations was denied: Herbert Hoover's 1930 nomination of John J. Parker was narrowly rejected by a 39 to 41 vote.

Parker's defeat is a matter of some controversy. His decisions as a circuit court judge had angered labor unions, and remarks he had made while running for office suggested a bias against blacks.[156] His later decisions on the Fourth Circuit Court of Appeals supported desegregation efforts, but at the time of his nomination, the National

Association for the Advancement of Colored People (NAACP) opposed him.

The rejection of Parker's nomination was the lone exception between 1874 and 1967; all the other fifty-four nominees (98 percent) to the Supreme Court were confirmed. By sharp contrast, from the Johnson through the Obama administrations, twenty-one of twenty-eight Supreme Court nominees, or 75 percent, won confirmation (Figure 2.3). Not surprisingly, this decline in confirmation rates corresponds with the increasing number of negative votes in the Senate and the slimmer victory margins. A good example of this trend is Clarence Thomas's narrow win in 1981 by 52 to 48.

Prior to the late 1960s, a confirmation battle like Thomas's hardly ever occurred.[157] About two-thirds of nominations before this time period were approved either

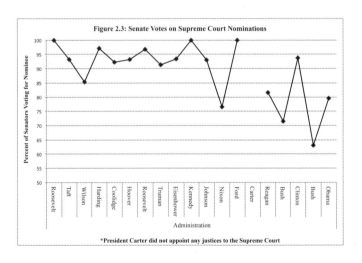

Figure 2.3: Senate Votes on Supreme Court Nominations

*President Carter did not appoint any justices to the Supreme Court

unanimously or simply by voice votes. But since then, the ratio has reversed. All four of the nominations that were withdrawn before a vote by the Senate (Homer Thornberry, Abe Fortas, Douglas Ginsburg, and Harriet E. Miers) have occurred since the late 1960s.

Confirmation Traditions: Competence, Propriety, and Temperament

> "I think that the standard has always been that character and professional qualifications are the fundamentals."[158]
> —Senator Arlen Specter, 2005

This is not the first time the judicial confirmation process has gone through a difficult period. Before and after the Civil War, confirmation hearings were politicized and divisive, though still nothing similar to our recent (and regular) drawn-out battles.[159] Excluding the five very quick confirmations during the war, the average confirmation from 1857 to 1888 lasted twenty-nine days, with the longest two taking sixty and eighty-two days. But by the beginning of the twentieth century, easygoing hearings had again become the norm, with members of the Senate focusing on a candidate's legal qualifications and integrity—not on his politics.[160] Reasons for rejecting a confirmation included a candidate breaking the law or holding a membership in a hate group, such as the Ku Klux Klan.[161]

Up until the end of the twentieth century, the Senate focused strictly on a nominee's competence, propriety, and temperament. "Competence" and "integrity" are fairly clear terms denoting whether a candidate understands the law and exhibits honesty and strong moral principles. "Judicial temperament" is less clear. The American Bar Association defines the term as a combination of "compassion, decisiveness, open-mindedness, sensitivity, courtesy, patience, freedom from bias and commitment to equal justice."[162] Such a focus largely eliminated the Senate's inquiries into candidates' personal ideologies and views on specific issues. Indeed, it would have appeared unseemly to inquire about a nominee's political views or possible future rulings.

As recently as 1977, the American Bar Association (ABA) stated that judicial nominees are to be rated solely on "professional qualifications: competence, integrity, and temperament."[163] But in 1980 the ABA signaled a change by adding the word "primarily" before "professional qualifications."[164] The ABA further opened the door into inquiries of personal philosophy and political views by stating: "The committee does not investigate the prospective nominee's political or ideological philosophy except to the extent that extreme views on such matters might bear on judicial temperament or integrity."[165]

The process itself originally involved fewer steps, as the Senate Judiciary Committee never held a single public hearing for a Supreme Court nominee until 1916 for Louis Brandeis. The next such hearing did not occur until

1925, when Harlan Fiske Stone was nominated by President Calvin Coolidge. Stone's career as a corporate lawyer stirred opposition from liberal senators, with one such senator accusing Stone of being a "tool of the House of [financier J. P.] Morgan" and of having spent "all of his life in the atmosphere of big business."[166] Stone himself proposed that he answer questions in person before the Senate Judiciary Committee.[167] After 1925, it gradually became more common to hold hearings. But it was not until 1946, when Truman nominated Fred Vinson to be chief justice, that Senate hearings became mandatory for all Supreme Court nominees.[168]

Televised hearings, which offered senators an outlet for political posturing, only began with Sandra Day O'Connor in 1981.[169] The senators' intentions may have been most evident during Samuel Alito's hearings. *The New York Times* even ran a page-one headline: "But Enough About You, Judge; Let's Hear What I Have to Say." During the most watched first day of hearings, when Alito was questioned, Senator Joseph Biden spoke 3,673 words, while Alito only uttered a mere quarter as much—1,013 words.[170] With its opportunity for national media exposure, television coverage may also have encouraged senators to ask more questions. Prior to televised hearings in 1981, it was quite common for only a few senators to ask the nominee questions. Yet, during Robert Bork's highly publicized 1987 hearings, all the Judiciary Committee senators asked questions.[171] Since that time, there has only been one single nomination hearing where a senator passed up an opportunity to question the nominee—in 1988, Senator Paul Simon (D-IL) didn't ask Anthony Kennedy any questions.

Still, television alone fails to explain the overall lengthening of confirmations, as no abrupt increase in the time to confirmation occurred when TV cameras began broadcasting the hearings. The average Senate Judiciary Committee confirmation hearing from 1900 to 1965 took just 1.2 days. From Thurgood Marshall's contentious hearing to that of John Paul Stevens, the average Judiciary Committee hearing took 4.4 days. After televised hearings began, hearings for all nominees from Reagan to Obama averaged 5.2 days; the two longest Senate Judiciary Committee hearings involved Robert Bork (fourteen days) and Clarence Thomas (eleven days).[172] That less-than-a-day change in the average pales in comparison to the thirty-seven-day change that took place in the total length of confirmations over that same period of time.

But what televised hearings may reflect is the increasing importance of judicial appointments. Television broadcasts programs that people want to watch; modern viewers may care more about who gets appointed to the Supreme Court because of the expanding role of the federal courts.

It is impossible to design a perfect system, and the practice that generally existed prior to the 1980s did not provide a guarantee against partisan battles. The changing rules are much more a symptom of an underlying problem than the cause. The big question is what changed to create these vicious battles.

Breaking with Convention

George Stephanopoulos: Well . . . except, sir, in 1967 when you were arguing for Thurgood Marshall. You warned colleagues they shouldn't take judicial philosophy into account. They shouldn't reject someone just because they disagree with [your] judicial philosophy. And you said that only background, experience, qualifications, and temperament should be considered. If it was the right standard in 1967, isn't it the right standard now?

Senator Edward Kennedy: No. Well, that, I think, has really changed and shifted, hasn't it, when the president sent Robert Bork to the Senate Judiciary Committee for nomination because it was very clear that he was selected primarily because of his judicial philosophy. They made it really an issue there and it became the issue before the Judiciary Committee and the country and I

think if someone is going to be selected just because of a judicial philosophy, then that is going to be an issue that's going to be before the Judiciary Committee.
—*This Week with George Stephanopoulos* (ABC News), July 3, 2005

"You wouldn't run for the United States Senate or for governor or for anything else without answering people's questions about what you believe. And I think the Supreme Court is no different."[173]
—Senator Evan Bayh, 2005

"This is especially true now that judges are largely nominated through an ideological prism by a president who has admitted that he wants to appoint justices in the 'mold' of Antonin Scalia and Clarence Thomas. To those who say ideology doesn't matter, they should take their quarrel to President Bush. I began to argue that a nominee's judicial ideology was crucial four years ago. Then, I was almost alone. Today there is a growing and gathering consensus on the left and on the right that these questions are legitimate, important, and often crucial.

Therefore, I—and others on both sides
of the aisle—will ask you about your
views."[174]

—Senator Charles Schumer, 2005

Confirmations became more difficult in the late 1960s, but it was not until the Reagan administration that long, drawn-out battles became a regular feature of the Supreme Court nomination process. The simultaneous confirmation hearings for William Rehnquist and Antonin Scalia in 1986 dragged out to eighty-nine and eighty-five days, respectively. As of 2012, only six justices ever waited at least as long for confirmation: Louis Brandeis (125 days in 1916); Robert Bork (114 days in 1987); Potter Stewart (108 days in 1958); Clarence Thomas (99 days in 1991); Samuel Alito (92 days in 2005-2006); and Elena Kagan (87 days in 2010).

Rehnquist's confirmation was not only long, but thirty-three senators voted against him for chief justice. He received more negative votes than any other justice confirmed to the High Court up to that point.[175] The attacks on Rehnquist in 1986 were vicious and personal and, at the time, quite shocking. Orrin Hatch remarked, "They've done everything they could to destroy this man's reputation."[176] Some of the remarks were scathing. Ted Kennedy's quotation at the beginning of the chapter insinuates that Rehnquist's brilliant mind could be used "in the service of racism and injustice."[177] Opponents claimed Rehnquist was a "John Bircher"—that is, a member of the

John Birch Society, a fairly radical right-wing group.[178] *The New York Times* noted: "Justice Rehnquist's opponents challenged his judicial ethics, his candor, his record on civil rights and individual liberty."[179] President Reagan described the charges against Rehnquist as nothing less than those of a "liberal lynch mob."[180]

Many senators couched their opposition to Rehnquist not in terms of the traditional qualifications—competence, propriety, and temperament—but through his alleged views on race. Take the 1952 memorandum that Rehnquist had written as a young law clerk for Justice Robert Jackson, which found nothing unconstitutional in racial segregation. That was two years before *Brown v. Board of Education*, and Rehnquist explained that those views were Jackson's, not his. Nevertheless, Senate Democrats seized on the memorandum as evidence of Rehnquist's racism.[181]

A particularly nasty attack—and one that temporarily posed significant problems for Rehnquist's confirmation—involved restrictive covenants on two houses that he owned in Vermont and Arizona. The covenants, which had not been enforceable for decades, were in the contract when Rehnquist bought the houses. The covenant for the Vermont home prohibited the owner from selling the house to Jews; for the Arizona home, sales to blacks were forbidden.[182] The charges over the covenants played into broad attacks against Rehnquist on civil rights issues, including accusations that he had harassed black and Hispanic voters in Phoenix during the 1960s.[183] However, those attacks on Rehnquist "lost some of [their] punch" when it was found that Joseph Biden, the ranking Democrat on the Senate Judiciary Committee, had also owned a house with a similar covenant.[184]

The issue of abortion can't explain the suddenly bitter confirmation battles under Reagan, either. During Rehnquist's confirmation process, which lasted from June 20 to September 17, 1986, there were almost three times as many news stories related to his nomination that mentioned race or discrimination than those that referenced abortion. Similarly, 70 percent more Scalia-related news stories mentioned race or discrimination over abortion during his hearings from June 23 to September 17, 1986.[185] The single hottest topic by far in the Supreme Court nomination process up through the 1986 nominations continued to be race—its effects on legal rulings, and even the nominee's own skin color, as was the case for Thurgood Marshall. The evaluation of race was also based on various statements on the part of the nominees as well as their behavior.[186] The recent opposition to Republican nominees has remained harsh even as the focal point of that opposition has evolved from race to abortion.

Scores of judges and legal scholars have questioned the 1973 Supreme Court decision in *Roe v. Wade*. As a result, many liberals were concerned that the confirmation of conservative justices placed that landmark decision at risk. For instance, Harvard University professor Laurence Tribe erroneously predicted that with Rehnquist's and

Scalia's confirmations, "In four or five years, I think *Roe v. Wade* will be overturned."[187] Pro-choice advocates such as Kate Michelman, executive director of the National Abortion Rights Action League, made similar claims.[188]

Fortunately for Scalia, the Democrats directed their fire primarily at Rehnquist, who was being elevated from associate justice to chief justice.[189] Scalia was a well-known conservative figure.[190] Before being placed on the Supreme Court, he had served as a judge on the U.S. Court of Appeals for the District of Columbia. He had also been a prominent conservative law professor and a presidential appointee during the Nixon and Ford administrations. Surely Scalia could have faced the same attacks on his ideology, but Democrats would have come across as heavy-handed and less credible if they'd gone after both Reagan nominees as being too extreme to sit on the court. Scalia also may have benefited from political calculations about offending Italian Americans, as he was the first Italian American nominated to the Supreme Court.[191] Although Scalia's confirmation was delayed, the Senate voted unanimously, 98–0, in favor of him.

When directly questioned about his ideological views, Scalia repeatedly refused to answer a long slew of questions about affirmative action, freedom of information, abortion, and the equal protection of individual rights. He managed to dodge the questions so well that Senator Biden became exasperated and asked: "Who are you, Judge Scalia? Let yourself go, because it's been pretty boring thus far." Scalia replied: "I have no agenda."[192]

However, as evidence that Scalia simply had lucky timing in 1986, one need only look at what happened when Rehnquist died in 2005. There was a brief consideration of nominating Scalia to fill the vacant chief justice position, but despite widespread acknowledgement of how bright he was, Democrats made clear that the nomination battle would be fearsome. Democratic Senate Minority Leader Harry Reid admitted at the time that Scalia was "one smart guy."[193] Biden acknowledged that Scalia was "completely competent."[194] Yet Biden also warned that appointing Scalia to succeed Rehnquist would "generate a firestorm on the Hill."[195]

Unfortunately, bitter and contentious Rehnquist-style hearings are now the norm. Following the November 1986 elections, what had been a 53–47 Republican majority dramatically reversed, becoming a 54–46 Democratic majority. The Democrats used their majority to insist for the first time that nominees answer their questions on ideology. This change in Senate control allowed for the brutal treatment of Robert Bork during his confirmation hearings to the Supreme Court. After 114 days, Bork's nomination was defeated with the largest number of "no" votes in American history.

Bork's qualifications were never in question. Senators on both sides of the aisle acknowledged that he was brilliant.[196] No one doubted that Bork had demonstrated the highest level of professional competence. He was one of the nation's best-known and best-regarded law professors, having spent seventeen years teaching at Yale Law School.

His book *The Antitrust Paradox* is one of the most influential law-and-economics books ever written,[197] a text that was used in graduate economics classes around the country. He had served with distinction as solicitor general of the United States and had been a federal appeals court judge. His opinions were notable for their occasionally elegant turn of phrase, but otherwise they were decidedly uncontroversial.

Bork had never been affiliated with any extremist groups, and his personal life did not raise any serious concerns, either. Political opponents of Bork were forced to go to great lengths to find potentially damaging material. They snooped through his video store rentals and produced a list that was leaked to the public. Unfortunately for Bork's adversaries, the worst that could be said about his rentals were that they were pretty bland fare: *Ruthless People*, *The Man Who Knew Too Much*, and *A Day at the Races*.[198] Nothing found could be used against him.

No matter how flawless and impressive his record, Bork's confirmation was a difficult sell from the beginning. His long, jargon-filled, complex answers during his hearing did not come across well on TV and his professorial style appeared condescending toward the senators. He had also made many enemies throughout his career, especially during his tenure as solicitor general for President Nixon. It was Bork who fired Archibald Cox, the special prosecutor who had been attempting to investigate the Watergate break-in. Two other political appointees, Attorney General Elliot Richardson and Deputy Attorney General William Ruckelshaus, had refused Nixon's orders to do so. Both Richardson and Ruckelshaus had promised during their confirmation hearings not to fire Cox.[199] Bork thus found himself next in line and reluctantly fired Cox. He had considered resigning, but decided that yet another top-level resignation would leave the Justice Department unable to function. Congressional Democrats used the incident to claim that Bork was engaged in a Nixon cover-up.

Opponents tried painting Bork as a dangerous right-wing extremist utterly out of touch with mainstream America. As soon as he was nominated, Senator Ted Kennedy infamously ripped into him: "In Robert Bork's America, women would be forced into back-alley abortions, blacks would sit at segregated lunch counters, rogue police could break down citizens' doors in midnight raids. School children could not be taught evolution."[200]

Even Alabama Democratic Senator Howell Heflin, normally temperate, used extreme language: "If the evidence shows that you are intelligent but an ideologue, a zealot, that you are principled but prejudiced, that you are competent but closed-minded, then there is considerable doubt as to whether you will be confirmed by the Senate."[201]

Of course, Bork was a conservative, but he was no more an extremist than Ronald Reagan, the president who appointed him. Yet the left felt threatened by him, and were sufficiently organized to stop Bork's confirmation.[202]

A number of organizations—the National Organization for Women, the American Civil Liberties Union, Planned Parenthood, and others—charged that Bork's "extremist" conservative ideology would undermine the judicial doctrines they embraced. Bork frightened opponents not just because he represented another vote, but because his brilliance had the potential to provide the intellectual ammunition that could shift the course of debates within the Supreme Court.[203, 204]

Abortion-rights advocates worried that replacing the retiring Justice Powell with Bork could tip the balance against them.[205] Yet abortion was more an excuse than a reason for Bork's defeat, as evidenced by the fact that the issue did not determine the fate of the two nominees who followed him. Douglas Ginsburg was viewed as a candidate who supported abortion, but that did not ensure his confirmation; similarly, Anthony Kennedy's opposition to abortion did not prevent his confirmation.[206]

Still, it is interesting to note how Bork, Ginsburg, and Kennedy compared on another dimension: intellect. As with Bork, Ginsburg's intelligence was highly touted. Liberal academic Alan Dershowitz, a former colleague of Ginsburg's at Harvard Law School, described Ginsburg as a "brilliant academic."[207] Former classmates referred to him as "absolutely brilliant."[208] Yet Ginsburg also failed to make it through the confirmation process. Some critics, such as Ralph Neas, president of People for the American Way, actually warned that Ginsburg's intelligence was one reason to keep him off the court.[209] Interestingly, Anthony Kennedy, the successful nominee who was confirmed unanimously by the Senate, was not the intellectual powerhouse of these previous nominations. Many lawyers agreed that Kennedy was "not brilliant in the way that Judge Robert H. Bork is"[210] and that he was "lacking Bork's brilliant reasoning."[211]

This was not the first time concerns had been raised about a potential Supreme Court justice's intelligence. Back in 1986, Aaron Director, the founder of the field of law and economics, personally told me that the main reason Judge Richard Posner, who is discussed at length in Chapter 5, would not make it to the Supreme Court was that he was simply "too brilliant."

The defeat of Robert Bork, whose brilliance was universally acknowledged, still to this day remains an open wound for some conservatives.

Confirmations after Bork

Confirmations have never been the same since the Rehnquist and Bork battles in 1986 and 1987. Some claim confirmation battles arise over nominees with strong views on controversial issues. Political commentator George Will has called this phenomenon the "Souterization" of public life,[212] referring to David Souter, whose views on the big polarizing issues were not clear, yet he was confirmed easily to the court.

One nomination, President Bush's selection of Harriet Miers in October 2005, shows that it is intelligence—not public views on controversial issues such as abortion—that has the largest impact on the chances of a successful confirmation. Bush said that he picked Miers over Fifth Circuit Court Judge Priscilla Owen in part because "[he] knew her better."[213] Miers had worked closely with the president while first serving as his deputy chief of staff for policy and then as the White House counsel. They had also known each other in Texas. But she had no real paper trail on most controversial issues. Bush appears to have viewed her as a "Souter"-type nominee, a largely "stealth" candidate.[214]

The one rare issue where Miers had taken a firm public stand—support for a constitutional ban on abortion except to save a mother's life—should have sent Democrats to the barricades. After all, it had become their signature issue during confirmation battles, and her opposition was clearer and stronger than that of other Republican nominees whom they had opposed.[215] Yet Democratic opposition to her was quite "muted."[216] Even though Republicans understood that Bush and some prominent conservatives would vouch for her political views,[217] it was Republicans who opposed her nomination, because they wanted a stronger, more influential candidate whose arguments might swing future Supreme Court decisions.

CBS's chief legal correspondent Jan Crawford Greenburg described Miers in her book, *Supreme Conflict: The Inside Story of the Struggle for Control of the United States*

Supreme Court, as someone Republican senators and lawyers considered very weak, who did not understand the law, and who could not express her views clearly.[218] Important Democrats actually supported her nomination. Senate Democratic Minority Leader Harry Reid pointedly announced: "I like Harriet Miers."[219] On the other hand, as National Public Radio noted, "Republican Opposition Made Miers Bid Untenable."

It was Republicans, not Democrats, who were planning on asking Miers tough questions designed to demonstrate her weaknesses. As *The Boston Globe* reported: "[Republicans] believe that a better strategy is to make her appear unqualified. Some of the questions from social conservative groups are similar to law school exams, aimed at testing Miers's knowledge of legal doctrines. Others demand specific information about her credentials, framed in a skeptical voice."[220] Six of the ten Republican senators on the Senate Judiciary Committee were described by *The New York Times* as opposing her nomination.[221]

With such strong opposition from Republicans over her lack of intelligence, as opposed to her conservative views, Miers's nomination collapsed very quickly, lasting just over three weeks. She was nominated on October 3, and she withdrew her nomination on October 27.[222]

Clarence Thomas provides yet another example of how a nominee's intelligence can affect the process. Thomas was nominated in 1991 by President George H. W. Bush to succeed Thurgood Marshall. Liberal interest groups and politicians savagely assaulted Thomas, a judge on the Court of Appeals for the District of Columbia Circuit.

Many spoke highly of Thomas's intellect. Take Armen Alchian, an economics professor at the University of California-Los Angeles, who lectured in a program that taught economics to federal judges during the 1980s and early 1990s. During that time he had a chance to teach some 300 judges,[223] including a then circuit court judge named Clarence Thomas. Alchian told me that Thomas was "very intelligent, very smart" and "while so many of them were extremely bright," Thomas was probably "one of the few brightest" students that he ever had.[224]

As noted earlier, one fear that opponents have is that a particularly bright justice might make arguments that sway other members of the Supreme Court. Indeed, in Thomas's case, that fear was well founded. In 2011, CNN's legal analyst Jeffrey Toobin wrote: "In several of the most important areas of constitutional law, Thomas has emerged as an intellectual leader of the Supreme Court. . . . when it comes to the free-speech rights of corporations, the rights of gun owners, and, potentially, the powers of the federal government; in each of these areas, the majority has followed where Thomas has been leading for a decade or more. Rarely has a Supreme Court justice enjoyed such broad or significant vindication."[225] Jan Crawford Greenburg relates a story in *Supreme Conflict* about how Thomas's strongly argued dissent in his third case on the court prompted both Scalia and Rehnquist to change their positions.[226] Others have made similar comments about Thomas's influence and intelligence.[227]

Thomas was undoubtedly a highly successful black conservative who strongly and publicly disagreed with the liberal and black political establishments on racial issues, economics, and abortion.[228] Liberals no doubt feared that Thomas would assault their causes. His brilliant mind only made him more of a threat.

As with Bork, left-wing groups tried hard to find something in Thomas's personal archives that would be damaging to his reputation and initially came up empty-handed. And then Anita Hill, a former colleague of Thomas's at the EEOC, came forward and publicly claimed that Thomas had made unwanted sexual comments to her. At first, members of the Senate Judiciary Committee did not pay the accusations much heed—after all, the alleged offenses had taken place years before, and Hill had since continued working for Thomas and received a promotion. Thomas adamantly denied every aspect of the accusations, and there were no witnesses or evidence to substantiate them. But so much was viewed to be at stake that these claims, which in previous nominations would never have seen the light of day, were granted a public investigation. The result was the surreal televised public hearings that transfixed the attention of the entire country. Thomas famously denounced the spectacle as a "high-tech lynching."[229]

Thomas was finally confirmed, after ninety-nine days, by a narrow 52–48 vote. The brutal hearing is long over, but scars remain. Several years later, a significant portion of Americans still believed that Thomas was guilty of "something."[230] Many assumed that surely where there was so much smoke, there was at least a little fire. Though Thomas narrowly escaped defeat, his hearings showed how far opponents were willing to go to overthrow a nomination.

A final contrast can be provided by President Obama's nominations to the Supreme Court. Given that Senate Democrats held large supermajorities when Sonia Sotomayor (sixty Democrats) and Elena Kagan (fifty-nine Democrats) were nominated, neither faced serious opposition during their confirmation battles. Yet it is generally understood that Kagan was significantly smarter than Sotomayor. For example, when David Souter's retirement from the court was announced in May 2009, Harvard Law Professor Laurence Tribe wrote to Obama: "Bluntly put, [Sotomayor is] not nearly as smart as she seems to think she is. . . . [Kagan] would be a much more formidable match for Justice Scalia than Justice Breyer has been—and certainly [more] than a Justice Sotomayor . . . ."[231] Consistent with the discussion here, Kagan faced more opposition than Sotomayor; thirty-seven and thirty-one senators voted against the two nominees respectively.

There are lots of examples where political opponents fight hardest against the smartest judicial nominees. Alas, any discussion of Supreme Court nominees cannot go beyond an anecdotal analysis as there have been too few nominations. Fortunately, circuit and district court nominations are plentiful enough for serious statistical analysis. That will be the subject of the next chapter.

3: THE FIGHT OVER LOWER COURT APPOINTMENTS

"We have reached the point in the
confirmation process where both sides of
the aisle consider intellectual distinction
a threatening characteristic in a judicial
nominee."[232]

—Judge J. Harvie Wilkinson, 2002

The highly publicized Supreme Court confirmation fights are the ones capturing national attention. But largely unnoticed are the everyday tussles over nominees appointed to the lower federal courts, even though these judges also play an important role in shaping the law. The lowest federal courts, the district courts (or "trial courts"), have a major impact on the application of law. District court judges make findings of fact that rarely form the basis of any appeal. For instance, the 1984 decisions made by District Court Judge Harold Greene in the antitrust suit against AT&T led to the breakup of the Bell Telephone System.[233]

At the next level, the circuit courts of appeals review the legal rulings of the district courts, and they shape the law for all the district courts within their circuit. Circuit court judges often look to other circuit courts for guidance.

Although the Supreme Court's verdicts affect the entire country, circuit courts are typically the final arbiter in their circuits, and few of their decisions are successfully challenged. Unlike the circuit courts, the Supreme Court gets to select which cases it will hear. Typically, it will hear 100 or fewer cases of the more than 60,000 circuit court decisions each year; that means that fewer than 1 out of every 600 circuit court decisions will be reviewed by the Supreme Court.[234] Circuit court decisions are virtually always the final word on legal doctrine in their circuit. As a result, circuit court judges have great power. In the years between Supreme Court judgeship vacancies, the Senate and interest groups pay even closer attention to the circuit judge nominations.

Placing Blame

Republicans and Democrats may not agree on much when it comes to confirming judges, but they do agree that a problem exists and that it is getting worse. While significant Supreme Court battles started occurring in the 1960s, nominees for all the federal courts faced consistently more difficult confirmations only from the 1980s on. Who is at fault? That debate has gone on for so long that many observers cannot even remember when it started or what triggered it. Alas, the debate has gone nowhere and the arguments put forth today are almost identical to the ones in the past. The partisan bickering continues predictably back and forth according to which party controls the presidency and the Senate. Consider the following examples.

- After Democrats took control of the Senate during the last two years of Reagan's second term, Republicans charged that Democrats had "stalled Reagan's nominees."[235] Democrats responded that the delays were really the Republicans' fault because of "tardiness in responding to committee information requests on nominees."[236]

- When Bill Clinton was president, he complained, "I don't want [judicial nominees] denied their opportunity to [be confirmed] because of their race. . . . [T]he quality of justice suffers when highly qualified women and minority candidates are denied the opportunity to serve."[237] Senator Orrin Hatch (R-UT) shot back that President Clinton's accusation of bias was "reckless and unfounded."[238]

- In 2005, former Senator Bob Dole (R-KS) noted, "President Bush has the lowest appellate-court confirmation rate of any modern president."[239] Somehow, using the same numbers, Senator Patrick Leahy (D-VT) came to the opposite conclusion, claiming, "We put through 208 of President Bush's nominees. We've held back 10. That's a 95 percent success rate. That's more than just about any president. That's more than President George Washington."[240]

- In April 2010, just over one year into the Obama administration, Senator Chuck Schumer (D-NY) was calling the delay in confirmations "just unpardonable, unexplainable."[241] By January 2011, *The New York*

Times complained: "Partisan obstruction was also the only plausible reason that Republicans declined to allow confirmation" for some nominees.[242]

A certain degree of differing partisan interpretations of data is surely unavoidable. However, the choice to include or ignore data often turns out to be blatantly partisan. Senator Leahy's claim that only ten Bush nominees were held back includes only nominees for whom a floor vote was held. He conveniently left out the fifteen judges who were never even allowed a final up-or-down vote. When Democrats complained about how their nominees were treated during Bill Clinton's administration, their data certainly included nominees who did not get a vote as a result of the nominee's home-state senator's disapproval or because another senator put a "hold" on the nomination. Another example of cherry-picking statistics is when circuit and district court judges are counted separately. In his statement, Dole focused only on circuit court nominees, whereas Leahy counted both.

It is easy to see why different politicians choose different statistics. District court appointments seldom get the attention that circuit court appointments do, but district court nominations are far more numerous. With 228 district and 51 circuit court nominees during George W. Bush's first term, Democrats like Leahy can argue that they have approved a large number of Republican judicial appointments. But that claim hides the real battles over the more important nominations.

What does the complete data tell us about the battles? Who faces the longest confirmation process? Who gets rejected and why? I have gathered a very large data set—just the information for circuit court judges is over six times larger than that used in previous research—to answer these questions.[243] The data examined here on the length of confirmations and the confirmation rate covers the period when judicial confirmation became more contentious. We have data on all nominations to circuit and district court judgeships during the past five administrations—those of Presidents Carter, Reagan, George H. W. Bush, Clinton, and George W. Bush. Data are also included for the first two years of Obama's administration.

Confirmation Delays

Time after time the nominees who I interviewed talked about the personal costs of the delays in their confirmations. The length of confirmations not only measures how long a nominee's life has been put on hold, but it also is related to how vicious the confirmations have been. Over the past three decades, the time it takes for federal judges to be confirmed has lengthened enormously. Figure 3.1 illustrates the length of confirmations, organized according to the session of Congress in which a person was first nominated.

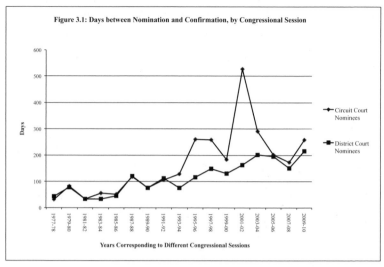

Figure 3.1: Days between Nomination and Confirmation, by Congressional Session

*To view a larger version of each graph, please refer to Supplement: Full-Page Graphs.

The data in Figure 3.1 show a definite upward trend, with the pattern changing at certain points. In general, three distinct periods for judicial confirmations can be discerned over the past thirty years.

The first period runs from the Carter administration through the first six years of the Reagan administration. During this time, the length of the confirmation process for district and circuit court nominees remained consistent at about fifty days.

The second period extends from the last two years of Reagan's second term through the first two years of Clinton's first term. With the Democratic takeover of the Senate in 1987, the confirmation process suddenly took more than twice as long. It took Reagan's nominees, for district and circuit courts, an average of 120 days to get confirmed.

The third and current period starts in 1995, when Republicans gained control of the Senate during the Clinton administration. Two things happened during this time. Confirmations for circuit court nominees for the first time began to take substantially longer than confirmations for the district courts. Also, the confirmation process slowed even more, though there were extremely large ups and downs over time. The confirmation process for circuit judges during the first two years of George W. Bush's first term took dramatically longer than it had during the last two years of the Clinton administration. It took about 527 days, more than twice as long as at the slowest period of the Clinton presidency, even though confirmations are typically at their speediest early in each presidential administration and at their slowest toward the end. So, not only was the confirmation process during the first two years of George W. Bush's presidency amazingly slow compared with any prior standard, they were particularly slow considering that it was the beginning of his term. As we will soon see, much of this gap can be explained as a result of different parties controlling the presidency and the Senate—in this case, a Republican president and a Democratic-controlled Senate.

Since the Obama administration isn't finished, it is possible, though exceedingly unlikely, that the graphs for the circuit court nominees might change. A couple circuit court nominees (Victoria Nourse and Caitlin Halligan) who were first nominated during the 111th Congress had not yet confirmed by August 2012, but they are very controversial nominees. All of Obama's district court nominees from the 111th Congress have already been decided on.

Nevertheless, it is clear that the confirmation of Obama's circuit court nominees is about as slow as the worst four years under the Clinton administration; only the Bush II administration during its first two years experienced significantly more trouble. The length of confirmations for Obama's district court nominees is also longer than every other president. Even though Democrats controlled the Senate during both Obama's and Clinton's first two years in office, the estimate for circuit court nominees for Obama's first two years is about twice as long as Clinton's first two years. On the other hand, it took George W. Bush's nominees about twice as long as Obama's to get confirmed.

The confirmation process has lengthened regardless of who is president or who controls the Senate. But having opposing parties control the presidency and the Senate plays an important role in adding to the delays. As we shall see in Chapter 4, when the same party controls both the presidency and the Senate, the confirmation process only takes about half as long. But, even after accounting for these differences, there is a clear trend over time: confirmations keep getting longer. The change seems to be a lasting one.

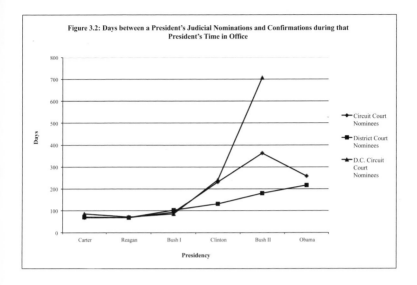

Figure 3.2: Days between a President's Judicial Nominations and Confirmations during that President's Time in Office

Figure 3.2 shows data on the time to confirmation by presidential administration rather than by congressional session. Not surprisingly, the pattern is similar to that portrayed in Figure 3.1. Assembling the information by presidential terms confirms the consistent lengthening of the confirmation process, at least since the first Bush administration.

As seen in Figure 3.2, the lengthening confirmations have been dramatic for circuit court nominees. Clinton's nominations took more than twice as long as those for his predecessor, George H. W. Bush. And George W. Bush's nominees took twice as long as Clinton's. The data for the first two years of the Obama administration indicates that his nominations took only 13 percent longer than Clinton's. Even these long delays likely underestimate the changes that have been occurring in the confirmation process; the figures won't capture those nominees who decided not to go through the process in fear of the battle to come.

Over the past five full administrations, the greatest change occurred for nominees to the U.S. Court of Appeals for the D.C. Circuit. As of this writing, no nominees to this court have been confirmed yet for Obama. The D.C. Circuit Court hears a large number of important cases involving the activities of the federal government. More than any other court, it has become the proving ground for future Supreme Court justices. Four recent members of the current Supreme Court were elevated from the D.C. Circuit: Ruth Bader Ginsburg, John Roberts, Antonin Scalia, and Clarence Thomas.

From 1977 to 1992, under Presidents Carter, Reagan, and George H. W. Bush, the average time from nomination to confirmation for the D.C. Circuit was less than eighty-seven days. In sharp contrast, under Clinton, the process took an average of 242 days. This figure rose still further to an astonishing 707 days under George W. Bush. The increase was not just a statistical fluke due to an unusual case, although there were not a huge number of nominees: Carter had four; Reagan, sixteen; George H. W. Bush, nine; Clinton, nine; and George W. Bush, six.

Looking at Figures 3.1 and 3.2 should put past debates into perspective. The delays in confirmations that so angered Republican partisans during the Reagan and first Bush administrations seemed major at the time, but appear trivial compared with the even longer delays experienced by later administrations.

Figures 3.3 and 3.4 provide another angle on the past political battles. A common perception was reflected in the following statement appearing in the *San Francisco Chronicle* in 2005: "It is important to remember that the source of this conflict is the handful of ideological extremists that President Bush insists on nominating to the federal judiciary."[244] But that simply was not so, as the delays were not confined to a few nominees. Instead, a broad-based pattern emerged of increasingly longer confirmation battles.

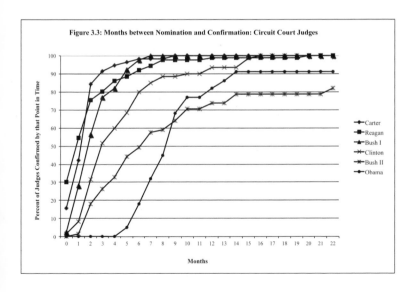

Figure 3.3: Months between Nomination and Confirmation: Circuit Court Judges

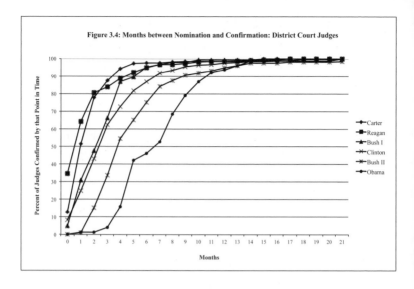

Figure 3.4: Months between Nomination and Confirmation: District Court Judges

Again, we can see in Figures 3.3 and 3.4 how the delay became most pronounced for circuit court nominees. For example, 55 percent of Reagan nominees to the circuit courts were confirmed within two months. But it took three months under George H. W. Bush to attain the same proportion of confirmed nominees. Then the delays got much worse during the next two administrations. It took four and a half months for Clinton; seven months for George W. Bush; and *eight* months for Obama. The ever-increasing delays can be seen in Figure 3.3.

Normally, with a filibuster-proof 60 Democrat Senators during part of Obama's first two years in office, Obama should have had no problem getting all of his nominees confirmed. Even when Democrats only had 59 Senators, they needed just one Republican to break a filibuster.

The long initial lag in confirming Obama's circuit and district court nominations is largely explained by two facts. First, the Senate Judiciary Committee was busy with two consecutive Supreme Court nominations. A similar delay was observed for George W. Bush's circuit court confirmations during the 109th Congress (2005-2006), when there were also two Supreme Court nominations.

Secondly, Obama was much slower than previous presidents in nominating judges. Five of Obama's twenty-five nominees for the circuit cou rt weren't announced until five months before the November mid-term elections, a time when it becomes difficult for any nominations to be considered. In contrast, George W. Bush was much quicker when he came into office, with only one out of thirty-two circuit court nominations during his first two years in office made that close to his first mid-term election.

One can quibble over whether, under President Obama, the percent of circuit court judges confirmed tops out at 91 or 95 percent after 14 months. It all depends on how one counts Caitlin Halligan's experience. Halligan's nomination to be a circuit court judge ended in a filibuster in December 2011, and the Senate could be viewed as having rendered its verdict at that time. Yet, Obama refused to accept "no" for an answer and renominated her for the same judgeship on June 11, 2012. Given how late she was renominated in a presidential election year, it is doubtful that Obama was serious about this renomination.

The delays at the district court level have been less severe, but differences are apparent there, too. For example, 35 percent of Reagan's district court nominees were confirmed within one month of nomination, whereas that proportion was not attained for nominees under Clinton, George W. Bush, and Obama until three, four, and six months respectively after judges nominations.

Confirmation Rates

The length of time to confirmation is not the only measure of how contentious nomination hearings have become. The confirmation rate—the percentage of nominees confirmed by the Senate—is just as important. If we are to believe that news coverage reflects public opinion, it's telling that a LexisNexis search of news stories appearing between June 30, 2004, and July 1, 2005, found almost the same number of news stories discussing both issues.[245] Generally mirroring the longer delays, a lower percentage of nominees were confirmed to the circuit courts up through George W. Bush's administration. Indeed, while confirmation lengths have gotten shorter during Obama's first two years, his confirmation rates have shot up even more dramatically.

The very high circuit court confirmation rates under Obama likely occurred for two reasons. First, with Democrats holding a massive majority in the Senate during 2009 and 2010, it was impossible for Republicans to actually defeat any of Obama's nominations. Secondly, any delays were not sufficiently long to cause nominees to withdraw their names from consideration. (Such withdrawals seldom occur unless the confirmation drags on over at least a couple of Congresses, and the data set for Obama only covers one Congress.)

Unlike the data for confirmation delays, confirmation rates for district and circuit court judges combined (Figure 3.5) reveal no real pattern. The confirmation rates for district court nominees in the 2003–2004 session were almost exactly the same as in the 1977–1978 or 2009–2010

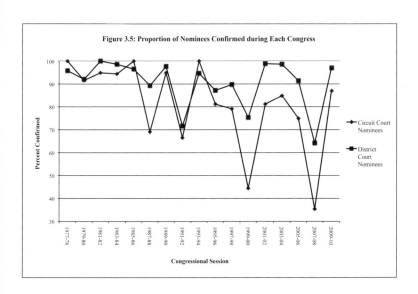

Figure 3.5: Proportion of Nominees Confirmed during Each Congress

sessions.

Even so, confirmation rates have fluctuated over time. During fourteen of the seventeen congressional sessions, district court confirmation rates were 87 percent or higher. But in the last two years of the administrations of George H. W. Bush, Clinton, and George W. Bush, the district court confirmation rates fell to 72, 75, and 64 percent respectively. These anomalies appear to be a "lame duck" effect, where opposition senators believe they can stop a nomination simply by delaying a vote until after the president is out of office. Nominations have to be renewed with every new Congress, and when a new president from a different party is elected, nominations made by the previous president simply die.

The impact of this effect is clear for both types of courts. However, once again, the effect is much more pronounced for the more important circuit courts than for the district courts. The line for circuit courts (Figure 3.5) shows dips before each presidential election. Interestingly, the two smallest changes occurred in 1984 and 1996, years in which an incumbent president was running for reelection and was fairly sure to win. Thus, there would have been little prospect of killing a nomination by delaying consideration until after the election.

There are also other patterns. Just as the confirmation process lengthened primarily for circuit court nominees, confirmation rates also dropped substantially for those same nominees. The circuit court confirmation rate ranged from 92 to 100 percent between 1977 and 1986 and reached 100 percent during the Clinton administration's first two years. Since then, however, the rate had not risen above 82 percent until the first two years of the Obama administration, when it reached 87 percent. But Republicans were only able to filibuster very controversial nominees who were appointed so late in 2010 that their confirmation votes were put off until the 122nd Congress when Democrats were reduced to holding only a 53- to 47-seat majority.

Political supporters of Bill Clinton and George W. Bush have complained that too many of their nominees were rejected. Although Clinton suffered his lowest two-year confirmation rate (44 percent) during his last two years in office, the data suggests that the decline in confirmation rates for circuit judge nominees continued under George W. Bush. His first term saw a lower confirmation rate (83 percent) than in Clinton's first term (91 percent), and his confirmation rate for his eight years in office was slightly lower than the confirmation rate for Clinton's (72 to 74 percent).

Excluding the preliminary data for Obama, the pattern across all congressional sessions is one of sharply declining confirmation rates for circuit judges. It falls from 100 percent during Carter's first two years to 71 percent during the first two years of George W. Bush's second term.

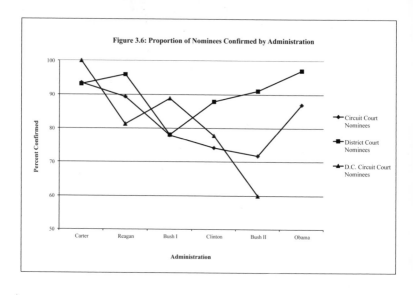

Figure 3.6: Proportion of Nominees Confirmed by Administration

The changes across administrations reveal a much clearer pattern than do changes across Congresses (Figure 3.6). The data show that, administration by administration, circuit court confirmation rates have fallen continuously since the Carter presidency. In sharp contrast, however, district court confirmation rates have actually risen substantially after George H. W. Bush was president. The stakes for circuit court appointments have apparently become much higher. Consequently, politicians who want to deflect criticism for rejecting circuit court nominees can point to the combined statistics for district and circuit courts.

Both parties clearly recognize the D.C. Circuit Court's special role and therefore make confirmation to that court especially difficult. During the Clinton administration, seven of nine nominees to the D.C. Circuit were confirmed, but George W. Bush was less successful, with only three of six nominations confirmed.

Comparing Judicial and Cabinet Nominations

> "[Michael Mukasey] is clearly smart, but sometimes smart can get you in trouble."[246]
> —Anonymous former high-ranking Republican Justice Department official discussing Mukasey's nomination to be attorney general, September 21, 2007

> "[Rice] uses her brilliance for, again, some very, very problematic, if not downright pernicious, ends and aims. That's what upsets me about Condoleezza Rice."[247]
> —Professor Cornel West, on NPR's *The Tavis Smiley Show*, November 17, 2004

The Senate is responsible for approving many other types of confirmations beyond judgeships. Thus we can also examine whether similar patterns exist for other high officials. The most important positions have the most at stake and ought to show the greatest contentiousness over confirmations—longer battles and lower confirmation rates. Further, positions that have gained increased power should also prove harder to attain. Comparing judicial confirmation battles to those for other nominations allows us to rank the relative changing importance of judges.

Besides judges, the most prominent confirmation battles involve cabinet secretaries. The number of cabinet positions varies during the six administrations that we study here, and there are sixteen for President Obama. These positions cover the secretaries of agriculture, commerce, defense, education, energy, health and human services, homeland security, housing and urban development, interior, labor, state, transportation, treasury, and veterans affairs, as well as the attorney general of the United States. The largest department is defense, with a budget of $664 billion in 2010 and over 3 million employees if one includes the 1.1 million reservists.[248] The smallest department is education, with only 5,000 employees in 2007, but it still had a budget of $107 billion in 2010.[249] Running even the smallest cabinet department is a very powerful job.

Surely, quick confirmation of the cabinet member is important, though departments can still run with other high-level political appointees. But, with a vacancy crisis frequently claimed for the judiciary, the same argument has been made for quickly confirming judges.[250]

Figures 3.7 and 3.8 illustrate a striking difference both in duration and in confirmation rates for cabinet positions. Despite their authority, the average cabinet position has nowhere near as contentious a confirmation as the average judicial appointment. Figure 3.7 shows the time between the announcement of a cabinet nominee and confirmation as well as the time between the Senate's official receipt of the nomination and confirmation; the latter time frame is most comparable to judicial confirmations as judicial nominations are forwarded to the Senate immediately after they are announced. The time to confirmation, counted from the date the Senate receives a cabinet nomination, has remained generally unchanged, varying by at most seventeen days. Circuit court confirmations under George W. Bush took over twenty times longer than the average for cabinet members. Surprisingly, even the relatively uncontroversial district court nominees under Bush took eleven times longer than the average.

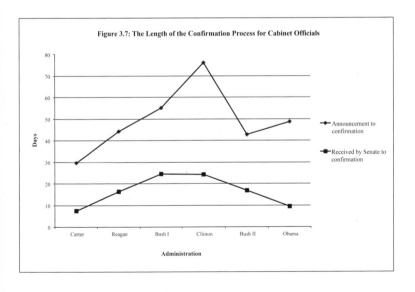

Figure 3.7: The Length of the Confirmation Process for Cabinet Officials

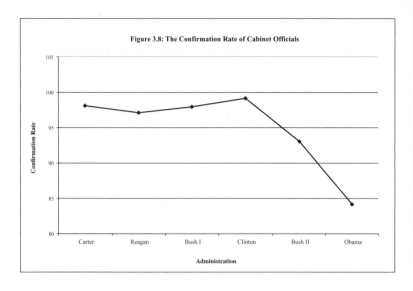

Figure 3.8: The Confirmation Rate of Cabinet Officials

The evidence in Figure 3.7 differs from the earlier evidence in another way. According to the figures presented earlier, judicial confirmations have become especially lengthy and contentious ever since the Clinton administration. Cabinet posts show quite a different pattern: Senate battles lengthened between the Carter and Bush I administrations, and then fell back near the level for Carter. During the Obama administration, the uptick in the number of days between when a nominee was announced and confirmed primarily represents something that the Senate had no control over: Obama announced most of his cabinet choices very soon after the November 2008 election. Nominations couldn't be officially forwarded to the Senate until Obama had been sworn into office, thus increasing the length of confirmation from announcement to confirmation. But once his nominees were forwarded to the Senate, confirmations followed very quickly, on average in just fifteen days.

Virtually all cabinet nominees up through Bush II were confirmed, and confirmation rates never fell below those for district or circuit court nominees until the preliminary figures for the Obama administration. One of Obama's three cabinet nominees, New Hampshire Republican Senator Judd Gregg, withdrew for reasons that had nothing to do with the confirmation process—he simply decided that he could not work with the Democratic Obama administration.[251] Indeed, for the Clinton and both Bush administrations, the gaps between cabinet and judicial confirmation rates are quite large, and the differences in confirmation rates between cabinet and circuit court nominees increased over time.

The length of confirmations as well as the decreasing confirmation rates indicate that senators regard circuit court nominations as generally much more important than cabinet nominations and that the courts' relative importance is increasing over time. Even the district court positions seem more important to senators than cabinet positions. Meanwhile, over time, the circuit court judges have been perceived as increasingly crucial.

Many factors correlate with difficult, delayed, or defeated judicial confirmations. Younger nominees have a harder time. After all, younger judges will have more of an impact since they will be on a court for more years. Candidates nominated by a president from a different party than one that controls the Senate are more likely to be delayed or defeated. The year of a president's term in office makes a difference, too: earlier nominees have a better chance of being confirmed before the political pressures of the next presidential campaign assert themselves. The number of nominations pending before the Senate also matters, with more nominations slowing down the process and lowering the confirmation rate.

The most politically explosive allegations during the confirmation process involve a nominee's sex, race, or religion. For instance, have Republicans particularly targeted blacks and women? Have Catholics faced more difficult confirmations because of their opposition to abortion?

To evaluate the accusation that increased "delays in approving Clinton's minority and female judges showed racist and sexist tendencies in the Senate," I constructed Figure 3.9.[252] (Since those claims were based on aggregating the confirmations for district and circuit judges, I have constructed this diagram for all District and Circuit court nominees.) Indeed, the figure reveals an increase in the length of confirmations for blacks, Hispanics, and women during the Clinton administration. But the length of confirmations of whites also increased, and it took Clinton's white nominees slightly longer to be confirmed than his black ones (148 to 141 days). Clinton's female nominees did take longer than his male ones (172 to 148), but George W. Bush's female nominees also faced relatively long confirmations (240 to 205).

It has taken George W. Bush's black or female nominees even longer to get confirmed than it did under Clinton—an average of 182 days versus 141 for blacks, and 240 versus 172 for women. Only Clinton's Hispanic nominees took much more time to be confirmed than his white nominees (234 versus 148 days), as did Bush's Hispanic ones (234 versus 188 days), but there is no evidence of systematic discrimination against Clinton's minority nominees as a whole. The Clinton administration's only legitimate complaint was that it was taking longer for every group to be confirmed.

Some Republicans have accused Democrats of discriminating against Catholics or evangelical Christians. Former Senate Republican Majority Leader Bill Frist argued in early 2005 that such discrimination exists.[253] On the other hand, President Bush was skeptical and said that

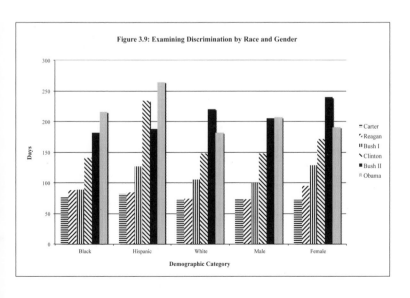

Figure 3.9: Examining Discrimination by Race and Gender

he did "not believe that Democratic opposition to his judicial nominees was based on religious discrimination ... I don't subscribe a person's opposing my nominations to an issue of faith. I think people oppose my nominees because of judicial philosophy."[254]

I collected data on the religious affiliation of circuit court nominees nominated up through 2004. This information came from news coverage of their confirmations and a search of their biographies in *Who's Who*. Unfortunately, for most nominees, no information was available, and for many faiths, there were too few nominees to study. I found the religious affiliation for 130 of the 345 circuit court nominees. It is unclear whether the rarity of these mentions is due to the media's dislike of publicizing the nominees' religious beliefs, or if they simply do not consider these beliefs to be important public knowledge. Except for the lack of an entry in *Who's Who*, which is determined by the person who is the subject of the entry, it is not clear how much of this lack of information is on the part of the nominee or the media. (For Supreme Court nominees, religious views are always reported, but so few Supreme Court nominees exist that it is hard to determine any patterns.)

Large differences do exist in the length of the confirmation process across different religions (Figure 3.10). The four religious groups with the longest averages are Mormons (463 days), Lutherans (349 days), United Church of Christ members (223 days), and Methodists (158 days). Caution should be used before drawing any conclusions, though, as the samples are very small—only four, three, two, and eight people respectively are associated with each of these religious groups. For the Mormons, a single nominee largely drives their high average: Richard Paez, a Clinton nominee to the Ninth Circuit, waited 1,505 days—over four years—to be confirmed by the Republican-controlled Senate.[255] It is hard to argue that there was discrimination against Mormons based on just this one nomination, but if there *was* discrimination against Mormons, it occurred against one single Democratic Mormon.

Still, despite the low numbers, there are some statistically significant differences.[256] On average, it took Jews 151 days to be confirmed—significantly more than the 118 days for Catholics, 106 days for Baptists, and 105

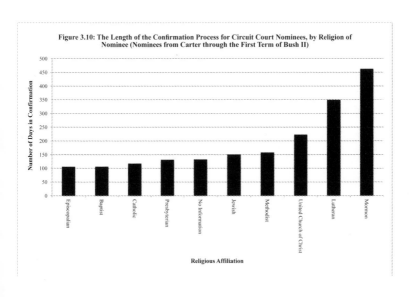

Figure 3.10: The Length of the Confirmation Process for Circuit Court Nominees, by Religion of Nominee (Nominees from Carter through the First Term of Bush II)

days for Episcopalians. The confirmation process for Christians as a group took 143 days, significantly shorter than that for Jews.

This implies that Christians as a group fared well over the five administrations studied, with Catholics, Baptists, Episcopalians, and Methodists all enjoying much shorter than average confirmations. Those whose religious views are not publicly known tend to take slightly longer than average to be confirmed. (Interestingly, no nominee was identified as an atheist.) The numbers cannot measure the intensity of religious fervor, which is what may really be at stake. But, at least using this rough data, it seems that President Bush has the stronger argument in the earlier quotation—that religious affiliation by itself doesn't make confirmations more difficult.

Huge changes have occurred over the last six presidential administrations in the judicial confirmation process. Increasingly, the more important the court, the greater the difficulty in getting a nominee confirmed. The confirmation rates have fallen and the length of the confirmation process has lengthened dramatically across the board. The next chapter will measure whether the smarter nominees have more difficult confirmations after accounting for other factors that might explain the length or rate of confirmations.

4: WHO HAS THE TOUGHEST TIME GETTING CONFIRMED?

> "The fact that neither party can predictably get its qualified people on the courts of appeals suggests that the problem of judicial nominations is more institutional than is acknowledged by partisans who play the blame game over judges. . . . And in the partisan war, the other side's talent is to be feared."[257]
> —*The Washington Post*, June 11, 2002

Can we establish a solid connection between the qualifications of judicial nominees and their chances for a smooth confirmation? To examine whether "smarter" or more persuasive nominees have a more difficult time being confirmed, we need to find some way to measure this. One way is by looking at information available at the time of their confirmation: did they go to a top law school, graduate at the top of their class, or clerk for prestigious circuit courts or the Supreme Court? Only those students at the top of their class serve on law reviews and the clerkships are very competitive.

A second way is to examine judges who have already been confirmed and see how influential they actually turned out to be. For example, did the judges' opinions influence the work of other judges, and possibly even the

Supreme Court? An entire academic literature has sprung up trying to measure the influence of judges based on how often their judicial opinions are cited. If political opponents are good at guessing the judges that will be the most influential, my prediction is that those judges had the most difficult time getting confirmed.

Of course, many other factors affect the confirmation process. As mentioned earlier, the specific year of a president's term is important, because during election years, particularly a presidential election year, the Senate does not vote as frequently on nominations. Thus, candidates nominated towards the end of a president's term are not going to get confirmed unless the president is reelected or another president from the same party is elected. If a president happens to put forward an unusually large number of judicial nominees during the end of his term, the confirmation rate would be low, but it would be a mistake to blame it on anything more than the timing of the nominations.

Whether the president's party controls the Senate is extremely important. The speed with which hearings are held, the rules under which nominations are considered (for example, whether it takes both home-state senators to block a nomination using so-called "blue slips"),[258] and even the likelihood that the nominee can muster a majority in committee and later on the floor are all affected by whether the same party controls the presidency and the Senate. Because the senators from the nominee's home state have a disproportionate influence on confirmation through the use of these blue slips, the estimates reported here also account for the possible party affiliation combinations of home-state senators and the president.[259]

As noted in Chapter 3, a widespread belief is that race or gender affects how cases are handled before the Senate. Other factors include: the quality of nominees (as measured by where they went to law school, for whom they clerked, or their ABA rating), whether the nominee already has served as a state or federal judge, whether the nominee engaged in private practice or worked in the government, the number of nominations in a year, and whether a nominee is renominated by a different president. The number of nominations in a year can affect how quickly nominations proceed simply because it takes time for senators and their staff to evaluate each nominee. Having many nominees lumped up in a particular year thus tends to slow things down.

Factors that Predict Who Will Be Confirmed

Data were collected on both district and circuit court nominees who were publicly announced from 1977 through the end of 2004. (See the data appendix for a detailed discussion.) Each nominee was described by the following statistics: date of nomination; hearing date; date of the final decision on the nomination; and whether the nominee was confirmed, defeated, or withdrawn. Presidents can also make what are called "recess appointments," which temporarily circumvent Senate approval. When Congress is out of session, the Constitution allows presidents to appoint people to serve as judges for the remainder of the current Congress. For these rare "recess appointments," the length of the confirmation process is defined as the time from the date of nomination to the date of appointment.

Biographies on federal judges, as well as searches of computer databases of news stories, provided the information on nominees' race, birth date, and political affiliation. Many different measures described a nominee's ability, including whether the nominee had graduated from a top ten law school, had served on a law review, or was a federal or state judge. For circuit court judges, curriculums vitae, biographies, and news databases provided information on whether the nominee had published in an academic journal, written books, or authored popular pieces, such as op-eds in newspapers or magazines. American Bar Association (ABA) ratings were collected for all nominees.

Two academic papers provide measures of judicial quality; one is by William Landes, Lawrence Lessig, and Michael Solimine.[260] They use the frequency that judges' opinions are cited by other judges as a measure of their *total influence*. *Average influence* is citations per published opinion. Obviously judges who have served longer get more citations, so these numbers adjust citations for such factors as the judge's tenure and whether the judge is a chief judge, on senior status, or retired. Landes and his co-writers found that federal circuit court judges from elite law schools and those who graduated with high honors produce a greater number of cited opinions.

The second academic paper measuring judicial quality is by Stephen Choi and Mitu Gulati. Their method is simpler but covers more characteristics. Their judicial rankings are based on how often judges are cited outside their circuit, the number of opinions they write, and their judicial independence (that is, whether a judge does not vote in accordance with other judges nominated by the same political party). Their composite index has eleven different components, among them citations by the Supreme Court, citations to the judge's twenty most cited opinions, where the opinion being cited was given a lot of weight (so-called invocations), and self-citations. Some judges might score highly in all these measures, some might only have opinions cited by the Supreme Court, and others might have more total citations.

These two indexes don't cover all six administrations. Landes and colleagues looked at federal appeals court judges who had at least six years of experience by 1995 (the Carter, Reagan, and George H. W. Bush administrations). Choi and Gulati examined judicial opinions published from 1998 to 2000 written by all judges appointed prior to January 1, 1998 (that is, the Carter, Reagan, and George H. W. Bush administrations, as well as through the first half of the second Clinton administration). Unfortunately, neither index goes beyond the Clinton administration. But the two measures have the advantage of examining how confirmed nominees actually performed as judges. Where someone went to law school or how well they did in school might be a pretty good indicator at predicting how well they will do as judges, but it doesn't work as well for seeing how judges actually do once they are in office. Yet the results we will examine find that both measures of judicial intelligence and influence—the measures before and after confirmation—show that better judges face significantly more difficult confirmation hearings.

Several other measures of nominee quality are available. The ABA rating uses an eleven-point scale ranging from "Not Qualified" to "Extremely Well Qualified." The different gradations include "Not Qualified/Qualified," "Qualified/Not Qualified," "Qualified," "Qualified/Well-Qualified," and so on. (Chapter 5 examines these ratings in depth.) These ratings try to measure the nominee's intellectual abilities; knowledge of the law, rules of evidence, and courtroom procedures; and their character, integrity, and judicial temperament.[261] Judicial temperament consists of "patience, courtesy, impartiality, even temper, a well-defined sense of justice, compassion, fair play, humility, tact, common sense and understanding."[262]

The *Almanac of the Federal Judiciary* provides detailed information on many nominees, such as where the judicial nominees clerked.[263] A clerkship on the U.S. Supreme Court is the most difficult to obtain, followed by clerkships on the federal circuit and district courts. Alas, since the number of clerkships has risen over time, having had a clerkship in later years may be less indicative of ability; as more clerkships are created, the quality of recipients may decline. The variables that I used for each administration may pick up some of this change.[264]

I also used the *Almanac's* survey of lawyers who have first-hand knowledge of a particular judge, as they have had cases heard by that judge. In that survey, respondents evaluate whether the judge was "smart" or not.[265] Just as with the measures of citations, these data are only available for those who have been confirmed and have served as a judge. Somewhat surprisingly, all the judges were described as at least smart. Any finer categorization seemed arbitrary, given the relatively imprecise statements made by the lawyers. Since all the judges were rated as at least smart, the results provide some evidence that even the judges who receive a Qualified/Not Qualified rating from the ABA were able to function intelligently on the bench.

The *Almanac* was more useful for obtaining information on judicial temperament and political views. The evaluations from lawyers provide fairly clear statements on whether a judge's temperament could be classified as "bad," "fair," or "good." The classification of a judge as having a bad judicial temperament is illustrated by lawyers' comments on A. Raymond Randolph and Richard F. Suhrheinrich, two of George H. W. Bush's nominees. Various lawyers said of Randolph: "No one will ever accuse him of excessive tact." "He can be difficult and nasty if he is against you in a case." "His questions can be tinged with sarcasm." "He can sometimes be a little surly." "He appears to be a little sour from the bench—not because he is displeased, or is going to vote against you—it is just the way he is." Of Richard F. Suhrheinrich they said: "His judicial demeanor leaves something to be desired." "His demeanor is a problem. He's not necessarily attorney friendly." "His interpersonal behavior is abysmal." "You need to wear armor when you have him on your panel." "Some people say he's mean-spirited. I would say he has a harsh streak." "He's a bully."

Assessments of judges classified as having "fair" judicial temperament contain phrases like: "He's gruff, but treats attorneys OK." "He is generally courteous and cordial and sometimes testy and argumentative." "His demeanor is all right." "She can actually be quite hostile on oral argument." By contrast, those discussed as "good" were described in the following way: "He has a fantastic temperament." "He treats lawyers very well." "There is no problem with his temperament."

As far as political views go, lawyers described judges as "liberal," "moderate," "conservative," "Libertarian," or "neutral." Some judges were categorized differently on the political scale by different lawyers. When that was the case, those judges were listed in multiple categories. Since not all nominees from a president have the same political views, using the *Almanac's* survey data can help further distinguish judges' political opinions.

Unfortunately, the *Almanac's* survey information is only provided with a multiple-year lag and thus covered few of George W. Bush's nominees when I originally collected this in 2005. Indeed, survey information covered only seven of his fifty-four circuit court nominees and fifteen of his 172 district court nominees.

As mentioned earlier, the political climate likely also matters. Beyond which party controls the presidency and the Senate, I am including the presidential approval ratings, the political affiliation of the senators from the state of the nominee, and the number of nominations in a year.

A Brief Overview: Ideology, Temperament, and Judicial Quality by Administration

A few simple figures can shed some light on the role that ideology, temperament, and judicial quality have on the increasing delays in the confirmation process.

Figure 4.1A suggests that the confirmation problems faced by George W. Bush's nominees were not a result of his nominees holding more extreme views. His circuit court nominees were actually much less likely to be classified as conservative than judges appointed by Reagan or George H. W. Bush. More than 57 percent of George W. Bush's circuit court judges were viewed as politically neutral by the lawyers who practice before them. That percentage is much higher than under any previous president. Twenty-eight percent of George W. Bush's nominees were classified as conservative and 14 percent were classified as liberal.

It must be emphasized that the *Almanac's* survey is taken by lawyers, who tend to be pretty liberal themselves.[266] For example, the Federal Election Commission requires that donors contributing more than $200 to federal campaigns must list their occupation. Data collected from fundrace.huffingtonpost.com allows donor searches by occupation. From January 1, 2007 to December 31, 2008, 80.5 percent of the $63 million that attorneys donated was given to Democrats.[267] A similar analysis of law professors found that 95 percent of their donations went to Barack Obama, with only 5 percent going to John McCain.[268] Thus, judges whom lawyers classify as moderate might be viewed by most people as liberal. Similarly, judges indicated as conservative in the survey might seem moderate to most people.

Given that warning, Bill Clinton's nominees also do not stand out as particularly extreme. The number of Clinton nominees classified as liberal is very low compared with Jimmy Carter's nominees (29 to 52 percent).

Figure 4.1B implies little change in the political views of district court judges across administrations. Again, whether it is the percentage of judges who are "conservative," "liberal," or "neutral," the judges of Clinton and George W. Bush do not stand out as extreme in any way. District court judges under both of them are viewed as more neutral than the judges for any previous president.

Thus, for both circuit and district judges, the lengthening of the confirmation process under Clinton and Bush aren't being driven by changes in judicial ideology. Indeed, the reverse appears to be the case. The length of the confirmation process has grown despite the fact that these judges, once they are on the job, are viewed by lawyers as increasingly politically neutral.

There is yet another possibility. It could be that a more contentious environment in the Senate hearings forced both presidents to nominate less objectionable candidates.

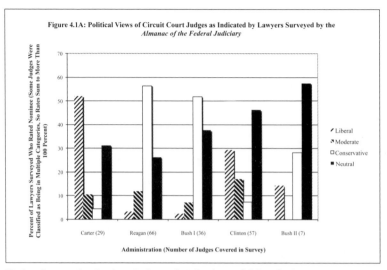

Figure 4.1A: Political Views of Circuit Court Judges as Indicated by Lawyers Surveyed by the *Almanac of the Federal Judiciary*

*To view a larger version of each graph, please refer to Supplement: Full-Page Graphs.

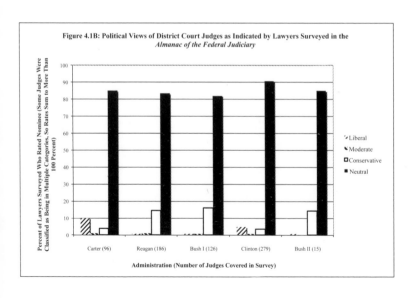

Figure 4.1B: Political Views of District Court Judges as Indicated by Lawyers Surveyed in the *Almanac of the Federal Judiciary*

Survey data are available only for judges who have been confirmed, so conceivably having more politically neutral circuit court judges on the bench in later administrations simply reflects that even if nominees are as extreme as before, the Senate may be becoming better at sorting out extremists. But the large rise in the percentage of judges who are classified as neutral, beginning with the Bush I nominees, is too large: even if all the defeated nominees were assumed to be "conservatives" or "liberals," there would still be a large net increase in the number of neutral nominees. The only reasonable explanation is that more "neutral" judges are being appointed to the courts by recent administrations.

Similarly, since the Reagan administration, a consistently growing proportion of circuit court judges are viewed as having a good judicial temperament. This corresponds closely with judges being perceived as more neutral (Figures 4.2A and 4.2B). For district court judges, the administration-by-administration pattern in good judicial temperament matches lawyers' views on the neutrality of the judges. Again, it is hard to view the data as providing any explanation for why circuit court nominations have become so much more contentious.

The percentage of circuit court nominees who attended top ten law schools and/or who served on a law review has been increasing across the past five administrations. Only about the top ten percent of students in a law school class are selected for the law review. Some students are

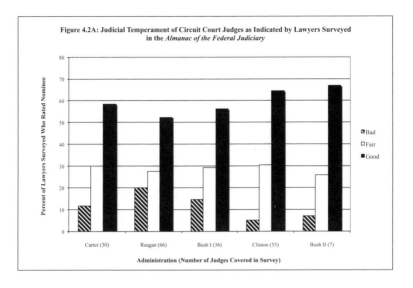

Figure 4.2A: Judicial Temperament of Circuit Court Judges As Indicated by Lawyers Surveyed in the *Almanac of the Federal Judiciary*

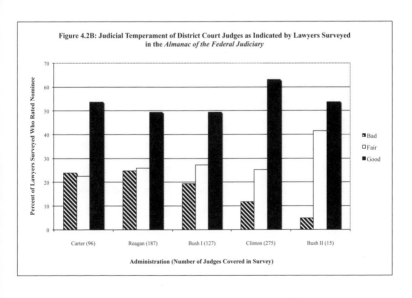

Figure 4.2B: Judicial Temperament of District Court Judges As Indicated by Lawyers Surveyed in the *Almanac of the Federal Judiciary*

selected by virtue of outstanding grades, and others are selected through a writing competition. Either way, when a student is appointed to the law review, it is regarded as a sign of distinction.

The next two figures illustrate nominees who distinguished themselves by being on a law review at a top ten law school. Figure 4.3 shows a surprising pattern: the most elite Republican nominees consistently are less likely to be confirmed than those with weaker records, whereas the most elite Democratic nominees are more likely to be confirmed than those with weaker records. So the confirmation process generally weeds out the smartest conservative Republicans, but not the smartest Democrats. Only 78 percent of George W. Bush's circuit court nominees who were on a law review at a top ten law school were confirmed during his first term, compared with 83 percent of his nominees without this background. The fifty-six percentage point gap between those who were on law reviews at top ten law schools and those who were not during George H. W. Bush's administration is even more striking.

For President Obama's first two years, with only one circuit court nominee who both graduated from a top ten law school and served on the law review, there is not really enough data to make much of a comparison and I am not going to make use of this data in the later regressions.[269] Yet, the pattern is the same as for other Democrats, it would show a higher confirmation rate for those with the more impressive academic record.

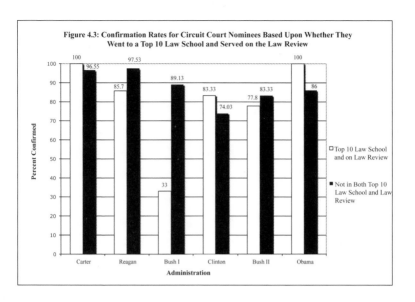

Figure 4.3: Confirmation Rates for Circuit Court Nominees Based Upon Whether They Went to a Top 10 Law School and Served on the Law Review

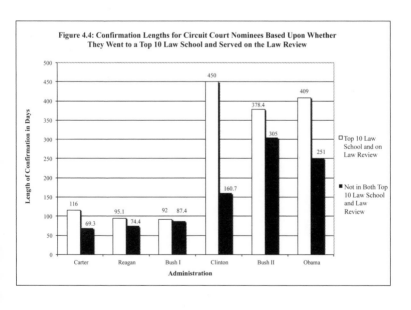

Figure 4.4: Confirmation Lengths for Circuit Court Nominees Based Upon Whether They Went to a Top 10 Law School and Served on the Law Review

Having served on a law review at a top ten law school appears to also set up circuit court nominees for significantly longer confirmation battles. That is true during each administration studied, but the gap varies tremendously—from just 4.6 days for George H. W. Bush to 289.3 days for Clinton. Except for the Bush I administration, the gaps are all statistically significant.

Citations to judges' opinions are presumably a better measure of quality and influence than information from their law school days. However, the Choi-Gulati and Landes et al. studies include different factors and the measures do not always show consistent patterns of change over time.[270]

Figure 4.5 shows how the Choi-Gulati rating varies for the first four administrations analyzed in this book. Remember that the Choi-Gulati judicial ranking includes more than citations and is based on the number of decisions produced by a circuit court judge, the citations to those decisions in circuits outside the judge's own circuit, and the judge's independence (that is, whether judges vote in accordance with other judges nominated by the same political party).[271] This measure does not explain the longer confirmation lengths or the lower confirmation rate. One interesting conclusion from their measure is that judges nominated by Carter and Clinton have the lowest quality ratings, whereas Reagan nominees have the highest rating.[272] In other words, Reagan's circuit court appointees turned out to be the most influential, Bush's fell in the middle, and Clinton and Carter appointees were the least influential.

The Landes et al. total influence indexes are depicted in Figure 4.6. The inside circuit citations are comparable to the Choi-Gulati rating and, likewise, demonstrate that judicial quality peaks with Reagan's nominees. However, Landes et al.'s outside circuit citations suggest that judicial quality and influence is declining over time across the three administrations shown.[273]

These hindsight measures of quality and influence are obviously not available to either the Senate or the president during the confirmation process. Nevertheless, they provide a rough estimate of how influential senators believed the nominee would later become. The Choi-Gulati and Landes et al. measures both suggest that the quality

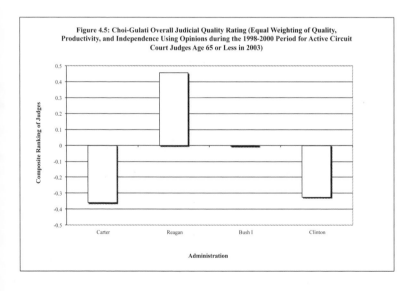

Figure 4.5: Choi-Gulati Overall Judicial Quality Rating (Equal Weighting of Quality, Productivity, and Independence Using Opinions during the 1998-2000 Period for Active Circuit Court Judges Age 65 or Less in 2003)

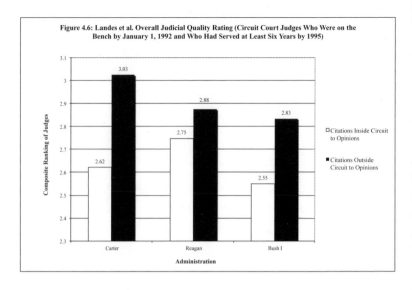

Figure 4.6: Landes et al. Overall Judicial Quality Rating (Circuit Court Judges Who Were on the Bench by January 1, 1992 and Who Had Served at Least Six Years by 1995)

of judges has declined since the Reagan administration. If correct, these measures raise concerns that the quality of judges has been falling even as the confirmation process has become increasingly difficult.

Increased Polarization

The increasingly polarized Senate can help explain why the battle over the courts has become more difficult (Figure 4.7). Not only is more at stake today, with courts having purview over a larger government and increased regulations, but Democratic and Republican senators agree on fewer issues. Decades ago, conservative Southern Democrats would work with Republicans. Liberal

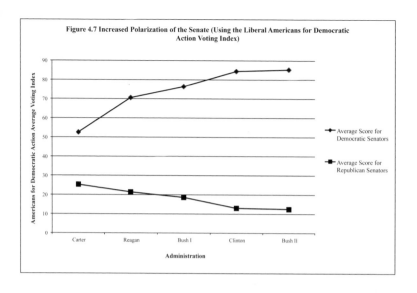

Figure 4.7 Increased Polarization of the Senate (Using the Liberal Americans for Democratic Action Voting Index)

Northeastern Republicans would find common cause with Democrats. Unlike a generation ago, "overlapping" senators are now a rare species. As the parties have diverged, it has become more difficult for senators to work together across party lines.

Americans for Democratic Action (ADA), self-described as "America's oldest independent liberal lobbying organization," is one of many interest groups that rank the voting records of senators and representatives.[274] In the Americans for Democratic Action system, a score of 100 represents a perfect liberal voting record; a zero means that the politician has a perfect conservative record. From the mid-1970s to the early 2000s, the changes in political views within parties have been huge. During the Carter administration in the late 1970s, the

Americans for Democratic Action believed that Senate Democrats were about equally divided between conservatives and liberals, with an average score of 53; by the time George W. Bush took office, the average Democratic rating had gone to 85. Meanwhile, the average score for Republicans had declined from 25 to 13. The average difference between the two parties had almost tripled over those three decades. Other interest group measures of voting show the same general pattern: the gap between Republicans and Democrats has become much larger.

Factors that Lengthen the Confirmation Process

If George W. Bush nominated the exact same person to be a judge as Ronald Reagan, with the same political conditions in terms of such influences as who controlled the Senate and the presidential approval rating, would confirmation be longer or shorter? To answer this, we need to simultaneously account for as many different factors as possible that measure differences across judicial nominees. While we have already looked at a lot of factors that may affect the length of confirmations, a word of caution is in order. What might appear to be important by itself may actually turn out to be irrelevant when other factors are accounted for. Figures 4.8 through 4.14 attempt to illustrate this.[275]

In the first estimates, the confirmation length—the number of days between nomination and confirmation—varies with the legal and professional background of the nominee (years in practice as a lawyer; attendance at a top ten law school; previous service as a federal or state judge; publications; type of clerkship, if any; and ABA rating), demographic background (race, gender, and age), and political environment (number of nominations during a year, presidential approval rating, party control of the Senate and presidency, and agreement on confirmation between the senators from the nominee's home state). I also account for whether nominees from different states have a more difficult time making it through the process.[276]

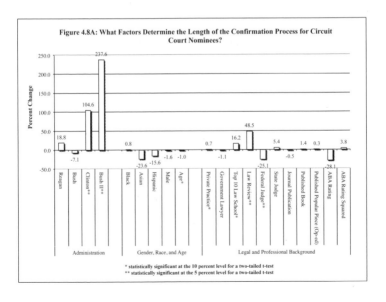

Figure 4.8A: What Factors Determine the Length of the Confirmation Process for Circuit Court Nominees?

* statistically significant at the 10 percent level for a two-tailed t-test
** statistically significant at the 5 percent level for a two-tailed t-test

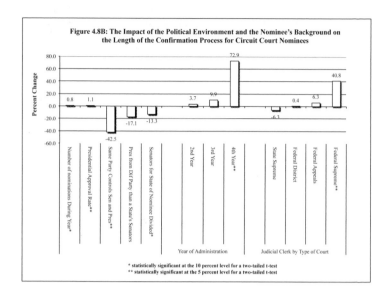

Figure 4.8B: The Impact of the Political Environment and the Nominee's Background on the Length of the Confirmation Process for Circuit Court Nominees

* statistically significant at the 10 percent level for a two-tailed t-test
** statistically significant at the 5 percent level for a two-tailed t-test

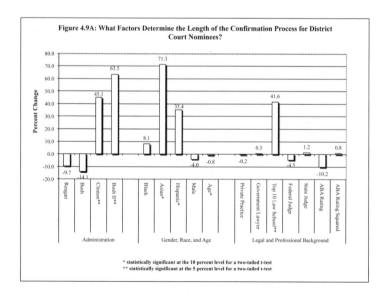

Figure 4.9A: What Factors Determine the Length of the Confirmation Process for District Court Nominees?

* statistically significant at the 10 percent level for a two-tailed t-test
** statistically significant at the 5 percent level for a two-tailed t-test

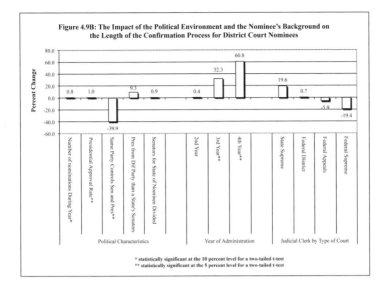

Figure 4.9B: The Impact of the Political Environment and the Nominee's Background on the Length of the Confirmation Process for District Court Nominees

* statistically significant at the 10 percent level for a two-tailed t-test
** statistically significant at the 5 percent level for a two-tailed t-test

Figures 4.8A-B present the estimates for circuit court nominees, and Figures 4.9A-B show the estimates for district court nominees. The patterns across administrations for district and circuit court judges are similar. The simplest regressions show that after the Carter administration, if the same individuals under the same political conditions as measured by everything that we are accounting for had been nominated, the length of time to confirmation would initially remain the same or shorten somewhat before increasing substantially. Under Bush I, the confirmation time fell significantly: by 14 percent for district court judges and by a smaller, not statistically significant, 7 percent for circuit court judges. The Clinton administration's district court judges took 45 percent longer and circuit court judges 105 percent longer to be confirmed than under Bush I. And compared to Clinton, Bush II's district court nominees took at least 64 percent longer and circuit court nominees 238 percent longer.

The results confirm the previous graphs and show that even after all the other factors noted previously are taken into account, the confirmation process takes much longer now than it used to. This process has become particularly long for circuit court judges: Bush II's circuit court nominees have taken about 2.8 times longer to be confirmed than nominees under his father. The differences between those first three administrations and either the Clinton or the Bush II administrations are statistically significant.[277]

As discussed, having the same party in control of both the presidency and the Senate dramatically shortens the confirmation process. According to the regressions, the effect is larger for the more contentious circuit court nominees. Having a unified government reduces the length of the confirmation process for district court nominees by 40 percent and for circuit court nominees by 43 percent.

Other variables provide consistent effects for both district and circuit court nominees. As expected, older nominees get through the process more quickly. Each one-year increase in a nominee's age reduces the length of the confirmation process for both district and circuit court nominees by about 1 percent. A large number of nominees in a single year slows the speed with which any nominee will be confirmed: each additional nominee increases the number of days by about 1 percent. Being nominated during the fourth year of a president's term increases the length of the confirmation process by about 73 percent for circuit courts and 61 percent for district courts. Possibly because they have already been through the confirmation process, those who have been a federal judge prior to nomination enjoy a speedier circuit court nomination process by about 26 percent.

The discrimination against smart nominees is substantial. Graduating from a top ten law school increases the length of the confirmation process by 16 percent; being on the law review adds another 49 percent to that length; having held clerkship at circuit court adds 6.3 percent; and clerking for the U.S. Supreme Court adds another 41 percent. Consequently, multiplying each of those probabilities together, someone who has accomplished all four will take 158 percent longer to be confirmed than someone who has accomplished none.

Despite all the battles over whether the American Bar Association should be given a formal role in rating judges,[278] their ratings have surprisingly little impact on the confirmation process and are not statistically related to the length of confirmations. Possibly the ABA simply does not do a very good job in rating nominees. The next chapter will examine the history of the ABA's role in judicial confirmations and its significant political biases in rating judicial nominees. Senators might be wise to disregard the ABA rating since it does not seem to accurately reflect a nominee's abilities.

Nomination battles also can differ as a result of the nominee's race and gender. And race matters differently for Republican and Democratic nominees. For example, although blacks take just as long as whites to be confirmed to district or circuit courts, there is a big difference between black Democratic and Republican nominees for the circuit courts. While black Democrats get through the process 17 percent faster than normal, the process for black Republicans takes 40 percent longer. Regardless of party, Asians and Hispanics take much longer to get confirmed to district courts than whites, but no similar statistically significant difference exists for circuit courts. For men, the results are not statistically significant, but the data suggest that men are confirmed faster than women for district courts, but slightly slower for circuit courts. Finally, having clerked for the Supreme Court slows the confirmation of circuit court nominees but has no effect on district court nominees.

For both types of judicial appointments, presidential approval ratings at the time of the nomination matter. Each 1 percentage point increase in the approval rate increases the length of the confirmation process by 1 percent; the effect is quite statistically significant. This result could have a logical explanation: presidents with strong approval ratings might be more willing to risk nominating judges who are more difficult to confirm than they would be if their popularity was weak.

Do Republican presidents nominate more conservative nominees as their approval ratings rise? And do Democratic presidents nominate more liberal ones? It would only seem logical. The analysis here indicates that this pattern indeed exists.[279] Increasing a Republican president's popularity by 1 percentage point increases the probability of a conservative being nominated by 1 percent and lowers the probability of a liberal being nominated by 6 percent. Similarly, for a Democratic president, a popularity increase of 1 percentage point increases the probability of a liberal being nominated by 3 percent and reduces the probability of a conservative being nominated by 3 percent.

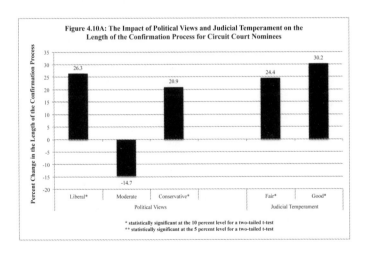

Figure 4.10A: The Impact of Political Views and Judicial Temperament on the Length of the Confirmation Process for Circuit Court Nominees

* statistically significant at the 10 percent level for a two-tailed t-test
** statistically significant at the 5 percent level for a two-tailed t-test

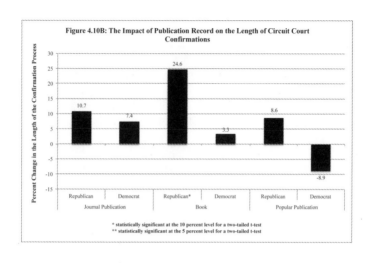

Figure 4.10B: The Impact of Publication Record on the Length of Circuit Court Confirmations

* statistically significant at the 10 percent level for a two-tailed t-test
** statistically significant at the 5 percent level for a two-tailed t-test

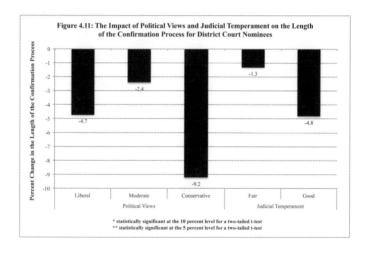

Figure 4.11: The Impact of Political Views and Judicial Temperament on the Length of the Confirmation Process for District Court Nominees

* statistically significant at the 10 percent level for a two-tailed t-test
** statistically significant at the 5 percent level for a two-tailed t-test

The survey information from the *Almanac of the Federal Judiciary* can also be included in these estimates to see how a judge's political biases and temperament change the length of confirmations; however, that survey information is not available for one-third of the nominees, so I calculated the results separately from those already reported.[280] To answer whether there is a partisan difference in how paper trails are treated, the circuit court analysis also examined whether publications have a different impact on Republicans and Democrats.

The results for the circuit courts in Figure 4.10A suggest that the nominee's judicial temperament and political views matter. Nominees who are confirmed and are eventually seen as being either liberal or conservative take over 20 percent longer than a neutral judge and over 35 percent longer than a moderate judge to be confirmed. However, the difference between liberal and conservative judges is not statistically significant. Similarly, the difference between neutral and moderate judges is not statistically different.

The results for judicial temperament are especially surprising: judges who have bad temperament are confirmed more quickly than judges with fair or good temperaments. Either senators are very poor at predicting how nominees will behave once they are confirmed, or the senators don't care very much about judicial temperament as a qualification. For example, having 10 percent more lawyers perceiving a judge as having a "bad" instead of a "fair" temperament implies it will take the "bad" judge about 2.3 percent less time to get confirmed. Nominees who turn out to be judges with a "bad" temperament take about 3 percent less time than those who turn out to have a "good" temperament.

While writing academic journal articles in Figure 4.10B (one measure of smartness) appears to make confirmations more difficult for both Republicans and Democrats, publishing a book or a popular piece such as an op-ed significantly delays the confirmation process for Republican circuit court nominees relative to Democrats. If a Republican and Democratic nominee both publish a book, the nomination for the Republican takes 21 percent longer than that for the Democrat. Similarly, potential Republican nominees should be advised not to publish newspaper op-eds. An op-ed increases the length of Republican confirmations by 9 percent. But Democrats who publish an op-ed actually *shorten* their confirmation by 9 percent. Democratic senators are more likely to oppose Republicans who have taken political stands, but Republicans are not equally concerned about Democratic nominees who have done the same thing.

Other factors might influence the length of Democratic and Republican nominees' confirmations in different ways. For district court nominees, there was nothing of interest showing up, so those results are not reported.[281] But at the circuit court level, the president's party mattered.

Among the statistically significant results, blacks nominated by a Democratic president took about 30 percent less time than blacks nominated by a Republican president. Republican nominees who went to a top ten law school and who served on law reviews both took at least 21 percent more time than Democrats to get confirmed. On the other hand, Republicans who had previously served as federal judges took about 40 percent less time for confirmation than did Democrats with the same background. Among those who clerked for federal judges after law school, only Democratic nominees got through significantly faster.

The figures in Chapter 3 suggest that nominees to the D.C. Circuit have faced more difficult confirmations in recent years than nominees to other circuit courts. Unfortunately, the regressions that we have been using cannot be used here since there are so many factors that we are trying to account for and so few observations—only thirty-seven D.C. Circuit Court and twenty-eight D.C. District Court nominees have been confirmed across the thirty-four years available from the Carter administration through the first two years of the Obama administration. Thus, in addition to looking at the differences across administrations, I can only account for the most basic variables: party control of the presidency and Senate as well as the age of the nominee (Figures 4.12 and 4.13).

When the same party controls both the presidency and the Senate, confirmation time for the D.C. District Court nominees is reduced by 55 to 61 percent compared with when the presidency and the Senate are controlled by different parties—a much bigger impact on confirmation speed than was found for all other circuit

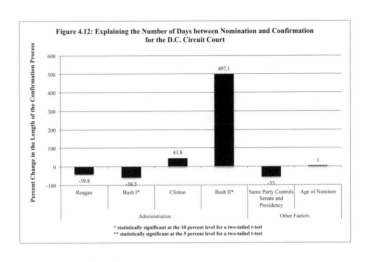

Figure 4.12: Explaining the Number of Days between Nomination and Confirmation for the D.C. Circuit Court

* statistically significant at the 10 percent level for a two-tailed t-test
** statistically significant at the 5 percent level for a two-tailed t-test

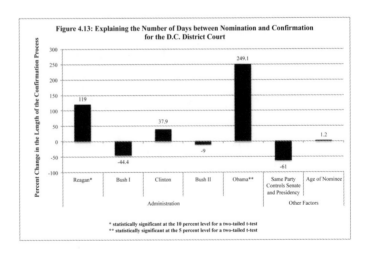

Figure 4.13: Explaining the Number of Days between Nomination and Confirmation for the D.C. District Court

* statistically significant at the 10 percent level for a two-tailed t-test
** statistically significant at the 5 percent level for a two-tailed t-test

or district courts. This result thus supports the idea that more is at stake with confirmations to this court, which has been a stepping stone to the Supreme Court for four of the current nine justices.[282] Since the D.C. Circuit Court has become a more important proving ground for Republican nominees than Democratic, it might explain why George W. Bush's nominees to that court faced the longest delays.

The estimates indicate no consistent pattern over time for the length of confirmation for D.C. District Court nominees, but the analysis for the D.C. Circuit suggests a lopsided V-shaped relationship: George W. Bush's nominees took a very statistically significant 497 days, more than 450 days longer than it took Clinton's nominees. The single Obama nominee to the D.C. Circuit had not been confirmed by early 2011, so that nomination was excluded from these estimates. Having the same party control the presidency and the Senate reduced the length of confirmations by between 55 and 61 percent, with the results being statistically significant.[283]

What about how smart the judges are? The thirteen Choi-Gulati and five Landes et al. measures of judicial quality found in Figures 4.14 and 4.15 depict the relationship between the various quality measures of the judge and the difficulty in confirmations. The most influential circuit court judges, the ones whose opinions were the most cited by other judges, experienced the most difficult time being confirmed. The Choi-Gulati total measure of quality ranges from −2.44 to 3.77.[284] Figure 4.14 shows that increasing the Choi-Gulati total measure by one standard deviation produces an extremely large 85 percent increase in the length of the confirmation process. Judges whose opinions ended up being given more weight when they were cited by others in so-called "invocations" also faced the most opposition when they were originally nominated.

But as noted in the introduction, citations are only one measure of intelligence. Smarter judges who went to elite law schools wrote not only more influential opinions, but they wrote more of them; this also served to increase a judge's influence.[285] Thus, not surprisingly, the Choi-Gulati measure of published opinions shows that those who wrote the most opinions had a more difficult time getting confirmed.

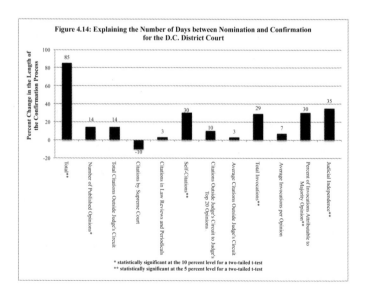

Figure 4.14: Explaining the Number of Days between Nomination and Confirmation for the D.C. District Court

* statistically significant at the 10 percent level for a two-tailed t-test
** statistically significant at the 5 percent level for a two-tailed t-test

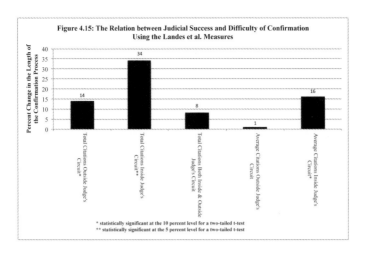

Figure 4.15: The Relation between Judicial Success and Difficulty of Confirmation Using the Landes et al. Measures

Percent Change in the Length of the Confirmation Process

- Total Citations Outside Judge's Circuit*: 14
- Total Citations Inside Judge's Circuit**: 34
- Total Citations Both Inside & Outside Judge's Circuit: 8
- Average Citations Outside Judge's Circuit: 1
- Average Citations Inside Judge's Circuit*: 16

* statistically significant at the 10 percent level for a two-tailed t-test
** statistically significant at the 5 percent level for a two-tailed t-test

Three brilliant judges need to be mentioned here as they completely dominate the measures of judicial quality: Frank Easterbrook, Richard Posner, and J. Harvie Wilkinson. Easterbrook and Posner have for decades produced a huge number of opinions and are extremely influential among judges across the country. In terms of their performance as measured in these indexes, Easterbrook and Posner are such extreme outliers that including them in the sample may skew the results. For example, on the Choi-Gulati measure, Posner's and Easterbrook's ratings (3.77 and 2.93 respectively) are twice or more than twice the rating of the third most highly ranked judge (J. Harvie Wilkinson, 1.51).[286] Wilkinson himself boasts twice the rating of the fourth-ranked judge. Other rankings tell the same story. For example, a recent ranking by *Legal Affairs*, a prominent bimonthly national magazine for lawyers, listed Easterbrook and Posner as two of the three most influential circuit court judges in the country.[287]

My analysis, however, finds that the problems facing the brightest judges are not merely the result of a few extreme examples. The results are unaffected even when Easterbrook and Posner are not included in the analysis; the highest quality judges still faced greater difficulty getting confirmed when they were nominated.

Long ago, however, such judicial stardom would have ensured a Supreme Court appointment regardless of political or personal factors. Herbert Hoover's appointment of Benjamin Cardozo to the Supreme Court in 1932 is such a case. Cardozo openly backed Hoover's opponent in the 1928 presidential election, writing that Republicans represented "all the narrow-minded bigots, all the Jew haters, all those who would make of the United States an exclusively Protestant government."[288] But Hoover thought "that the Supreme Court should have a strong minority of the opposition's party and that all appointments should be made from experienced jurists" and felt Cardozo was the smartest Democrat he could nominate.[289]

It is possible that both low- and high-quality nominees have difficulty being confirmed. Senators may not want to let their opponents place the brightest lawyers as judges, yet weak nominees might also be rejected. In statistical terms, the relationship would be nonlinear,[290] but looking at it in that way did not change the result.[291] At least for the judges that we could study, the less influential the judge, the easier it was for him to get confirmed.[292] A president's political opponents are not going to stop a nominee who will not make much difference in the long run.

As mentioned before, Choi and Gulati not only calculated an overall quality index, but they provided eleven other measures of quality that compose their total measure. Figure 4.14 examines how the total index and each of the eleven component parts relate to the length of the confirmation process. Higher, more desirable scores on eleven of the indexes correlate with longer confirmation processes, and six measures—total invocations and the percent of invocations attributable to majority opinions (measures of how important the decision was when the judge's name is mentioned), number of published opinions, self-citations, and judicial independence—are statistically significant. The relationship with self-citations is picking up that smarter judges are more likely to cite their own past opinions. The one anomaly involves citations in law reviews: more citations (and, thus, higher quality) are associated with shorter confirmation times, but it is not statistically significant.[293]

Using the five Landes et al. measures yields similar results, again indicating that the most successful judges face the most difficult confirmation battles. The measures of a judge's influence within his circuit using both total and average citations are significant, as are the total citations outside the circuit.[294]

By most citation measures, higher quality judges face a more difficult confirmation process. To be precise, a 1 percent increase in judicial quality increases the length of the confirmation process by between 1 and 3 percent.[295] I originally thought that not just the highest quality judges but also the lowest might face the most difficulty, but indeed it is not so—the lower the quality of the judge, the faster the confirmation. It is possible that those who are especially weak candidates simply fail to be nominated in the first place.

Are Republican and Democratic nominees treated differently based on whether they will be influential judges? To analyze this question, we can look at the Choi-Gulati overall quality index and the five Landes et al. measures. The pattern is clear no matter which index is used: Republican nominees tend to face a longer confirmation process than Democrats. Some of the measures suggest that the difference in the length of confirmations is quite long, up to a 63 percentage point difference. But the evidence only shows that Democratic Senators made life particularly more difficult for Republicans whose average judicial opinion was expected to be influential outside his home circuit. Democratic Senators seem to be more concerned about stopping potentially powerful Republican nominees who would have a national impact.

As mentioned earlier, the long-term upward trend in confirmation battles can, at least in part, be explained by the increased polarization in the political process.[296] As

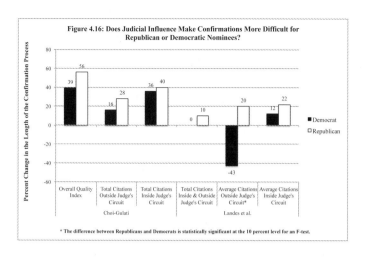

Figure 4.16: Does Judicial Influence Make Confirmations More Difficult for Republican or Democratic Nominees?

* The difference between Republicans and Democrats is statistically significant at the 10 percent level for an F-test.

the parties diverge, the battles simply become longer and nastier. Polarization has been widely studied by political scientists and economists.[297] Indeed, my results indicate that polarization is also an important factor for judicial appointments. The Americans for Democratic Action index for 1977 to 2004 shows that increased polarization lengthens the confirmation process. A one percentage point increase in the gap between the Americans for Democratic Action index lengthens the confirmation process for district court judges by 1 percentage point and for circuit court judges by 3 percentage points. This also implies that the same party controlling the presidency and the Senate will be more important over time since the gap between a president's views and those of the opposing party will also likely be larger.

How the Characteristics of Individual Nominees Determine Confirmation Rates

Confirmation rates can be examined in the same way as the length of the confirmation process.[298] When analyzing what factors are at play, the results are very similar.[299] Again, no clear pattern across administrations emerges for district court nominees, but there is a consistent and statistically significant decline over time in the confirmation rate for circuit court nominees.

Unsurprisingly, what affects the length of confirmations also affects the confirmation rate. Thus, for circuit court nominees, the most important factor for getting the nominee confirmed are either having unified party control of the presidency and the Senate or having the nominee renominated by a different president.

Similarly, factors suggesting higher intelligence and quality as a lawyer make confirmation less likely. Graduating from a top ten law school reduces the probability of confirmation by 20 percent, and having a judicial clerkship on the Supreme Court reduces it by another 5 percent. Being nominated during the last six months of a president's term reduces the confirmation rate by a whopping 88 percent. Being nominated at any time during the fourth year of a presidency makes it much more difficult to be confirmed for the circuit court, but it does not have a statistically significant effect for district courts. Nor can we discern a difference in the confirmation odds for African Americans and whites of confirmation to either the district or circuit courts.

One caveat should be mentioned about the merits of going to a top law school: once a person is nominated, being from a top ten law school substantially lowers the probability of being confirmed, but it is also true that graduating from a top law school increases the chances of being nominated in the first place. Although 29 percent of judicial nominees graduated from a top ten school, only 8 percent of practicing lawyers in 2004 did so.[300] Going to a top ten school thus more than triples one's chances of getting nominated, but cuts the subsequent chances of confirmation by 20 to 60 percent.[301]

Some other surprising differences were found between circuit and district court nominees. Graduating from a top ten school had a large impact on being approved as a district court judge, reducing that probability by 60 percent. Although being a state judge improved the odds of a nominee being confirmed for a district court, being a federal judge lowered the odds of getting onto the circuit court.

The measures of quality once a judge is on the bench did not show up significantly here. Nevertheless, they lend some additional support—however weak—to the hypothesis that smarter judges have a tougher time getting confirmed. Increased polarization is significantly related to a lower probability of confirmation for circuit court judges, though not for district court judges. In my estimates for circuit court nominees, a one percentage point increase in the gap between Republican and Democratic senators results in at least a 7 percent decline in the probability of confirmation.[302]

I also analyzed the estimates separately for Republicans and Democrats to see in what ways the different factors affected their nominees. There is again some evidence that smart Republicans face more difficulty getting confirmed, as graduating from a top ten law school decreases the confirmation rate for Republicans more than for Democrats. Other factors that tend to increase the confirmation of Democrats more than Republicans include higher ABA ratings, high presidential approval ratings, and unified government. The relative impact of unified government on Democrats is small, just eight percentage points, but it indicates that Democrats remain relatively effective in blocking Republican nominations even when they are in the minority. Being a federal or state judge is more important for Republican nominees, and male Republicans are not as disadvantaged as male Democrats.

How the Characteristics of Individual Nominees Determine Supreme Court Confirmations

It is much more difficult to make similar systematic comparisons for Supreme Court nominees, as there are so few. Even going back decades still yields few nominees and suffers from comparing candidates under radically different circumstances. For example, only thirty-two confirmation battles have occurred since World War II and only nineteen since Abe Fortas's 1968 nomination to Chief Justice. It is very questionable to estimate regressions with such small samples and even harder to put a lot of weight on those results.

Still, with those qualifications in mind, a few simple estimates provide some insight into the confirmation process. In arriving at these estimates, I attempted to account for various factors that would affect confirmations: whether the same party controls the Senate and presidency; age at confirmation; race; gender; attendance at a top ten law school; law review participation; previous federal judicial clerkships; and the number of published journal articles, books, and articles in popular publications. White Supreme Court nominees took thirty-six fewer days to be confirmed than African American nominees, and going to a top ten law school and/or serving on a law review increased the length of confirmations by twenty-three and thirty days respectively; all these effects were statistically significant.[303] Being male added fourteen days to the process, whereas having clerked for both the circuit and the Supreme Court added a total of nine days, although these last effects were not statistically significant.[304]

Similar to work by Charles Shipan and Megan Shannon (2003), my results found that split party control between the presidency and the Senate as well as the age of the nominee do matter for lower court judges. Shipan and Shannon examined Supreme Court nominees over a longer period of time (from 1866 to 1994), but they had fewer control variables and do not address the general questions discussed here on the quality of the nominee.

There is a common claim that recent nominees have shorter paper trails—that longer paper trails are thought to offer opponents more opportunities to defeat a nominee. This is the so-called "Souterization" of nominees discussed earlier. To test this, I compiled a list of publications for Supreme Court nominees who were confirmed from 1946 to 2010. Using a simple regression to account for any nonlinear trends[305] and accounting for the nominee's political party, published journal articles and books peaked for those confirmed in 1986, and op-eds and other more popular publications peaked earlier in 1978.[306] Coincidently, that is the same time that William Rehnquist was elevated to be Chief Justice and Antonin Scalia was confirmed to be an associate justice. The estimated average drop in the number of published academic journal articles for Republicans from 1986 to 2005 was quite large, about 42 percent or 3.4 articles. For Democrats, from 1993 when Ruth Bader Ginsburg was confirmed to 2010 when Elena Kagan was confirmed, the estimated drop was 30 percent or 5.2 articles.

Based on the results that we obtained for circuit court nominations, Chief Justice John Roberts's own history suggested that he would face tough confirmations. He was first nominated to the circuit court in 1992 during George H. W. Bush's administration, but Democrats controlled the Senate and no vote was held on his nomination. Republicans renominated Roberts again in 2001, but his confirmation wasn't much easier this time. Of the 278 circuit court judges confirmed from 1977 through 2004, only ten nominees took longer than the 729 days that it took Roberts to secure his circuit court confirmation. As indicated in Figures 4.8A and 4.8B, this was not surprising given his record: he graduated from a top ten law school, served on the law review, clerked for both the circuit and Supreme Courts, and published scholarly as well as popular pieces. Being male and relatively young also suggested a longer confirmation process would be in store.

Yet, at seventy-two days, Roberts's confirmation to the Supreme Court was not unusually long by contemporary standards. This puts him almost exactly equal to the average confirmation length for the Reagan through Obama administrations, even though based on this data, one would have expected him to face a longer confirmation process. Having the same party controlling both the White House and the Senate helped, but something else was going on, most probably Rehnquist's death prior to Roberts's confirmation hearings. As with the overlapping Rehnquist and Scalia nominations in 1986, the Democrats concentrated their fire on only one nominee. In this case, they went after the replacement for Sandra Day O'Connor, Samuel Alito. As a conservative, he would be replacing a swing vote on the court and his confirmation dragged on for ninety-two days.

As we have seen, lower-quality nominees to the circuit courts are, generally, more easily confirmed. Nevertheless, there are instances where presidents go too far in appointing weak nominees. Bush, suffering from low poll numbers after Hurricane Katrina and from the battle he faced over John Roberts (his nominee to replace Rehnquist), decided to nominate Harriet Miers to replace Sandra Day O'Connor. Miers seemed like one of the safest choices President Bush could have made for a Supreme Court justice. She was an older white female who had a short paper trail. Yet, consistent with the findings that opponents primarily oppose the brightest nominees, it was Republicans, not Democrats, who were most concerned about her competency and expected lack of influence.[307]

Miers's replacement was intellectually much stronger, and not surprisingly, Alito's confirmation hearings in 2005 and 2006 were more contentious than Roberts's. Even though Alito was probably no more conservative than Miers, Democrats were much more upset over his nomination. As President Bush described the nomination process: "They tried to paint him as a racist, a radical, a bigot. . . ."[308] The Choi-Gulati rankings provide a somewhat mixed picture of Alito's abilities. He rated very high in terms of judicial independence—Choi and Gulati found that Alito was the twelfth most politically independent Republican of the fifty-five they studied. This would normally reduce the degree of opposition.

On the other hand, in Alito's fifteen years as a circuit court judge, his judicial opinions covered a lot of today's hot button issues, including abortion; affirmative action; age, disability, racial, religious, and sexual discrimination; freedom of speech and freedom of religion; gun control;

health and worker protection; and immigration issues.[309] And his opinions had some influence, ranking him about in the middle of the circuit court judges based on how frequently the Supreme Court cited his decisions. He also placed in the top 30 percent based on the number of opinions he had written. His legal background was stellar: a graduate of Yale Law School, he served on the law review, clerked for the circuit court, and was widely published in law journals. His legal background did not make him the intellectual threat that Robert Bork posed, but he was still likely to be influential and faced a relatively difficult battle. Still, with a 55–45 Republican majority and a Republican president—as well as John Roberts's confirmation hearings creating some distraction—Alito's relatively narrow 58–42 confirmation vote showed that Democrats still viewed him as a threat.

Confirmation Battles over Cabinet Members

The confirmation battles over cabinet nominees are very short in comparison to those for judges. Nevertheless, can we detect a similar pattern, where the same factors explain which nominees face the toughest battles? To answer this, I looked at 196 cabinet nominations from the Carter administration, starting immediately after the 1976 general election through 2005 during the Bush II administration. Almost all the factors examined for judges can similarly be examined for cabinet nominations: administration, gender, race, age, professional background, political characteristics, and the year of the administration. The main difference is that for judges, measures of quality are more readily available.[310] This arises partly from the vastly different jobs from which cabinet nominees are drawn; they are not all lawyers as judges are, and there are too few nominees for any particular cabinet post to discern any real pattern.

Overall, the results were indeed similar to those shown for judges, though the effects were small—a matter of only a couple of days. (Figures 4.17A-C show the results for one regression.) Graduate school per se doesn't seem to matter, but going to a top ten undergraduate school increased the confirmation process by 10 percent; going to a top ten graduate school increased the confirmation process by 8 percent, though this last effect was not statistically significant.

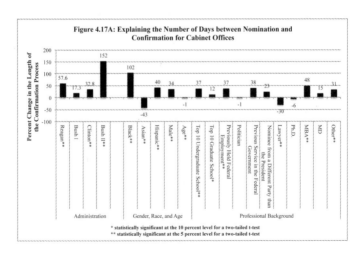

Figure 4.17A: Explaining the Number of Days between Nomination and Confirmation for Cabinet Offices

* statistically significant at the 10 percent level for a two-tailed t-test
** statistically significant at the 5 percent level for a two-tailed t-test

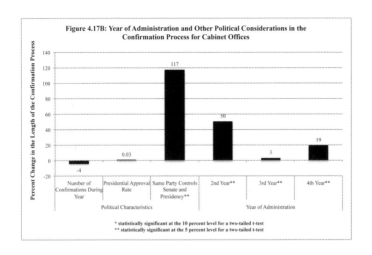

Figure 4.17B: Year of Administration and Other Political Considerations in the Confirmation Process for Cabinet Offices

* statistically significant at the 10 percent level for a two-tailed t-test
** statistically significant at the 5 percent level for a two-tailed t-test

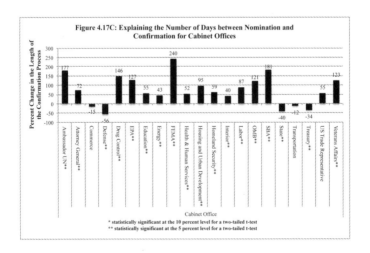

Figure 4.17C: Explaining the Number of Days between Nomination and Confirmation for Cabinet Offices

* statistically significant at the 10 percent level for a two-tailed t-test
** statistically significant at the 5 percent level for a two-tailed t-test

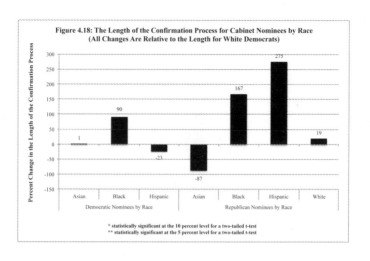

Figure 4.18: The Length of the Confirmation Process for Cabinet Nominees by Race
(All Changes Are Relative to the Length for White Democrats)

* statistically significant at the 10 percent level for a two-tailed t-test
** statistically significant at the 5 percent level for a two-tailed t-test

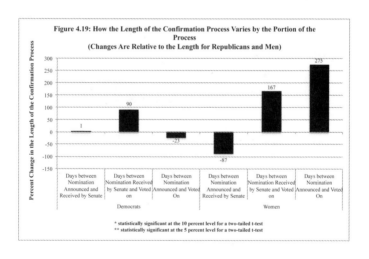

Figure 4.19: How the Length of the Confirmation Process Varies by the Portion of the Process
(Changes Are Relative to the Length for Republicans and Men)

* statistically significant at the 10 percent level for a two-tailed t-test
** statistically significant at the 5 percent level for a two-tailed t-test

Conclusion

For cabinet posts there is no significant difference in the length of confirmations by race (Figure 4.18) or by party or gender (Figure 4.19).

The key factor seems to be that the more important the court, the more difficult the confirmation. With confirmation rates falling and the length of the confirmation process getting dramatically longer, the quality of circuit court judges has been declining over time. The most troubling results strongly indicate that the most successful circuit court judges, as measured by Choi-Gulati or Landes et al., faced the most difficult confirmation battles. The effect was large: a 1 percent increase in judicial quality increased the length of the confirmation process by between 1 and 3 percent. Similarly, nominees who attended the best schools or served as clerks for the Supreme Court also faced difficult nominations to the circuit court. While demonstrating brilliance increases the probability of nomination, it makes it much harder to get confirmed. Again, my results underestimate the difficulty of the confirmation process because I don't know how many potential nominees turned down the chance to go before the Senate.

The length of the confirmation process has increased during recent Republican and Democratic administrations while the opposition party controlled the Senate, so it is difficult to blame the problem on any particular party. The major lengthening of the confirmation process for circuit court judges started in 1995, under Clinton, when the Republicans controlled the Senate. The process continued to accelerate out of control when Bush II was president and the Democrats controlled the Senate; it has continued at a higher rate with the introduction of judicial filibusters during the 108th Congress (2003-04). In return, Republicans filibustered against President Obama's nomination of Goodwin Liu to the Ninth Circuit Court, with Liu withdrawing his name for consideration after thirteen months.[311]

Judicial confirmation rates have fallen and the length of the process has increased dramatically since the 1970s, but not all nominees were affected equally. The smartest nominees who would be the most influential, most cited judges suffered the most difficult time getting confirmed.

Major changes have been occurring. Just take the drop in the percent of nominees who attended top 10 law schools. For circuit court nominees, during the end of the 1970s, more than half—54 percent—went to a top 10 law school. That fell to 47.5 percent during the 1980s, 42.4 percent in the 1990s, and 41.8 percent in the 2000s.

Among the other results that stand out, Democratic senators make confirmations difficult for Republican picks who are black or who have achieved a high average impact per opinion outside their circuit. Similarly, Republican senators resist Democratic circuit court nominees who have previously served as federal district court judges.

5: ABA RATINGS: WHAT DO THEY REALLY MEASURE?

"Posner . . . formerly a professor of law
at the University of Chicago, is by all
accounts brilliant; according to critics,
dangerously brilliant."[312]
—Nicholas D. Kristof, 1982

For more than fifty years, the American Bar Association (ABA) has played a central role in determining who has been appointed to the federal courts. The ABA has advised every president since Eisenhower in 1953 and the Senate Judiciary Committee since 1948.[313] Using a scale that ranges from "Extremely Well Qualified" to "Not Qualified," the fifteen-member ABA committee assigns ratings to judicial nominees. The ABA is quietly told which nominees a president is considering and then provides the president with an advisory opinion before the nominee's name is ever made public. The goal of this is to protect potential nominees from having to go through a public and painful humiliation of facing a negative rating from the country's top association of lawyers. Potential nominees who have failed to meet the ABA's criteria have never had their names formally put forward.[314]

The idea of having an independent, nonpolitical review is quite appealing. Besides the possibility of catching substandard nominees whose flaws have been overlooked by the president's staff, such a review could be attractive for nominees themselves. After all, it could in theory help ensure that their confirmations go smoothly and make the process less political. In fact, in addition to legal aptitude, experience, and integrity, the ABA criteria explicitly tries to screen out nominees who would potentially let their politics influence their judicial decisions as well as those who do not have the right judicial temperament. All of these different factors are considered equally in evaluating the nominee.

At least since the Reagan administration, Republicans have grumbled that the ABA has a bias against conservatives. Bork was rated "Well Qualified" by a majority of the ABA panel, but four committee members actually voted to find him "Unqualified," despite no specific problems during his term on the powerful D.C. Circuit.[315] As *Time* magazine put it, "The most surprising blow to Bork was dealt by the [ABA], which damned him with divided praise."[316] The flames were fanned further during Clarence Thomas's confirmation, when he was rated only as "Qualified"; two committee members even claimed that he was "Unqualified."

Many Republicans viewed Bork's and Thomas's ratings as merely the most visible among many cases of bias. The three most influential circuit court judges from the Carter to Clinton administrations were all appointed by Ronald Reagan: Richard Posner, Frank Easterbrook, and James Wilkinson. Yet, all three were rated only as "Qualified/Not Qualified" by the ABA, and they received the most "Not Qualified" votes of any confirmed circuit court nominees from Carter through George W. Bush.

Chapter 4 noted that while higher ABA ratings for circuit and district court nominees speed up the process, the effect is not statistically significant. The ratings might be useful for broader political debates over nominees, but the Senate does not seem to pay much attention to ABA scores. It's possible that, despite what senators say publicly, they know the ABA ratings are biased. Alternatively, the Senate may recognize that the ABA does a poor job of predicting the type of judge a nominee will become. This chapter examines both possibilities.

Of the 345 circuit court nominees over the five administrations from Carter through the first term of Bush II, the ratings of "Qualified/Not Qualified" were the lowest ever given out by the ABA. As Figure 5.1 shows, 306 of the 345 nominees (89 percent) received higher ratings than Posner, Easterbrook, and Wilkinson and were ranked at least as "Qualified." For district court nominees (Figure 5.2), 1,092 of the 1,215 nominees (90 percent) were given at least a "Qualified" rating. The small number of ratings of "Well Qualified/Extremely Well Qualified" and higher arises because they were only given out during the Carter administration and part of the Reagan administration.

A few quotations illustrate how questionable the ABA ratings are considered within judicial circles. Judge Terence Evans of the Seventh Circuit was appointed by President Clinton, but he describes Posner as "absolutely off-the-wall brilliant" and Easterbrook as "absolutely bril-

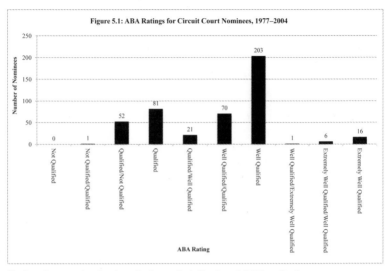

Figure 5.1: ABA Ratings for Circuit Court Nominees, 1977–2004

*To view a larger version of each graph, please refer to Supplement: Full-Page Graphs.

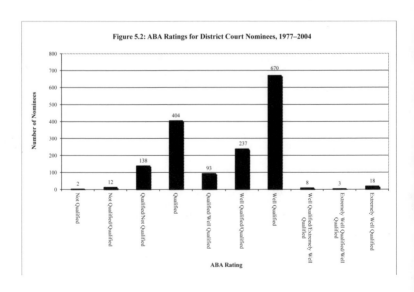

Figure 5.2: ABA Ratings for District Court Nominees, 1977–2004

liant. A certified genius—his mind is like a computer. He must know a thousand names of cases and their citations by heart."[317] Another Reagan appointee on the Seventh Circuit, Dan Manion, said of both Easterbrook and Posner that they are "two really brilliant judges."[318] District Court Judge Brian Duff noted that "Judge Easterbrook is a brilliant man and an excellent writer who believes his strength is as the strength of 10 because his heart is pure."[319] *The American Lawyer* called Easterbrook "brilliant."[320]

The extraordinary abilities of Easterbrook, Posner, and Wilkinson were known long before they were appointed to the circuit court. Easterbrook and Posner were extremely successful professors at the University of Chicago Law School, which was ranked at the time as one of the top three or four law schools in the country. Wilkinson had been a professor at the University of Virginia Law School, one of the top ten schools in the country.

Prior to his nomination to the court in October 1981, Posner had authored nine books and more than ninety-three academic journal articles, an output that few academics match over an entire career but which Posner had accomplished by age forty-two.[321] He had been president of the *Harvard Law Review* and graduated first in his law school class. Well before his nomination he had been the founding editor of the *Journal of Legal Studies*, a journal that applied economic analysis to every aspect of the legal system. Shortly before his nomination, the journal was ranked as one of the top four most influential economics journals. More important than his volume of work was its importance. His early work was path-breaking and was widely recognized as extremely important. His first book, *Economic Analysis of Law*, is considered by many to be a "pioneering" work and has had a huge impact on academia.[322] It has become a classic textbook in law schools and economics departments throughout the country.

Meanwhile, Easterbrook had published thirty-one journal articles and two books at the time of his nomination in 1984, at age thirty-six.[323] His 1981 article "The Proper Role of a Target's Management in Responding to a Tender Offer" in the *Harvard Law Review* was the most heavily cited corporate law article in legal scholarship. Easterbrook had also had a distinguished career outside of academia. In 1974 he served as Assistant to the Solicitor General, and in 1978 he was Deputy Solicitor General for the Carter administration Justice Department. Few people have managed such success in academia while practicing law in the real world.

Although Wilkinson's career prior to his judicial nomination had not reached the heights of the careers of Easterbrook and Posner, his career had been highly successful by most standards. He had served as the Deputy Assistant Attorney General in the Civil Rights Division of the Department of Justice and clerked for the U.S. Supreme Court. He had published academic articles as well as two books.

The writings and impact of these three individuals on academia and the law are significant enough that one could go on with a long list of accolades, but the point is simple: it is hard to believe that the members of the ABA committee who scored Easterbrook, Posner, and Wilkinson as "Qualified/Not Qualified"—the lowest rating they were giving to anyone—could really have believed that these judges were weaker than 90 percent of the nominees over nearly three decades. The comparison is even worse when one considers that Easterbrook and Posner appear to have received six or seven "Not Qualified" votes, the most "Unqualified" votes of anyone confirmed to the circuit courts during the period studied in this book.

In a search of news stories from the period, I found few complaints that could have motivated a low ABA rating.[324] The Chicago Council of Lawyers found Easterbrook's trial experience lacking, but the ABA rule that nominees be a practicing lawyer for at least ten years had been met by all but the most strained definitions. Easterbrook graduated from law school in 1973, eleven years before his nomination; during that time he had worked in government for five years presenting cases before the Supreme Court and had handled private cases while teaching. The charge looks even more ridiculous once one considers the positions he held. For example, Easterbrook's positions in the Office of the Solicitor General were ideal for someone doing the type of appellate work handled by circuit courts. This office supervises and conducts two-thirds of the litigation before the Supreme Court each year.[325] In addition, when Easterbrook was not in government, he argued a number of important cases in private practice, though he lost one before the Supreme Court in which the National Collegiate Athletic Association's multimillion-dollar contracts with ABC and CBS were voided.[326] In the twenty cases that he argued before the Supreme Court, some viewed him as "one of the very top advocates appearing before the Supreme Court in his days at the bar."[327]

For Wilkinson, the left-wing magazine *The Nation* claimed that his nomination faced "bitter opposition from civil rights groups," but the magazine did not mention any professional shortcomings.[328] Similarly, a LexisNexis search found no mentions of Posner's supposed short-comings that could explain his low ABA rating.

Three academics nominated by Democrats provide a useful contrast. Guido Calabresi of Yale is probably the most similar to Easterbrook and Posner in terms of his academic success, but he was rated as "Well Qualified/ Qualified." Calabresi has long been known as a partisan Democrat. It was even reported that he "notoriously told a liberal group in June that Bush's election was like Mussolini's rise to power—the president had been installed by the 'illegitimate acts of a legitimate institution.'"[329] Diane Wood, also a University of Chicago professor and an appointee to the Seventh Circuit (the same circuit as Easterbrook and Posner) and a Clinton appointee, is not remotely similar to Easterbrook and Posner in terms of influence, yet was rated "Well Qualified."

Goodwin Liu, a Berkeley Law professor, was nominated on February 24, 2010, at age thirty-nine. On the positive side, like Posner, Liu had clerked on the Supreme Court. But besides being young, he had a number of strikes against him. At the time of his nomination by President Obama, Liu had only a small fraction of the academic output of Easterbrook or Posner with just seventeen law review publications. He had also not argued any cases before the Supreme Court. Unlike Easterbrook or Posner, he had engaged in a lot of political activity, writing eleven op-eds advocating partisan liberal positions on affirmative action, gay marriage, and school funding, and attacking Samuel Alito's nomination to the Supreme Court. Yet the ABA unanimously rated Liu as "Well Qualified."

With cases such as these, some Republicans, including Senator Bob Dole, labeled the ABA as just "another blatantly partisan liberal advocacy group."[330] This debate holds a certain irony for Posner: despite the conservative label that he had because of his association with the Chicago Law School and his strong interest in law and economics, Posner is a long-time registered Democrat.[331] But because Posner was one of Reagan's initial circuit court nominations, Democrats were unconvinced that his views would be sympathetic to theirs.

Although most Democrats publicly point to the ABA as unbiased evaluators of judicial quality, for some Democrats the evidence is equally obvious that the ABA is biased against them. Talking about district court nominees who were rated as "Not Qualified," Senator Patrick Leahy said in March 2001:

> The group, though, that does the screen-
> ing has really kept themselves out of
> partisan politics. Otherwise, I think

Democrats would be the ones first
against it, because I think it's something
like twenty-five or twenty-six nominees
where they've said they were not qualified. Twenty-two or twenty-three of them
were Democrats. Only three or four were
Republicans. So it's hard to see any kind
of a Democratic bias there.[332]

In this case, Senator Leahy isn't just cherry-picking numbers—his statement is false. As shown in Figures 5.1 and
5.2, there simply aren't that many nominees who are classified as either "Not Qualified" or "Not Qualified/Quali-
fied," with only one circuit court nominee and fourteen
district court nominees all the way from Carter through
Obama who fall into those categories. Even including
those who are "Qualified/Not Qualified" does not help
his claim because, as we will see in the next section, most
of those who were classified as "Not Qualified" in any way
are Republicans.

Former U.S. attorneys general are divided on whether
the ABA keeps politics out of its decisions. Those against
the ABA include Richard Thornburgh (Bush I), William
Barr (Bush I), and Ed Meese (Reagan). Democrat Griffin
Bell (Carter) supported removing the ABA from the process as early as 1996.[333] Conversely, Elliot C. Richardson
(Nixon), Benjamin Civiletti (Carter), and Nicholas Kat-
zenbach (Johnson) maintain that the ABA provides an
important service in evaluating nominees.

The debate over the ABA's role in the confirmation process heated up after George W. Bush's election in 2000. In March 2001, he ordered his Department of Justice to stop consulting with the ABA before the administration made its nominations public; the Republican-controlled Senate announced that it would also stop requiring ABA evaluations before proceeding. Democrats were quite angry. Senator Joseph Biden called Bush's action "outrageous," and Senator Barbara Boxer declared "It's war."[334] But this brief experiment was temporarily undone when the Democrats gained control of the Senate just two months later, after Vermont Senator Jim Jeffords bolted the Republican Party. Democrats announced that confirmations would not proceed until after the ABA had conducted its rating. When Republicans regained control of the Senate in 2003, the ABA again lost its central role of evaluating candidates.

Yet, the ABA was never more than partially sidelined, even with Republicans running the show from 2003 to 2006. The ABA still kept on publicly announcing its evaluations, even though nominees were no longer vetted through the ABA before nomination. Indeed, in the two years from May 2003 to May 2005, a LexisNexis search found more than 602 news stories that discussed the ABA ratings of Bush's judicial nominees.[335] Virtually all the stories simply reported what a nominee's ABA rating was without commenting on any possible bias in the evaluation. Under Obama, with Democrats again controlling the presidency and the Senate, the ABA regained its traditional place in the confirmation process.

Consistent with Republican accusations, the American Bar Association remains unabashedly liberal. The organization has taken stands supporting affirmative action, abortion, and single-payer national health care; bans on semiautomatic assault weapons; and funding for the National Endowment for the Arts with no restrictions on content or subject matter.[336] It has also opposed policies generally supported by conservatives, such as restrictions on welfare benefits, the prohibition of government benefits for illegal immigrants, and mandatory minimum prison sentences for certain crimes.[337]

It is difficult to find a position that does not toe the liberal Democratic line. Still, the ABA rejects the liberal label and claims that there is a "high wall" between its policy positions and its evaluation of judges.[338] Surely, it is possible that despite such liberal activism, the ratings could be politically unbiased. However, these concerns raise several questions. Are the ABA judicial ratings systematically biased against Republican or conservative judges? Does the threat of a "Not Qualified" rating prevent Republican judges from being nominated while a judge with the same qualifications but proposed by a Democrat would be confirmed unchallenged? Does the ABA evaluate candidates equally with regard to other categories, such as race? With the ABA again being used by the Obama administration and the Democratic Senate to evaluate judges, the issue of political bias is quite relevant.

Determining ABA Scores for Judicial Nominees

The following sections look at what factors determine ABA scores for circuit and district court nominees.

Circuit Court Nominees. Few judicial nominees have been examined in previous research on possible ABA bias. One of my earlier studies analyzed 114 circuit court nominees, still a rather small sample from a statistical point of view.[339] The next largest study by another author looked at just forty-nine circuit court nominees.[340] The evidence was mixed, and the results were extremely sensitive to how the data were studied.[341] This is hardly surprising given the small samples, which also limited what differences could be accounted for among the nominees.

In contrast, the research described here is based on the ABA scores for 324 circuit court and 1,216 district court nominees. It is valuable to compare how the ABA treats both types of nominees. As we saw in Chapter 3, circuit court nominees have a much more difficult time being confirmed than do district court nominees. Following the same logic, it would be quite plausible that the ABA is most biased toward the more important circuit court nominations.[342]

Figures 5.3 and 5.4 depict the percentage of different administrations' nominees who were given the various ABA ratings. The graphs do suggest that the ABA treats Republicans and Democrats differently for circuit court nominations. Carter and Clinton nominees clearly received the greatest number of "Well Qualified" ratings and the fewest low scores.

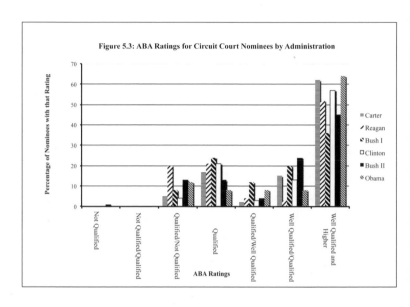

Figure 5.3: ABA Ratings for Circuit Court Nominees by Administration

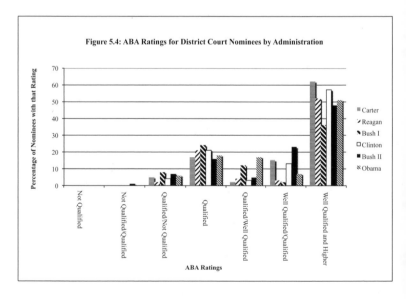

Figure 5.4: ABA Ratings for District Court Nominees by Administration

In contrast, there is no apparent pattern for district courts. For example, Reagan nominees got a "Well Qualified" rating slightly more frequently than Obama's nominees. George W. Bush's nominees also received that rating virtually as frequently as Obama's. In addition, an almost identical share of Carter administration nominees received "Well Qualified," "Qualified/Not Qualified," and "Not Qualified" ratings as did Bush II nominees.

Other factors must be taken into account, of course. After all, Republican circuit court nominees might be of a lower quality than Democratic nominees and thus deserve the lower ratings. To account for that possibility, I relied on the factors discussed in the previous chapter: attendance at a top ten law school; service as a federal or state judge; at least ten years of experience in the practice of law (as well as length of time in private or government practice); previous clerkships; political factors (party control of the presidency and Senate, the president's approval ratings as given by Gallup, and the number of nominations made that year); race, age, and gender of the nominee; and the administration in which the nomination took place.

The variables on legal background are included because they are used by the ABA in rating nominees. The political factors also could be important in explaining the ABA's behavior. After all, the ABA may bias ratings very strategically. If the nomination is going to be successful no matter what the ABA does, the organization has little reason to bias the score. For example, ABA ratings probably do not matter as much when the same party controls both the Senate and presidency. If bias exists, the greatest return for the ABA is to bias the ratings for nominations that it anticipates will be the most contested. Of course, selectively targeting certain nominees also makes it somewhat more difficult to detect bias than if all members of a party face lower ratings.

Consider the ratings given to Easterbrook, Posner, and Wilkinson as opposed to the ratings given to other circuit court nominees. If the ABA had been unbiased and applied the factors listed above consistently across all nominees (and if one excludes the factors measuring systematic bias across administrations), there should have been only a 24 percent probability of the ABA giving Easterbrook a "Qualified/Not Qualified" rating, a 20 percent probability for Posner, and a 16 percent probability for Wilkinson. The odds of all three being rated as "Qualified/Not Qualified" would have been less than 1 percent.

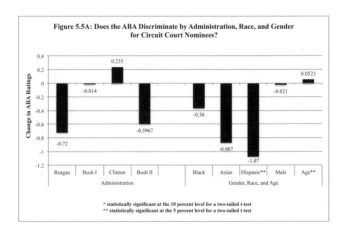

Figure 5.5A: Does the ABA Discriminate by Administration, Race, and Gender for Circuit Court Nominees?

* statistically significant at the 10 percent level for a two-tailed t-test
** statistically significant at the 5 percent level for a two-tailed t-test

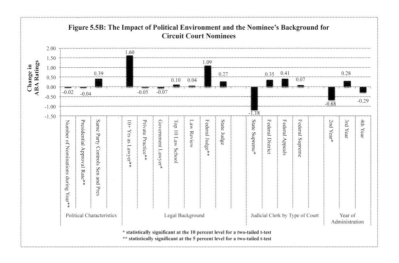

Figure 5.5B: The Impact of Political Environment and the Nominee's Background for Circuit Court Nominees

Figures 5.5A and 5.5B show how the different factors are related to the ABA score for circuit court nominees. Figure 5.5A shows the ratings across administrations as well as the impact of differences in race, gender, and age after all the other factors are accounted for. A value of one in the figures implies a one rating level change.

In interpreting the results, two things should be kept in mind. First, think of each of the ten different ABA ratings (shown in Figures 5.1 and 5.2) as being its own ten-point scale. A coefficient value of "one" implies one point on the ten-point scale. Second, when comparing outcomes for administrations or other factors, we must always exclude one administration or factor to be used as the baseline. For example, in Figure 5.5, the Carter administration is the baseline that other administrations are compared to. Thus, the –0.72 value shown for the Reagan administration means that his nominees, everything else being equal, received about three-quarters of one rating level less than the baseline Carter administration.

Put differently, the average Carter circuit court nominees received an ABA score that was slightly less than "Well Qualified/Qualified." A Reagan or Bush II nominee who had the same experience and background as the average Carter nominee would have received an ABA rating of "Qualified/Well Qualified." Accounting for different combinations of the factors used in these regressions doesn't change the fact that Reagan and George W. Bush's circuit court nominees faced consistently lower ABA scores than those for Carter or Clinton. (See the Appendix for Chapter 5.)

One of the other findings in Figure 5.5A is particularly startling. Even after accounting for education and career achievements, Hispanics were given a rating one level lower than whites. In other words, while the average white nominee received a weak "Well Qualified/Qualified" rating, a similar hypothetical Hispanic nominee received a weaker "Qualified/Well Qualified" rating. The estimates in Chapter 4 imply that these lower ABA scores lengthen Hispanics' confirmation process by about 6 percent. Yet Democrats are silent on how the ABA treats Hispanics.

Another finding is that older nominees are given higher ABA ratings. Each twenty-year increase in a nominee's age raises the rating by 1.5 levels, and having been a lawyer for at least ten years and having been a federal judge raise the rating by one level. The higher rating from age exists even after taking into account whether they have been in practice for at least ten years and the number of years they have been in private or government practice. The effect, though, is relatively small per additional year of age. As will be shown later, the effect is driven by higher scores for older Republicans. Having already been a federal judge (but not a state judge) also seems to ensure a much higher ABA rating.

As discussed in the previous chapter, the *Almanac for the Federal Judiciary* surveys lawyers about circuit court judges' political views and judicial temperament. Along with competence, the ability to separate political views from judicial decisions and judicial temperament are two factors that the ABA says it explicitly takes into account when evaluating nominees. Those factors are analyzed here in separate regressions because information is not available for all nominees. Presumably if the

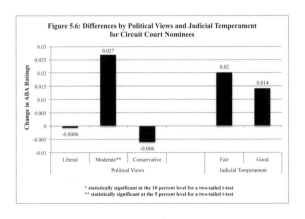

Figure 5.6: Differences by Political Views and Judicial Temperament for Circuit Court Nominees

ABA does its job correctly, the judges with the best judicial temperament and the least political bias should have received the highest ABA ratings when they were nominated.

Because the lawyer surveys only provide information for those who have been confirmed, examining whether judicial temperament correlates with positive ABA ratings necessarily involves a small sample. The evidence implies that even after accounting for many other factors, ABA ratings do a poor job of predicting how well judges will perform in terms of judicial temperament. If the ABA ratings were useful predictors, those nominees who got low ABA ratings should also do poorly in terms of these different survey results once they become judges. But nominees who end up getting classified as having "fair" judicial temperament once they are on the court were given higher ABA ratings than nominees who ended up being classified as having a "good" temperament. In this case, it is fortunate that these perverse results are not statistically significant: the ABA ratings don't help senators pick nominees who will have the right temperament.

ABA ratings are more strongly correlated with political biases. Judges who were rated as moderate resulted in significantly higher ABA ratings than did nominees whom the survey found to be neutral, liberal, or conservative. The possible problem here is that what may be moderate to practicing lawyers might be quite liberal to non-lawyers.[343] Conservative nominees actually received just slightly lower ABA ratings than liberal ones, but the difference is not statistically significant.

The impact of publications on ABA ratings was tested in several ways. As described in Chapter 4, publications were divided into three categories: journal publications, such as law reviews; books; and popular writings, such as opinion pieces in newspapers or magazines. I first looked for correlation between the type of publication and the ABA rating. Presumably, writing a law review article indicates a nominee's expertise in that area. The same would be true of books and even popular pieces, although the ABA might look with concern on nominees who have been too politically active.

Surprisingly, publishing books or journal articles don't appear to affect the ABA rating. According to Figure 5.7, Democrats seem to get a slightly bigger increase in their ABA rating from book publications than do Republicans, but the differences are not statistically significant.

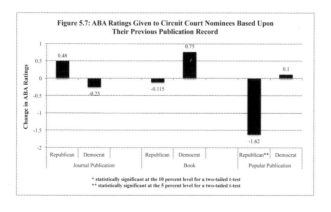

Figure 5.7: ABA Ratings Given to Circuit Court Nominees Based Upon Their Previous Publication Record

* statistically significant at the 10 percent level for a two-tailed t-test
** statistically significant at the 5 percent level for a two-tailed t-test

By contrast, the statistical tests reveal a huge and significant difference in how Republicans and Democrats are treated if they publish op-ed and popular pieces. The average Democratic circuit court nominee who published in newspapers or popular magazines had an average ABA rating that was right in the middle, between "Well Qualified/Qualified" and "Well Qualified." Those nominees received a rating that was just slightly higher than similar Democratic nominees who had not published in popular publications and almost 1.75 levels higher than similar Republicans who had also published in those outlets. For similar Republicans and Democrats who had published in popular media outlets, the difference translates to being ranked as between "Well Qualified/Qualified" and "Well Qualified" and between "Qualified" and "Qualified/Not Qualified." Thus, potential Republican nominees who express their political or legal views in the popular press risk getting much lower ABA ratings.

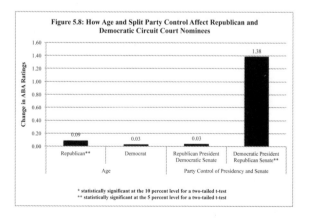

Figure 5.8: How Age and Split Party Control Affect Republican and Democratic Circuit Court Nominees

* statistically significant at the 10 percent level for a two-tailed t-test
** statistically significant at the 5 percent level for a two-tailed t-test

Each factor in ABA ratings was then broken down to see if the ABA treated Republicans and Democrats differently when calculating their ratings. For most factors, there was no difference. As with past research by Shipan and Shannon (2003), the two factors for which I found a difference were the nominee's age at nomination and split party control between the presidency and the Senate. The results in Figure 5.8 show that ABA ratings increase with the age of Republican nominees, whereas for Democratic nominees age is unrelated to their rating. The results also demonstrate that Democratic nominees receive much higher ratings when the Senate is controlled by Republicans than Republican nominees receive when the Democrats control the Senate.

These key results indicate that the ABA biases its ratings when they matter most. Democrats don't mind putting older Republicans on the courts because they will not be on as long as younger Republicans. By giving an older Republican a higher ABA rating, the ABA can make it look like they are behaving fairly towards Republicans on average without having to worry about the consequences of having that person on the court for too long.

The reasoning is no different for the second finding on split party control. Giving Republican nominees low ratings when the Republicans control both the presidency and the Senate exposes the ABA to charges of bias with no benefit because Republicans control the process and will get their confirmations through. Republican nominations only stand to be defeated when the Democrats control the Senate, and it is then, when the ratings matter, that the ABA shows its true bias. Similarly, there is no reason to bias ratings in favor of Democratic nominees when the Democrats control both the presidency and the Senate.

Both the age and the split party control effects are fairly important: a fifteen-year increase in a nominee's age raises the ABA rating for a Republican relative to that for a Democrat by one level. The age for Republican circuit court nominees ranges from thirty-two to sixty-nine, and for Democrats it ranges from thirty-three to sixty-six. If the ABA is biased against Republicans, giving higher ratings to older Republicans is one way to raise the average Republican ABA rating without helping younger Republican nominees who would be on the court for a longer amount of time if confirmed. Since we account for political views, this result can be explained away as older Republicans being perceived as more moderate than younger ones. The result is strongest when the Democrats control the Senate and the Republicans control the presidency.

Democratic nominees with a Republican Senate receive a rating that is about 1.35 levels higher than do Republican nominees under a Democratic Senate. Again, if the ABA favors Democratic nominees, the greatest return occurs when there is split control; if the ABA wants to help out Democrats, they will do so when the president is a Democrat with a Republican Senate.

District Court Nominees. The next four figures in this chapter (Figures 5.9A to 5.11) are based on the same methodology being applied to district court nominees. There seem to be no differences at the district court level between Republicans and Democrats, which is consistent with the theory that the ABA only biases ratings when it matters to avoid charges of biases for relatively unimportant positions. Carter and Reagan nominees have similar scores, as do Clinton and Bush II nominees.

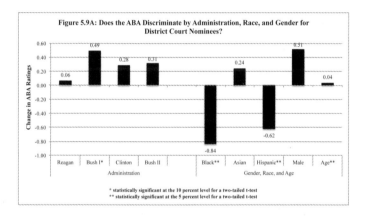

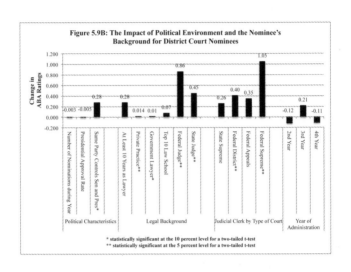

Figure 5.9B: The Impact of Political Environment and the Nominee's Background for District Court Nominees

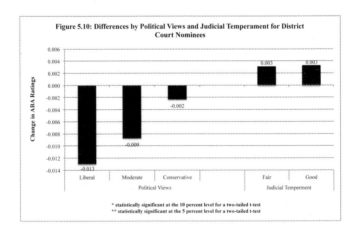

Figure 5.10: Differences by Political Views and Judicial Temperament for District Court Nominees

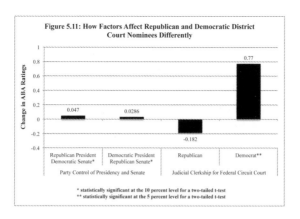

Figure 5.11: How Factors Affect Republican and Democratic District Court Nominees Differently

A few other significant results are similar, too. Hispanics again receive lower ABA ratings than whites and older nominees even for the same apparent qualifications. All nominees who had served as a federal or state judge or who had clerked for the Supreme or district courts also received higher ABA ratings than those without such experience.[344]

ABA Scores and Judicial Influence

In Chapter 4, we went to great lengths examining different measures of judicial quality. Going to an elite law school or being on a law review may make circuit court confirmations more difficult, but these factors are unrelated to ABA ratings. As mentioned earlier, work by Landes, Lessig, and Solimine as well as by Choi and Gulati provides additional judicial quality measures ranging from

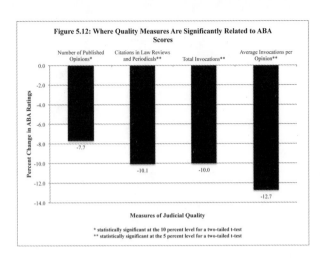

Figure 5.12: Where Quality Measures Are Significantly Related to ABA Scores

the number of different types of citations to the number of opinions written.

Yet looking separately at each of their seventeen indexes shows that they are either unrelated or negatively related to ABA ratings. Four of the Choi and Gulati measures show that higher judicial quality results in significantly lower ABA ratings. Of particular interest, invocations (a judge's citations that are given the most weight in other judges' opinions) indicate that each additional invocation or average invocation per opinion lowers the ABA rating by 10 and 13 percent respectively. On average, ABA ratings not only do a poor job predicting judicial temperament and bias, they also serve as very poor predictors for how well a judge's opinions will be valued by other judges.

The ABA ratings can also be shown separately for Democratic and Republican judges. Doing so gives an interesting result: the ratings are positively associated with the influence of Democratic judges and negatively associated with the influence of Republican ones. The results clearly indicate a bias on the part of the ABA. It is obviously trying to get more influential Democrats on the federal bench. And it favors potentially less influential Republicans over stronger ones. While the ABA ratings might have originally been set up to alert presidents to potential problems with nominees, the actual process has become quite political.

6: INCREASING TENURE

The longer a judge is on the bench, the more opportunities he or she will have to shape the law. A member of a president's cabinet will have his or her position for a maximum of eight years; a federal judge is on the bench for life.[345] With people living longer, tenure may increase and, with more at stake, confirmation battles could intensify. Some politicians, such as Senator Rick Santorum (R-PA) and Representative Lamar Smith (R-TX), have proposed term limits for judges.[346] And a group of law professors has called for a constitutional amendment to limit the term of Supreme Court justices to eighteen years.[347]

The United States is the only democracy in the world that grants judges life tenure without a mandatory retirement age.[348] France, Germany, Ireland, Italy, Malta, Spain, and Austria appoint their justices to fixed terms.[349] Yet the United States is fundamentally different from these other countries in that our Constitution was designed to make it difficult to institute change. Not only does our Constitution have a Senate and House that represent different constituencies and a presidency with yet a different mixture of voters to make changes difficult, but the federal courts represent past presidents and Senates from up to decades earlier and help put an additional brake on change. Even if judicial tenure was increasing, it is quite possible that the constitution's framers would view longer tenures as a benefit.

Advocates for term limits argue that it is simply undemocratic and wrong if "powerful officials hold office for an average of 25.6 years with some of them serving for 35 years or more."[350] Yet some benefits may exist along with the "costs." For example, long terms for judges can ensure stability. Individuals and corporations value certainty in legal decisions, whether the case involves how contracts will be interpreted or the size of punitive damages. Decisions on what to do in the future are often difficult enough, but when one does not know what rules will be in place, many projects that would otherwise be profitable simply will not be worth the risk.

There is no proof that one system is worse than another. But what should be examined is whether district, circuit, and Supreme Court judges have been staying on the bench longer than their predecessors.

Does length of tenure affect confirmation battles? As shown in previous chapters, the battles over circuit court nominees have been much more bitter than battles over district court nominees. Is the bitterness due to differing tenures for circuit court judges and district court judges? Is the length and intensity of battles during the confirmation process related to increasing lengths of service on the courts?

Judges' tenure has increased with the increase in average life expectancy: the growth in tenure for district and circuit court judges actually slightly exceeds the growth in lifespan. The reasons for longer tenure vary for different types of judges. Supreme Court justices are staying longer on the bench because they are retiring slightly later. In contrast, circuit court judges under Bush II were retiring at virtually the same age as under Carter, and district court judges were retiring just one year later than under that administration. The longer tenures for circuit and district court judges almost entirely arose from appointment at increasingly younger ages.

Americans' life expectancy has increased significantly over the past century. People who make it to age fifty-five can expect to live almost eight years longer than they would have one hundred years ago. Given that Supreme Court justices are confirmed at an average age of fifty-four, one might assume that they have experienced the same increase in life expectancy. But, surprisingly, that is not true. The life expectancy for judges has remained virtually constant over the past century. Most likely the living standards for justices on the High Court were superior to those of much of the population in 1900, so their life expectancy was already higher than that of the average person.

Some notable examples include the famous Oliver Wendell Holmes, who was nominated to the Supreme Court in 1902 and served thirty-one years until 1932. He died at the age of ninety in 1935. Charles E. Hughes joined the Supreme Court in 1910 and served for thirty years until 1941. He died at the age of eighty-six in 1948. Willis Van Devanter also joined the court in 1910, where he stayed for twenty-six years. He died in 1941 at the age of eighty-one.

Indeed, the justices who retired between 1900 and 1979 died at remarkably similar ages. Justices who retired between 1900 and 1909 died, on average, at age seventy-nine. By the 1970s, that number had increased by only one year. It was only during the last two decades of the twentieth century that the life expectancy of Supreme Court justices began to rise. In the 1980s, the average age of death for Supreme Court justices rose to eighty-three, and it was as recently as the 1990s that it shot up to eighty-seven. Rehnquist's recent death at age eighty falls below the average over the past couple of decades.

There is a clearer increase in tenure than in life expectancy, although tenure first falls during the 1940s, 1950s, and 1960s before rising and eventually becoming about thirteen years longer during the 1990s than it was at the beginning of the century. The rise in tenure starts during the 1970s, before any increase in lifespan for Supreme Court justices (Figure 6.1).

Possibly the most surprising fact is that despite extensive variation in the justices' retirement ages from 1900 to 1979, the changes in how long they spent on the job are small. During this time, justices spent eleven to fourteen years on the bench no matter what their age at confirmation.

From the Carter presidency through George W. Bush's first term, virtually no change occurred in retirement age for circuit court judges—it rose only from age 65.7 to 65.8 (Figure 6.2). The retirement age for district

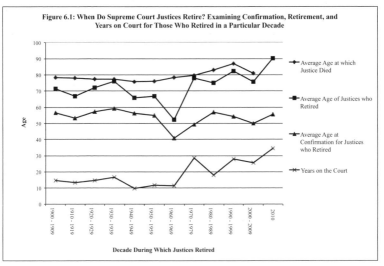

Figure 6.1: When Do Supreme Court Justices Retire? Examining Confirmation, Retirement, and Years on Court for Those Who Retired in a Particular Decade

Legend:
- Average Age at which Justice Died
- Average Age of Justices who Retired
- Average Age at Confirmation for Justices who Retired
- Years on the Court

Y-axis: Age

X-axis: Decade During Which Justices Retired
1900 - 1909, 1910 - 1919, 1920 - 1929, 1930 - 1939, 1940 - 1949, 1950 - 1959, 1960 - 1969, 1970 - 1979, 1980 - 1989, 1990 - 1999, 2000 - 2009, 2010

*To view a larger version of each graph, please refer to Supplement: Full-Page Graphs.

judges rose only slightly more: less than 1.5 years over that twenty-eight-year period (Figure 6.3). Retirement ages for both types of judges remain stuck within a year or so of age sixty-five over the past five administrations. From the 1970s through the 1990s, the retirement age for Supreme Court justices increased from 78 to 82.5.

The length of tenure for circuit and district court judges remained largely unchanged from the Carter administration to the Bush I presidency, but they changed in opposite directions after that. From the Bush I administration to the first term of Bush II, circuit court judges' tenure declined an average of 0.6 years while district court judges' tenure rose by 3.3 years—changes in tenure of about 4 and 25 percent. Those changes appear at odds with the changes in the confirmation process, particularly

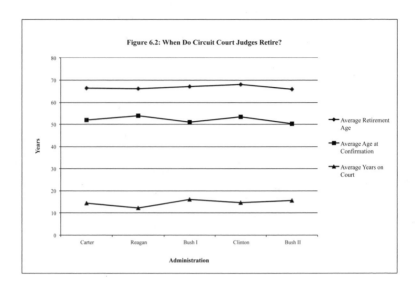

Figure 6.2: When Do Circuit Court Judges Retire?

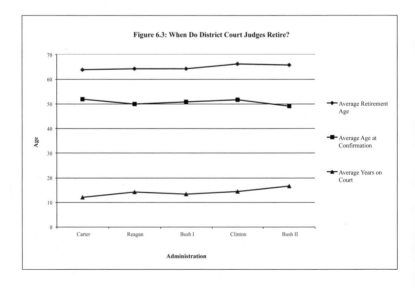

Figure 6.3: When Do District Court Judges Retire?

198   JOHN R. LOTT, JR.

the lengthening of the process for circuit court judges relative to district court judges that took place between those two administrations.

The numbers suggest that mandatory retirement ages will have little impact on the length of tenure. About 80 percent of all circuit court judges and 86 percent of all district court judges retire by age seventy. By age seventy-five, the proportion of judges who have retired rises to 93 and 97 percent respectively.

Is there a connection between length of tenure and certain groups of judges? Women, for instance, live longer than men, and whites live longer than blacks. White women who were fifty-five years old in 2002 could expect to live another twenty-eight years. Fifty-five-year-old black men could expect to live just twenty-one more years.

But it seems that differences in life expectancy due to sex or race are not accurate indicators of tenure. White women live longer and get appointed to the circuit courts at a younger age than white men, but they spend about one year less on the circuit courts than white men do, retiring considerably earlier. White women spend about five months longer on circuit courts than do black men, but that is entirely due to being confirmed at a younger age (Figure 6.4).

The small differences in tenure are unrelated to changes in life expectancy and largely unrelated to the difficulty of the confirmation process (Figure 6.5). Although black women served on circuit courts longer

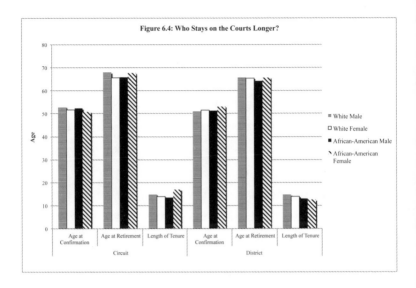

Figure 6.4: Who Stays on the Courts Longer?

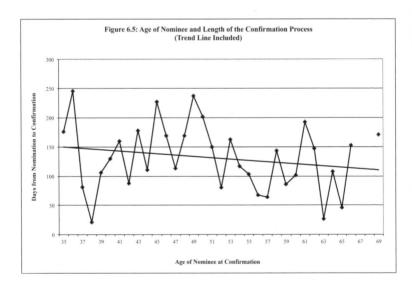

Figure 6.5: Age of Nominee and Length of the Confirmation Process
(Trend Line Included)

than white women, from 1977 to 2005 it took an average of 164 days to confirm a white woman as a circuit court judge; that is sixty-seven more days than it took to confirm black women, on average. Whatever roles life expectancy and tenure play, they do not appear related to the difficulty of the confirmation process. One would think that the increased importance of District and Circuit Court judges would cause them to stay on as judges longer, but the compensation scheme for retirement has prevented that from occurring. By contrast, you see an increase in tenure for Supreme Court judges; that increase corresponds with when judicial confirmations started getting more contentious.

Tenure largely seems dependent on the age at which judges are appointed, and the confirmation process seems to reflect that. It is for this very reason that younger men often face a longer confirmation process than older men. But the most important issue is the growing range of subjects that federal judges are asked to rule on these days and the growing possibility that they will decide a case in a way that will greatly enrage interest groups with political clout.

CONCLUSION

"We've become a trial, not a hearing."
—Senator Lindsey Graham, 2006, discussing the Senate Judiciary Committee's confirmation hearings[351]

The whole confirmation process seems backwards. Those who turn out to be the very best judges—at least in terms of how influential their opinions are—face a particularly tough time. Résumé items that usually confer prestige have become more of a millstone than an advantage for those seeking judgeships on the circuit courts. The gold standards of the legal world—graduating from a top ten law school, serving on a law review, and clerking for the Supreme Court—may be useful for getting a job in a private firm or the government generally, but those rules do not apply here. Those caught in the crossfire also tend to have more "patience, courtesy, impartiality, even temper, a well-defined sense of justice, compassion, fair play, humility, tact, common sense and understanding."[352]

Are those really the type of nominees that we most want to prevent from being judges? In the political battlefield of judicial confirmations, characteristics that we normally associate with the ideal judge such as judicial temperament and impartiality appear to take a backseat. With the extremely complicated legal issues facing courts, there is a real cost of keeping the brightest lawyers from becoming judges.

Major changes have occurred in the judicial confirmation process. The key factor seems to be that the more important the court, the more difficult the confirmation. With confirmation rates falling and the length of the confirmation process getting dramatically longer, the judicial performance of circuit court nominees has been declining over time. It is surprising how the "predictive" measures of quality are so adversely related to the difficulty of the confirmation process. For any given nomination, where one went to a top law school, whether one was on the law review, or whether one served as a judicial law clerk does make confirmation significantly more difficult, significantly lengthening and lowering the probability of confirmation.

The bitterness and personal toll of failed confirmations comes through in the personal stories of those who have gone through the process. Even many who have survived the process regret having gone through it. Charges in the press of racism or evaluations by other lawyers claiming that a nominee is "unqualified" must surely sting, especially when confirmation rules prevent nominees from being able to defend themselves. No data is available on potential nominees who turned down offers of potential appointments and those who did turn down inquiries hardly want to go public with the difficulties they expected to face.

A pretty simple economics idea states that if something becomes more costly, people do less of it. In this case, the cost of the very brightest people becoming judges has increased dramatically over time. The simultaneous drop in the number of very influential judges found by William Landes, Larry Lessig, and Michael Solimine as well as Stephen Choi and Mitu Gulati raises real concerns that this impact may be quite large.

The most troubling results strongly indicate that circuit court judges who have turned out to be the most successful judges faced the most difficult confirmation battles. The effect was large: a 1 percent increase in judicial quality increased the length of the confirmation process by between 1 and 3 percent. Similarly, nominees who attended the best schools or served as clerks for the Supreme Court also faced difficult nominations to the circuit court. While being brilliant increases the probability of nomination, this quality makes it much harder to get confirmed. Clearly nominees want to be bright, but revealing too much brightness to the other party's senators and political supporters until they get confirmed makes them vulnerable. Again, my results underestimate the difficulty of the confirmation process because I don't know how many potential nominees turned down the chance to go before the Senate.

Possibly senators of the party opposite the president only really care about preventing the best judges who are "better able to push the agendas" from being on the circuit court because they will have the most impact.[353] Circuit courts can overrule strong district court judges. Opponents might not much care about weak nominees to circuit courts because they are on three-judge panels and the brighter panel members will dominate the weaker judges. Alternatively, confirmation delay may be a way to prevent a judge from doing as much damage as he would do if he were appointed immediately.[354]

As the federal government has extended its reach into our lives by taking over areas previously reserved to the states and even going beyond what the states used to do, and as the courts have become more aggressive in asserting their own role in making policy, it is hardly surprising that each side wants to get its own people on the courts. When the range of regulatory questions taken to the courts was relatively limited and judges did their best to figure out what the existing law meant rather than follow their own policy preferences, it did not matter quite as much which party appointed the judges.

As Robert Bork once declared, our country's federal courts have become political institutions, replacing our desire for impartiality and intelligence with political considerations of whether someone can help or hurt a political cause. Because a nominee's political affiliation may predict how he will vote on the many controversial issues facing the court, it is not surprising that judicial nominations have become political contests. Even in areas where only small differences exist between Republican and Democratic nominees on multiple-judge panels (whether it is for the circuit courts or the Supreme Court), what are small differences for any individual judge make a big difference for the positions taken by the panel's majority.

Long confirmation battles with high rejection rates discourage presidents from nominating the "best and brightest" and, perhaps just as important, discourage the best and brightest from accepting nominations. If true, the results described in this book underestimate the impact of the confirmation process on judicial quality.

Maybe Americans dislike the bitter confirmation battles and view Senate leaders of both parties as "spoiled children,"[355] but if they want this changed, they will have to rethink the type of government that they want. Maybe Americans do not want the smartest, most influential people with the best judicial temperament. But the next time you hear opponents claim that a president's nominees are "extremist," consider whether they mean "smart" and "influential" instead.

APPENDIX FOR CHAPTER 4

Existing Literature

Three papers have systematically analyzed the length of the judicial confirmation process and associated confirmation rates.[356] These three papers concentrate on circuit court nominees. Lauren Bell looks at the nomination process of federal circuit court nominees from 1979 to 1998; Sarah Binder and Forrest Maltzman study the period from 1947 to 1998; and David Nixon and David Goss examine the period from 1892 to 1996.[357] All of the authors find that divided political control of the Senate and presidency has an important impact on how long it takes to confirm a judge. For example, Binder and Maltzman find that the confirmation rate at any point in the confirmation process doubles when the same party controls both the presidency and the Senate.

There are some differences in what these studies examine. Bell finds that the impact of a presidential election year and importance of interest groups, as well as how well female and minority nominees do, all have different effects when government is divided. Binder and Maltzman also claim (p. 197) that the Senate "does not treat critical nominations differently than other nominations, all else equal." They measure how critical a nomination is by looking at how ideologically divided a circuit court is. Nixon and Goss claim that female and minority nominees, as well as nominees to fill a vacancy created by a death, take considerably less time for confirmation.

The three papers are interesting, but none of them systematically examine how the confirmation process is changing over time, nor do they account for the nominees' quality beyond the American Bar Association (ABA) rating, which, given the perceived biases of the ABA, could mean something quite different for Republican and Democratic nominees. Also, none of the estimates account for geographical or time differences in the confirmation process.[358]

Nolan McCarty and Rose Razaghian studied the confirmation process for non-judicial executive branch nominations from 1885 to 1996.[359] For cabinet officials, the length of the nomination process is affected by divided government and the size of the ideological gap between the two parties in the Senate; divided government also greatly lengthens the process for lower-level positions. They also found that nominations are processed more quickly early in a president's term and that Republican as well as Justice Department nominations in general tend to take longer than other nominations. In a rough comparison between the pre- and post-New Deal periods, they do not find any long-term changes in the length of the confirmation process.

Some research has examined how the confirmation rate has changed over time. For example, R. E. Hartley and L. M. Holmes find that the proportion of lower court nominees confirmed does not change under divided government, although they do not account for other factors that may affect judicial selection.[360]

APPENDIX FOR CHAPTER 5

All the results show that Reagan and George W. Bush's circuit court nominees face consistently lower ABA scores than those for Carter or Clinton. Most estimates also show that George H. W. Bush's nominees were given lower ABA scores than were Democratic nominees.

Table 1 for the Appendix for Chapter 5: How Sensitive Are the Regression Results by Administration shown in Figures 5.5 and 5.6 to Different Combinations of Control Variables (t-statistics are in parentheses)

Additional Variables Being Accounted for	Administration			
	Reagan	Bush I	Clinton	Bush II
No Other Variables	-.7179 (2.18)	-.8126 (2.30)	-.1858 (0.57)	-.8362 (2.38)
	N = 345 LR chi^2 = 11.08			
Whether Same Party Controls Presidency and Senate	-.7342 (2.17)	-.8658 (1.95)	-.2252 (0.59)	-.8679 (2.24)
	N = 345 LR chi^2 = 11.12			
Race and Sex	-.7558 (2.27)	-.8306 (2.34)	-.1471 (0.45)	-.8310 (2.35)
	N = 345 LR chi^2 = 12.63			

Political Information on Confirmation (Nominations in one year, presidential approval rating, whether same party controls presidency and Senate, whether the nominee comes from a state where the state's senators are both from a different party than the president, dummies for the year of the presidency)	-.7708 (1.85)	-.3740 (0.69)	-.0022 (0.00)	-.8310 (1.71)
	N = 341 LR chi^2 = 28.42			
Nominee's Professional Characteristics and Age at Nomination (Practice for more than ten years, private and government practice dummies, top ten law school, served on law review, previously served as federal or state judge, and clerkships nominee may have held)	-.8696 (2.37)	-.8606 (2.11)	-.2500 (0.69)	-1.1166 (2.77)
	N = 327 LR chi^2 = 53.84			

Variable	Obs	Mean	Std. Dev.	Obs	Mean	Std. Dev.
Table 2 for the Appendix for Chapter 5: Data Summary Used in Regressions (Data covers period from Carter administration through first term of George W. Bush)						
ABA Rating (6 = Well Qualified, 5 = Well Qualified/Qualified, 4 = Qualified/Well Qualified, 3 = Qualified, . . .	345	4.73	1.51	1215	4.50	1.52
Nomination during Carter Administration	348	0.18	0.38	1224	0.18	0.38
Nomination during Reagan Administration	348	0.27	0.44	1224	0.25	0.43
Nomination during Bush I Administration	348	0.14	0.35	1224	0.15	0.36
Nomination during Clinton Administration	348	0.26	0.44	1224	0.28	0.45
Nomination during Bush II Administration	348	0.16	0.36	1226	0.14	0.35
Nominations during that Year	344	79.56	35.50	1221	77.04	34.78
Presidential Approval Rate	344	54.01	11.30	1222	53.88	12.49
Same Party Controls Both the Senate and Presidency	348	0.51	0.50	1226	0.52	0.50
State that Nominee Is from Is Represented by Senators from Different Parties	345	0.20	0.40	1224	0.24	0.42
Black	348	0.09	0.29	1224	0.10	0.30
Asian	348	0.01	0.08	1224	0.01	0.09
Hispanic	348	0.05	0.23	1224	0.07	0.25
Male	348	0.81	0.39	1226	0.82	0.38

Age at Nomination	340	50.89	6.54	1206	49.58	6.46
Dummy for Whether the Nominee Has Been a Lawyer for Ten Years	344	0.77	0.42	1223	0.86	0.35
Years in Private Practice	348	10.95	9.28	1143	13.62	9.35
Years as Government Lawyer	348	3.33	4.82	1132	3.79	5.03
Went to Top Ten Law School	340	0.45	0.50	1190	0.25	0.43
Served on Law Review	348	0.19	0.39	1226	0.11	0.31
Previously Served as a Federal Judge	345	0.35	0.48	1207	0.12	0.33
Previously Served as a State Judge	345	0.28	0.45	1207	0.39	0.49
Served as a State Supreme Court Clerk	335	0.03	0.17	1175	0.03	0.18
Served as a Federal District Court Clerk	335	0.10	0.30	1174	0.10	0.30
Served as a Federal Circuit Court Clerk	335	0.17	0.37	1174	0.07	0.26
Served as a Federal Supreme Court Clerk	335	0.12	0.33	1174	0.02	0.15
Nominations during the Second Year of a Presidential Term	345	0.20	0.40	1223	0.24	0.43
Nominations during the Third Year of a Presidential Term	345	0.37	0.48	1223	0.36	0.48
Nominations during the Fourth Year of a Presidential Term	345	0.17	0.37	1223	0.20	0.40

DATA APPENDIX

Data were collected on nominees who were publicly announced, whether they were confirmed, defeated, or withdrawn. The Lower Federal Court Confirmation Database provided the nomination date, whether the nominee was confirmed, the confirmation date, and the court to which the nominee was appointed, as well as the nominee's gender and race for district and circuit court judges from 1977 to 2000.[361] The Office of Legal Policy in the U.S. Department of Justice provided information on the judicial nominees from 2001 through the end of 2004.[362] Although nominations are treated as open until a final decision is made, the data in the appendix shows what happens if one assumes that George W. Bush's initially unconfirmed nominees who were renominated during his second term were confirmed on December 31, 2004. For all recess appointments, the length of the confirmation process is defined as the time from the date of first nomination to the date of the recess appointment.

Biographies on federal judges from the Federal Judicial Center provided information on race and on whether the nominee had been a federal or state judge, a graduate of a top ten law school, or a member of a law review. The Center provided information on incumbent judges from 2001 on; Center data was used to fill in gaps prior to 2001.[363] American Bar Association (ABA) ratings for judges from 1989 through early 2004 were provided by the ABA itself.[364] Ratings data for earlier years is available from the Lower Federal Court Confirmation Database. The data for the last part of 2004 was obtained from the Senate Judiciary Committee.[365] Short biographies of all Clinton nominees (including those not confirmed) are available from the Clinton Presidential Materials Project.[366] LexisNexis searches were relied upon extensively when race and political affiliation were not readily available from other databases. Such searches were also extensively used to find information on nominees who were not confirmed.[367] The writings of circuit court nominees were obtained from Westlaw's biographical information on each nominee. Not all nominees had a "published works" section listed in their biography on Westlaw's legal directory of judges. We attempted to fill in any blanks by searching on both Westlaw and LexisNexis for any journal articles or popular newspaper pieces that those nominees had written. We used Amazon.com to determine whether the nominees had written any books.

Information on the senators from each state at the time of nomination and their political affiliation was obtained from the Congressional Biographical Directory.[368] The presidential approval rate was provided by the Gallup survey.

Details on each source follow:

Lower Federal Court Confirmation Database (1977–2004) http://www.constitutionproject.org
- The original database was created at the behest of the Constitution Project's Courts Initiative (http://www.constitutionproject.org/ci/) by Wendy L. Martinek, Binghamton University.

Office of Legal Policy (www.justice.gov/olp/)
- Biographies of nominees from the 107th Congress to present (previous information was obtained from the Lower Federal Court Confirmation Database)
- Dates nominated, hearing, confirmation
- Information on service as a federal or state judge, attendance at a top ten law school, law review membership, and clerkship

Federal Judicial Center (http://www.fjc.gov/)
- Biographies of federal judges since 1789 (used to fill in gaps previous to 2000 and for all judges from 2000 to the present)
- Information on race; identified the incumbent judge whom the nominee was replacing
- Information on service as a federal or state judge, attendance at a top ten law school, law review membership, and clerkship

ABA ratings (http://www.abanet.org/scfedjud/home.html)

- Ratings from the 101st Congress to present (previous data for each Congress was obtained from the Lower Federal Court Confirmation Database)

Senate Judiciary Committee

Nominations clerk[369] (202) 224-5225

LexisNexis

- This database was used when race and political affiliation were not readily available from other sources. Race is available for about 95 percent of confirmed judges who are in the Federal Judicial Center biographical database. When race was not available, I used the search terms: "Name, white or Caucasian or African American or black or Asian or Hispanic." Political affiliation is not part of the questionnaire completed by judicial nominees; unless mentioned in a biography under affiliations and activities (from the *Almanac of the Federal Judiciary*), this information is not readily available. I used the following LexisNexis search terms: "Name, Republican or Democrat or conservative or Republican, date of nomination" to find out political affiliation. This approach was used for all Bush II nominees. I was successful about 50 percent of the time. I did not assume party affiliation was the same as the affiliation of the president who nominated the person. When much was written about a nominee, it was easier to find this information.

Searched all newspapers to find information on race and political affiliation

Congressional Biographical Directory (http://bioguide. congress.gov/biosearch/biosearch.asp)
- Identified senators from the nominee's home state at the time of nomination as well as political affiliation

Senate reference information (http://www.senate.gov)
- Under reference, then statistics and lists: sessions of Congress information
- http://www.senate.gov/pagelayout/reference/ two_column_table/stats_and_lists.htm

Gallup Presidential Approval Ratings (Alec M. Gallup, Jr., *The Gallup Poll Cumulative Index: Public Opinion, 1935-1997* (Lanham, MD: SR Books, April 28, 1999). Westlaw was used for judicial citations.

After creating a list of decisions for each circuit court judge, I identified whether the judge authored the opinion and whether it was a majority opinion or a dissent; I then counted the number of times that particular part of the decision was cited in other decisions by other judges.

HeinOnline, LegalTrac, and ArticleFirst were used to determine the number of publications authored by each Supreme Court justice.

Westlaw, LexisNexis, and Amazon.com were used to locate publications by the circuit and district judges.
- Three categories of publications: journal articles, books, and popular works (that is, newspaper and magazine articles)

Almanac of the Federal Judiciary

Lawyer evaluations (used to obtain data for all lower court judges and the appeals court judges not covered in my dataset as well as all Bush II confirmed judges where lawyer evaluation information was provided).
- Information is compiled three or four times per year, but it takes up to three years for a complete evaluation of a particular judge. I do not have in-

formation on judges who retired (or whose status changed to limited caseloads or no new cases) prior to December 2003 (when I began to look at lawyer evaluations) because that information is no longer available. (The Library of Congress does not maintain old versions of the *Almanac*.)

- Attorneys are asked about elements of performance such as a judge's level of legal ability, demeanor, management of courtroom proceedings, and philosophical leanings. The evaluations are updated approximately every three years. A new judge is usually evaluated after at least three years on the bench.

- The evaluations are the result of the collective opinions of the attorneys interviewed, and they do not impart to the reader any specific facts concerning the judges evaluated.

BIBLIOGRAPHY

Bell, Lauren Cohen. "Senatorial Discourtesy: The Senate's Use of Delay to Shape the Federal Judiciary." *Political Research Quarterly* 55 (September 2002): 589–607.

Binder, Sarah A., and Forrest Maltzman. "Senatorial Delay in Confirming Federal Judges, 1947–1998." *American Journal of Political Science* 46 (January 2002): 190–9.

Caldeira, Gregory, Marie Hojnacki, and John R. Wright. "The Lobbying Activities of Organized Interests in Federal Judicial Nominations." *Journal of Politics* 62 (February 2000): 51–69.

Chase, Harold W. *Federal Judges: The Appointing Process*. Minneapolis: University of Minnesota Press, 1972.

Choi, Stephen, and Mitu Gulati. "Choosing the Next Supreme Court Justice: An Empirical Ranking of Judicial Performance." UC Berkeley Public Law Research Paper No. 141; Georgetown Public Law Research Paper No. 473281; Georgetown Law and Economics Research Paper No. 473281. http://repositories.cdlib.org/boaltwp/66/ (accessed December 12, 2005).

Choi, Stephen, and Mitu Gulati. "Mr. Justice Posner?
Unpacking the Statistics." *NYU Annual Survey of
American Law* 61 (2005): 19–44.

Choi, Stephen, and Mitu Gulati. "A Tournament of
Judges?" *California Law Review* 92 (2004):
299–345.

Edwards, George C., III. *Presidential Approval: A
Sourcebook*, with Alec M. Gallup. Baltimore:
Johns Hopkins University Press, 1990.

Gaille, S. Scott. "Publishing by United States Court
of Appeals Judges: Before and After the Bork
Hearings." *Journal of Legal Studies* 27 (June
1997): 371–6.

Goldberg, Steven. "Federal Judges and the Heisman
Trophy." *Florida State University Law Review* 32,
no. 4 (2005).

Goldman, Sheldon. "Assessing the Senate Judicial
Confirmation Process: The Index of Obstruction
and Delay." *Judicature* 87 (March-April 2003):
251–7.

Goldman, Sheldon. "Picking Federal Judges." *Lower
Court Selection from Roosevelt through Reagan*.
New Haven: Yale University Press, 1997.

Grossman, Joel B. *Lawyers and Judges: The ABA and
the Politics of Judicial Selection*. New York: John
Wiley & Sons, 1965.

Hammond, T. H., and J. S. Hill. "Deference or
Preference? Explaining Senate Confirmation of
Presidential Appointments to Administrative
Agencies." *Journal of Theoretical Politics* 5 (1993):
23–59.

Hartley, R. E., and L. M. Holmes. "Increasing Senate
Scrutiny of Lower Federal Court Nominees."
Political Science Quarterly 117 (2002): 259–78.

Jones, David R. "Party Polarization and Legislative
Gridlock." *Political Research Quarterly* 54 (2001):
125–41.

Kang, Michael S., and Joanna Shepherd. "The Partisan
Price of Justice: An Empirical Analysis
of Campaign Contributions and Judicial
Decisions." *New York University Law Review*,
April 2011.

Kemper, M., W. L. Kemper, and S. R. Van Winkle. "To
Advise and Consent: The Senate and Lower
Federal Court Nominations, 1977–1998."
Journal of Politics 64 (2002): 337–61.

Landes, William M., Lawrence Lessig, and Michael
E. Solimine. "Judicial Influence: A Citation
Analysis of Federal Courts of Appeals Judges,"
Journal of Legal Studies 27 (1998): 271–332.

Levin, Mark R., *Men In Black: How the Supreme Court Is
Destroying America*. Washington, D.C.: Regnery
Publishing, Inc., 2005.

Lindquist, Stefanie A., David A. Yalof, and John A. Clark. "The Impact of Presidential Appointments to the U.S. Supreme Court." *Political Research Quarterly* 53 (2000): 795–814.

Lott, John R., Jr. "The American Bar Association, Judicial Ratings, and Political Bias." *The Journal of Law and Politics* 17 (2001): 41–62.

McCarty, Nolan, and Rose Razaghian. "Advice and Consent: Senate Responses to Executive Branch Nominations 1885–1996." *American Journal of Political Science* 43 (1999): 1122–43.

McGinnis, John O., and Michael B. Rappaport. "Supermajority Rules and the Judicial Confirmation Process." *Cardozo Law Review* 26, no. 2 (2005): 543–78.

Nixon, D. C., and D. L. Goss. "Confirmation Delay for Vacancies on the Circuit Court of Appeals." *American Politics Quarterly* 29 (2001): 246–274.

Posner, Eric, and Miguel De Figueiredo. "Is the International Court of Justice Biased?" Working paper, University of Chicago Law School, December 2004.

Shipan, Charles R., and Megan Shannon, "Delaying Justice(s): A Duration Analysis of Supreme Court Confirmations." *American Journal of Political Science* 47, no. 4 (October 2003): 654–668.

Sunstein, Cass R., David Schkade, and Lisa Michelle
        Ellman. "Ideological Voting on Federal Courts
        of Appeals: A Preliminary Investigation."
        Working paper no. 198, John M. Olin Program
        in Law and Economics, University of Chicago
        Law School, September 2003.
Theriault, Sean M. "The Case of the Vanishing
        Moderates: Party Polarization in the Modern
        Congress." Working paper, University of Texas at
        Austin, May 2, 2004.

NOTES

1   Greg Mankiw, "Jury Duty," Greg Mankiw's blog: Random observations for students of economics, June 23, 2009 (http://gregmankiw.blogspot.com/2009/06/jury-duty.html).

2   Robert Christensen and John Szmer, "Examining the Efficiency of the U.S. Courts of Appeals: Pathologies and Prescriptions," IEL Paper in Comparative Analysis of Institutions, Economics and Law, May 2011.

3   Charlie Savage, "Picking Judges a Disorderly Affair," *Boston Globe*, May 8, 2005.

4   *Dred Scott v. Sanford*, 60 U.S. 393 (1857).

5   American Enterprise Institute, "The Supreme Court: Lochner at 100—Still Crazy After All These Years?" conference summary, 2005. David E. Bernstein, *Rehabilitating Lochner: Defending Individual Rights against Progressive Reform*, University Of Chicago Press: Chicago, Illinois, 2011.

6   *Roper v. Simmons*, 543 U.S. ___ (2005). *Kelo v. City of New London*, 545 U.S. ___ (2005). *McCreary County v. American Civil Liberties Union*, 545 U.S. ___ (2005).

7   *Brown, Governor of California, et al. v. Entertainment Merchants Association et al.* (No. 08-1448) 556 F. 3d 950, affirmed, decided June 27, 2011.

8   *Wal-Mart Stores, Inc. v. Dukes* (No. 10-277) 603 F. 3d 571, reversed, decided June 20, 2011.

9   *Hosanna-Tabor Evangelical Lutheran Church v. and School Equal Employment Opportunity Commission* (No. 10-553) (October term 2011) http://www.law.cornell.edu/supct/pdf/10-553.pdf.

10 *Mayo Foundation for Medical Education and Research v. United States* (No. 09-837) 568 F. 3d 675, affirmed, decided January 11, 2011.

11 *Massachusetts, et al. v. Environmental Protection Agency et al.* 549 U.S. (2007). http://www.law.cornell.edu/supct/pdf/05-1120P.ZO.

12 *Kennedy v. Louisiana*, 554 U.S. (2008). http://www.law.cornell.edu/supct/pdf/07-343P.ZO.

13 *United States v. Jones*, No. 10-1259 U.S. (October 2011) http://www.law.cornell.edu/supct/pdf/10-1259.pdf.

14 *Yaser Esam Hamdi and Esam Fouad Hamdi v. Donald H. Rumsfeld*, 542 U.S. (2004). http://www.law.cornell.edu/supct/pdf/03-6696P.ZO.

15 Jonathan Turley, "10 Reasons the U.S. Is No Longer the Land of the Free," *Washington Post*, January 15, 2012.

16 *City of Rancho Palos Verdes v. Abrams*, 544 U.S ___ (2005). *National Cable &Telecommunications Association v. Brand X Internet Services*, 545 U.S. ___ (2005).

17 MarketWatch notes: "Until Wednesday's ruling [June 29, 2011], the lower court findings were split right along party lines." Steven Ertelt writes: "All three judges listening to two legal challenges were appointed by Democrats—Judge Diana Motz, the senior member of the panel, is a Clinton appointee while Judges Andre Davis and James Wynn were appointed by Obama." Russ Britt, "Appeals Court Rules in Favor of Health Reform: Says Affordable Care Act 'Valid Exercise' of Congressional Power," MarketWatch, June 29, 2011. (http://www.marketwatch.com/story/appeals-court-rules-in-favor-of-health-reform-2011-06-29). Steven Ertelt, "Appeals Court Panel Dismisses Virginia Obamacare Lawsuit," LifeNews.com, September 8, 2011 (http://www.lifenews.com/2011/09/08/appeals-court-panel-dismisses-virginia-obamacare-lawsuit/).

18 Further investigation into this data would be most illuminating. Other factors may also provide interesting correlates, such as how closely divided the legislatures being battled over are, or the closeness of individual races, or even simple growth in personal income. But all those factors have been shown in various studies to be secondary to the growth of government.

19 Government expenditures are only a rough measure of what is at stake in campaigns. The remainder is probably related to the growth in regulation and the concomitant need to influence that regulation. The gains and losses from regulations can be just as large as the impact from government spending programs.

20 Ibid.

21 Dana Milbank, "Word from O'Connor Sets Off Pre-Fourth Fireworks," *Washington Post*, July 2, 2005.

22 Ibid.

23 A Google News search between the first day of hearings and the final Senate vote finds 44 percent more news stories on Thomas's than Alito's confirmation. More news stories were found for Thomas's confirmation even though relatively few news stories from the early 1990s were available on the Internet.

24 "The Thomas Nomination," *New York Times*, Sunday, October 13, 1991 (http://www.nytimes.com/1991/10/13/us/thomas-nomination-hearing-captures-big-tv-audience-lp-television-audience-for.html).

25 Ibid.

26 John Corry, "Evaluating Bork on TV: Message or the Image?" *New York Times*, September 17, 1987 (http://www.nytimes.com/1987/09/17/arts/evaluating-bork-on-tv-message-or-the-image.html).

27 Dena Bunis, "Alito Confirmation Questioning Begins," *The Orange County Register*, January 10, 2006 (http://www.ocregister.com/articles/alito-32502-coverage-gavel.html).

28 Michael S. Kang and Joanna Shepherd. "The Partisan Price of Justice: An Empirical Analysis of Campaign Contributions and Judicial Decisions." *New York University Law Review*, April 2011.

29 Robert Bork, interview by Jim Lehrer, *MacNeil/Lehrer NewsHour*, PBS, July 23, 1990.

30 Barbara Jordan, interview by Jim Lehrer, *MacNeil/Lehrer NewsHour*, PBS, July 23, 1990.

31 U.S. Department of State International Information Programs, Information USA, "Basic Readings in U.S. Democracy: Marbury v. Madison (1803)," http://infousa.state.gov/government/overview/9.html.

32 *Dred Scott v. Sanford.*

33 American Enterprise Institute, "The Supreme Court."

34 *Brown v. Board of Education of Topeka*, 347 U.S. 483 (1954).

35 http://mason.gmu.edu/~berkowit/theprofessorsandbushvgore.htm.

36 *Griswold v. Connecticut*, 381 U.S. 479 (1965).

37 *Roe v. Wade*, 410 U.S. 113 (1973).

38   John R. Lott, Jr. and John Whitley, "Abortion and Crime: Unwanted Children and Out-of-Wedlock Births," *Economic Inquiry*, Vol. 45, no. 2, (April 2007): 304-324.

39   *Lawrence v. Texas*, 539 U.S. 558 (2003).

40   http://www.answers.com/main/ntquery;jsessionid=4j9bv32f 8p3o3?method=4&dsid=2222&dekey=Goodridge+v.+Depa rtment+of+Public+Health&gwp=8&curtab=2222_1&sbid=l c08a&linktext=Goodridge%20v.%20Department%20of%20 Public%20Health.

41   Michelle Mittelstadt, "Courts Have Mixed Reactions to Right to Sexual Privacy Ruling," *Dallas Morning News*, March 13, 2005.

42   *Lawrence and Garner v. Texas*, 539 U.S. 558 (2003).

43   Editorial, "Why Not Civil Unions?" *Washington Post*, February 6, 2004.

44   Ibid.

45   *Roper v. Simmons*.

46   Ibid. See also Levin (2005).

47   Breyer wrote: "I can find nothing in the Second Amendment's text, history, or underlying rationale that could warrant characterizing it as 'fundamental' insofar as it seeks to protect the keeping and bearing of arms for private self-defense purposes." *Otis McDonald et al., Petitioners v. City of Chicago, Illinois, et al.* (No. 08-1521) 567 F. 3d 856, reversed and remanded, June 28, 2010.

48   Quotes from personal e-mail correspondence with Judge Frank Easterbrook.

49   This can be seen in part from the earlier discussion on the number of unanimous decisions for circuit courts.

50   Charles E. Schumer, "Ideological Balance on the D.C. Circuit Matters," press release, September 24, 2002. See also: New York State Democratic Committee, U.S. Senator Charles E. Schumer, http://www.nydems.org/html/ electedofficials/schumer.html; Katherine Marsh, "Ideology Matters," *Legal Affairs*, July/August 2003 (http://www. legalaffairs.org/issues/July-August-2003/story_marsh_ julaug03.msp).

51   Charles E. Schumer, "Ideological Balance."

52   My research assistants examined the cases from 2000 to 2003 to determine the percentage of cases that involved dissents.

Opinions are available at http://www.cadc.uscourts.gov/bin/opinions/allopinions.asp. This point was first made to me by Frank Easterbrook. See also Ronald A. Cass, "The D.C. Circuit: Considering Balance on the Nation's Second Highest Court," Statement of Ronald A. Cass submitted to the subcommittee on Administration Oversight and the Court of the Senate Committee on the Judiciary, September 24, 2002.

53   My research assistants examined the cases from 2000 to 2003 to determine the percentage of cases that were unpublished. The source for the cases was Administrative Office of the U.S. Courts, "Judicial Business of the United States Courts: Annual Report of the Director, 1997–2004," http://www.uscourts.gov/judbususc/judbus.html.

54   Cass Sunstein, David Schkade, and Lisa Ellman, "Ideological Voting on Federal Courts of Appeals: A Preliminary Investigation," (working paper no. 03-9, University of Chicago Law School, September 2003).

55   Joshua Kaminsky and Gregory Shaffer find that about 40 percent of the Supreme Court cases between 1953 and 2003 were decided unanimously. Jennifer Nicoll says that 39 percent of cases between 1946 and 1968 were decided unanimously. Lee Epstein, et al. find that about 40 percent of the cases from 2005 to 2009 were decided unanimously, thought there rates during the 1950s and 1960s seem to be lower than for Kaminski and Shaffer. Joshua Kaminski and Gregory Shaffer, "Unanimity and the Supreme Court: Anatomy of a Judicial Blowout," University of Maryland Working Paper, April 29, 2005 (http://www.bsos.umd.edu/gvpt/apworkshop/kaminski-shaffer.pdf). Jennifer E. Nicoll, "A Study of Unanimity on the Court," Washington University in St. Louis Department of Political Science Working Paper, undated (http://www.pitt.edu/~jnvictor/Papers/unanimous.PDF).

56   Epstein, et al., "Unanimous Decisions."

57   Jennifer E. Nicoll, "Study of Unanimity."

58   Frank B. Cross, "The Justices of Strategy," *Duke Law Journal*, (1998): 554.

59   Judge Richard Posner writes that this effect, while it exists, might not be large: "Judges don't like to be reversed, but I do not think that aversion to reversal figures largely in

the judicial utility function. It is nonexistent in the case of Supreme Court justices, and fairly unimportant in the case of court of appeals judges because reversals of appellate decisions by the Court have become rare and most reflect differences in judicial philosophy or legal policy rather than mistake or incompetence by the appellate judges. Hence they are not perceived as criticism." He also noted that there can sometimes be costs to not being reversed: "The fact that Judge Bork had never been reversed by the Supreme Court was actually used as an argument *against* his confirmation, as indicating that he was in too close sympathy with a Court viewed as excessively conservative by many senators." However, this last point doesn't seem very strong because Bork's opponents would have used it against him if he had been reversed many times. Richard A. Posner, "What Do Judges Maximize? (The Same Thing Everybody Else Does)," University of Chicago Law School Working Paper, 1993 (http://www.law.uchicago.edu/files/files/15.RAP_.Judges.pdf).

60   Lee Epstein, Bill Landes, and Richard Posner provide evidence that the discussion in the text might significantly underestimate the swing in votes on the court from replacing one party's nominees with another. They show that disagreement between judges is much more prevalent than dissent. They argue that judges have an aversion to openly disagreeing with their colleagues. Thus replacing one party's nominees with another might produce an even larger swing in votes because some of the remaining judges will swing their votes with the majority. Lee Epstein, William M. Landes, Richard A. Posner, *The Behavior of Federal Judges: A Theoretical and Empirical Study of Rational Choice*, Harvard University Press, 2012. The ten non-unanimous decisions are: *Planned Parenthood v. Casey*, 505 U.S. 833 (1992); *Stenberg v. Carhart*, 530 U.S. 914 (2000); *Rust v. Sullivan*, 500 U.S. 173 (1991); *Ohio v. Akron Center*, 497 U.S. 502 (1990); *Hodgson v. Minnesota*, 497 U.S. 417 (1990); *Bray v. Alexandria Women's Health Clinic*, 506 U.S. 263 (1993); *Scheidler v. National Organization For Women, Inc.*, 537 U.S. 393 (2003); *Madsen v. Women's Health Ctr.*, 512 U.S. 753 (1994); *Schenck v. Pro Choice Network*, 519

U.S. 357 (1997); and *Legal Services Corp. v. Velazquez*, 531 U.S. 533 (2001).

61   Alexander Bickel and other scholars have made similar suggestions. Alexander M. Bickel, *The Least Dangerous Branch: The Supreme Court at the Bar of Politics* (New Haven: Yale University Press, 1986).

62   *Bush v. Gore*, 531 U.S. 98 (2000).

63   http://en.wikipedia.org/wiki/Environmental_Protection_ Agency.

64   http://www.epa.gov/epahome/aboutepa.htm.

65   Miguel Bustillo, "States Sue EPA over Mercury Emissions," *Los Angeles Times*, March 30, 2005.

66   http://en.wikipedia.org/wiki/Equal_Employment_ Opportunity_Commission.

67   http://en.wikipedia.org/wiki/Title_IX.

68   http://go.reuters.com/-helpSection.jhtml?p=stockData.

69   http://en.wikipedia.org/wiki/Sarbanes-Oxley.

70   *City of Rancho Palos Verdes v. Abrams*.

71   Michael W. Kahn, "Posters Discourage Eating, Drinking, Loud Talking on Phones in Subway," Associated Press, December 3, 2004.

72   Lyndsey Layton, "Between Metro and Cell User, a Disconnect," *Washington Post*, September 28, 2004 (http://www.washingtonpost.com/wp-dyn/articles/A55325-2004Sep27.html).

73   http://www.lewrockwell.com/roberts/roberts24.html.

74   Chris Smith, "McNab to continue serving Federal prison sentence for lobster smuggling, US Supreme Court denies a writ of certiorari in regard to U.S. vs. McNab et al.," NOAA News Release, March 22, 2004.

75   The case was *McNab v. United States*, some violations occurred both before, during and after his brief tenure with the company, but had no direct authority over the actions that were viewed as criminal. Overcriminalized.com, "Case Studies: Hansen v. United States," Overcriminalized.com (November 2003) (http://www.overcriminalized.com/CaseStudy/Hansen-Over-Regulation.aspx).

76   Gary Fields and John R. Emshwiller, "As Criminal Laws Proliferate, More Are Ensnared," *Wall Street Journal*, July 23, 2011. (http://online.wsj.com/article/SB1000142405274870

3749504576172714184601654.html). Heritage Foundation, "Growth in Federal Criminal Offenses: Supporting Information," n.d., http://www.overcriminalized.com/federalcrimes.htm.

77 Gary Fields and John R. Emshwiller, "As Criminal Laws Proliferate, More Are Ensnared," *Wall Street Journal*, July 23, 2011. (http://online.wsj.com/article/SB1000142405274870 3749504576172714184601654.html).

78 Overcriminalized.com, "When Art Becomes a Crime," Overcriminalized.com (November 2009) (http://www.overcriminalized.com/CaseStudy/When-Art-Becomes-a-Crime.aspx).

79 United States Sentencing Commission Guidelines Manual, amended January 15, 1988.

80 United States Sentencing Commission Guidelines Manual, effective November 1, 2004.

81 James Lindgren, "Examining the American Bar Association's Ratings of Nominees to the U.S. Courts of Appeals for Political Bias, 1989-2000," *The Journal of Law and Politics* 17 (2001): 1–40; John R. Lott Jr., "The American Bar Association, Judicial Ratings, and Political Bias," *The Journal of Law and Politics* 17 (2001): 41–62.

82 On August 23, 2011, a simple news search over the previous month found Robert Bork's 1987 confirmation battle mentioned in the *Washington Post*, CNN, *Politico*, *Boston Globe*, *Deseret News* (Salt Lake City, UT), and the *Huffington Post*. Over the last two months, Clarence Thomas's confirmation was discussed in *The New York Times*, *Chicago Tribune*, *New Yorker*, Charlotte (NC) *Observer*, Reuters, Forbes, *Toronto Star*, *Seattle Post Intelligencer*, Adweek, and Bloomberg News.

83 *Chicago Daily Law Bulletin*, "Illinois Judge among 4 OK'd by Senate," October 4, 2000, 1; Dan Carney, "More Challenges to Clinton Nominees Cause Judicial Stalemate," *Congressional Quarterly Weekly Report* 22 (1997): 2912–14. Orrin G. Hatch et al., "Judicial Nominees Have Waited Long Enough, Senator," *Washington Times*, November 29, 2001.

84 Charles E. Schumer, "Press Conference to Release a Letter Calling on Republicans to Denounce Statements Against Judges and React to Votes in the Senate Judiciary Committee," Federal News Service, April 14, 2005.

85   John Cornyn, Charles Schumer, interviews by Chris
      Wallace, *Fox News Sunday*, Fox News Channel, April 10,
      2005.

86   Ed Hornick, "Democratic Senators Urge Action Now on
      Obama's Judicial Nominees," CNN, April 13, 2010 (http://
      articles.cnn.com/2010-04-13/politics/obama.judicial.
      nominees_1_judicial-nominees-senate-democrats-up-or-
      down-vote?_s=PM:POLITICS).

87   Alexander Bolton, "Reid plans to hold extra sessions to
      move stalled judicial nominees," *The Hill*, April 13, 2010
      (http://thehill.com/homenews/senate/91881-reid-to-hold-
      extra-sessions-to-move-judicial-nominees).

88   U.S. States News, "Name That Filibuster," U.S. Fed News,
      April 27, 2005. See also Michael Barone, interview by Jim
      Angle, *Special Report with Brit Hume*, Fox News Network,
      April 22, 2005.

89   Donald Lambro, "Democrats Flip-Flop on Filibusters,"
      Washington Times, May 23, 2005, http://www.washtimes.
      com/national/20050522-115721-3263r.htm.

90   Ibid.

91   Trish Turner, "Senate GOP Marks a First: Blocking an
      Obama Judicial Nominee," Fox News, May 19, 2011 (http://
      politics.blogs.foxnews.com/2011/05/19/senate-gop-marks-
      first-blocking-obama-judicial-nominee). Republicans had
      previously used filibusters to stop non-judicial nominations
      when the other party controls the White House and the
      Senate. Orrin Hatch (R-UT), says that it is "unprecedented,
      unfair, dangerous, partisan and unconstitutional" to filibuster
      a president's judicial choices. How different are filibusters
      over judicial nominees from filibusters over other nominees?
      In 1980, Hatch was accused of filibustering President
      Jimmy Carter's nominee for general counsel of the National
      Labor Relations Board. *The New York Times* notes that
      then Republican Senators Rick Santorum of Pennsylvania
      and Mike DeWine of Ohio filibustered in 1995 to block
      President Clinton's nominee for surgeon general. Yet, when
      George W. Bush was president, they deplored the same
      tactic used by Democrats against Bush's judicial picks. (See
      Robert Landauer, "50% + 1 Not Always Ample Majority,"
      The Oregonian, March 29, 2005; Jeffrey Lubbers, "A Wasteful,

and Not Unprecedented, Filibuster," Letters, *Washington Post*, November 21, 2003, http://www.washingtonpost.com/ac2/wp-dyn?pagename=article&contentId=A2123-2003Nov20&notFound=true; and Editorial, "Mr. Smith Goes Under the Gavel," *New York Times*, November 28, 2004. The *Times* also attacked Senator Bill Frist for supporting a filibuster of a judicial nomination, although the Senate Majority Leader, Trent Lott, pointed out, "Senate Democratic Leader Tom Daschle and I, as the Senate's majority leader, actually used cloture petitions in 2000 to overcome Senators' holds and move forward on the nominations of Richard A. Paez and Marsha L. Berzon to the 9th Circuit, that was unlike the situation we have experienced over the last 2½ years where the Democratic leadership is using filibusters to block nominations from up-or-down votes." http://lott.senate.gov/index.cfm?FuseAction=PressReleases.Print&PressRelease_id=135&suppresslayouts=true).

92   William P. Marshall, "The Judicial Nomination Wars," *University of Richmond Law Review*, March 2005 (Vol. 39, No. 3), footnote 46, p. 825. For similar changes by Senator Orrin Hatch, compare also Brian Blomquist, "Lott Won't Use Rulings to Topple Federal Judges," *Washington Times*, March 18, 1997, p. A4 and in News Conference with Republican Senators, Federal News Service, April 12, 2002.

93   Alexander Bolton, "Senate hands Obama his first defeat on a judicial nominee," *The Hill*, May 19, 2011 (http://thehill.com/blogs/floor-action/senate/162191-senate-hands-obama-his-first-defeat-on-a-judicial-nominee).

94   Sonya Ross, "Clinton Bypasses Congress, Appoints Civil Rights Chief," Associated Press, August 4, 2000; Jesse J. Holland, "Senate Approves Last Clinton Judges," Associated Press, October 4, 2000.

95   Joan Biskupic, "Politics Snares Court Hopes of Minorities and Women," *USA Today*, August 22, 2000.

96   Roger Hartley, "Gender, Maybe; Race, Seems Not," *National Journal*, September 4, 2000. An irony for these last judicial nominees who were approved by Congress was the following report: "In an end-of-session twist, Democrats are holding up President Clinton's federal judicial nominations in the Senate hoping to win additional approvals for

other judges." Jesse J. Holland, "Dem Holds Clinton Nominations," Associated Press, September 18, 2000.

97 Editorial, *Chattanooga* (TN) *Times Free Press*, March 6, 2005; *Special Report with Brit Hume*, Fox News Network, April 12, 2005.

98 Ibid.

99 Ed Hornick, "Democratic Senators Urge Action Now on Obama's Judicial Nominees," CNN, April 13, 2010 (http://articles.cnn.com/2010-04-13/politics/obama.judicial.nominees_1_judicial-nominees-senate-democrats-up-or-down-vote?_s=PM:POLITICS).

100 David G. Savage, "Senate face-off is due over judicial nominee," Los Angeles *Times*, November 16, 2009 (http://www.latimes.com/news/nationworld/nation/la-na-judges16-2009nov16,0,1183259.story).

101 Alec Gallup, *The Gallup Poll: Public Opinion 2005* (New York: Rowman & Littlefield, 2007), 190.

102 Michael S. Kang and Joanna Shepherd, "The Partisan Price of Justice: An Empirical Analysis of Campaign Contributions and Judicial Decisions," *New York University Law Review*, April 2011.

103 Susan Jones, "Dobson Says He Didn't Discuss Roe v Wade with Karl Rove," CNSNews.com, October 12, 2005.

104 Neal Conan, "Politics of Judicial Nominations," *Talk of the Nation*, National Public Radio, September 9, 2002.

105 DeWayne Wickham, "Judicial Nominee Takes Parting, Partisan Shot," *USA Today*, December 14, 2004.

106 "Candidate Withdraws," *Washington Post*, September 10, 1987.

107 Charles Pickering, interview by Neil Cavuto, *Your World with Neil Cavuto*, Fox News Network, May 10, 2005. Transcript available at http://www.foxnews.com/story/0,2933,156138,00.html.

108 Robert H. Bork, "The Theorists of Conservative Constitutional Revisionism," in *The Tempting of America* (New York: Free Press, 1990), 223–7.

109 Mitchel A. Sollenberger, "The Law: Must the Senate Take a Floor Vote on a Presidential Judicial Nominee?" *Presidential Studies Quarterly* 34, no. 2 (June 2004): 420–36.

110 Bernard Siegan, telephone interview by author, May 7, 2005. All quotes from Siegan are from that interview.

111 Robert H. Bork told me that Siegan's book was "both valorous and superior to most constitutional theory." Robert H. Bork, telephone interview by author, May 10, 2005. All quotes from Judge Bork that are not explicitly attributed to another source are from that interview.

112 Mark Gitenstein, *Matters of Principle: An Insider's Account of America's Rejection of Robert Bork's Nomination to the Supreme Court* (New York: Simon & Schuster, 1992), 212.

113 The Prowler, "Debate and Delay," *The American Spectator*, May 20, 2005, http://www.spectator.org/dsp_article. asp?art_id=8193.

114 Siegan, interview.

115 Lawrence Baum, "The Selection and Confirmation of Justices: Criteria and Process," in *The Supreme Court*, 7th ed. (Washington, D.C.: CQ Electronic Library, CQ Supreme Court Collection, 2001), http://www.cqpress.com/incontext/SupremeCourt/the_selection.htm.

116 Kathy Barks Hoffman, "Three of Michigan's Four Judicial Nominees Finally Moving," Associated Press State and Local Wire, May 26, 2005.

117 Liz Marlantes, "Alito Grilling Gets Too Intense for Some," ABC News, January 11, 2005. George W. Bush, *Decision Points* (New York: Crown, 2010), 102.

118 Two well-known Clinton nominees, Ronnie White and Kent Marcus, did not return my calls.

119 Robert S. Raymar, telephone interview by author, June 21, 2005. Raymar went out of his way many times during the interview to emphasize the honor that he had in being nominated and that he did not hold any animosity against anyone in the process, though he did think that Clinton, through his infidelities, had thrown away a rare opportunity as president. Raymar also emphasized that the opposition was against Clinton, not against him.

120 Ibid.

121 Ibid.

122 Lillian R. BeVier, telephone interview by author, June 17, 2005.

123 BeVier, interview. Obviously, this is not just a problem for judicial nominees. Administrations are concerned about endless questions to various nominees. Condoleezza Rice complained about endless information requests being directed to John Bolton during his confirmation process to be confirmed as ambassador to the United Nations. Condoleezza Rice, interview by Chris Wallace, *Fox News Sunday*, Fox News Channel, June 20, 2005. Transcript available online at http://www.foxnews.com/story/0,2933,160008,00.html.

124 BeVier, interview.

125 Byron York, "The Next Big Fight," National Review Online, February 6, 2002, (http://www.nationalreview.com/york/york020602.shtml).

126 Mary-Jayne McKay, "Judge Pickering Denies Racism," CBS News, February 11, 2009 (http://www.cbsnews.com/stories/2004/03/25/60minutes/main608667.shtml).

127 Byron York, "The Cross Burning Case: What Really Happened," National Review Online, January 9, 2003.

128 Charles Pickering, telephone interview by author, June 20, 2005.

129 Ibid.

130 Ibid.

131 Raymar, interview.

132 Ibid.

133 Clarence Thomas, *My Grandfather's Son: A Memoir* (New York: Harper, 2007), Chapters 8 and 9.

134 Clarence Thomas's "Statement Before the Senate Judiciary Committee," October 11, 1991 (http://www.americanrhetoric.com/speeches/clarencethomashightechlynching.htm).

135 Clarence Thomas, *My Grandfather's Son: A Memoir* (New York: Harper, 2007), 268-9.

136 Clarence Thomas, *My Grandfather's Son: A Memoir* (New York: Harper, 2007), 245.

137 Clarence Thomas, *My Grandfather's Son: A Memoir* (New York: Harper, 2007), 239.

138 Clarence Thomas, *My Grandfather's Son: A Memoir* (New York: Harper, 2007), 236.

139   Scott Horton, "Doubting Thomas," *Harpers*, October 2, 2007 (http://harpers.org/archive/2007/10/hbc-90001339).

140   Henry J. Reske, "Rehnquist Court Convenes Today," United Press International, October 6, 1986.

141   Richard A. Posner, "A Political Foreword," *Harvard Law Review* 119, no. 1 (November 2005): 32–102. (http://www.harvardlawreview.org/issues/119/Nov05/PosnerFTX.pdf).

142   Comments made immediately before the committee vote on Judge John Roberts on September 22, 2005, http://www.nytimes.com/2005/09/22/politics/politicsspecial1/22text-roberts.html?pagewanted=all.

143   Jim Angle, James Rosen, and Megyn Kendall, "O'Connor's Career; Possible Replacements," *Fox Special Report with Brit Hume*, Fox News Network, July 1, 2005.

144   Marc Ambinder, "The Curious Case of Goodwin Liu," *The Atlantic Blog*, March 24, 2010 (http://www.theatlantic.com/politics/archive/2010/03/the-curious-case-of-goodwin-liu/37980/). Liberals have also raised this point about Liu being "too smart," though given that they are his supporters this isn't particularly surprising. "The other side is worried. They're not worried that [Goodwin Liu is] bad. They're worried that he's too good. They're worried that he's too smart . . .," Nan Aron, president of the liberal Alliance for Justice, claimed. David Ingram, "Democrats Push to Confirm Appeals Court Nominee Goodwin Liu," The Blog of the Legal Times, May 17, 2011 (http://legaltimes.typepad.com/blt/2011/05/democrats-may-push-to-confirm-appeals-court-nominee-goodwin-liu.html).

145   One concern is that the number of days the Senate is in session has been changing over time and that might explain the changes in the length of the confirmation process. Yet, it is hard to see any pattern in the number of days that the Senate is in session, at least since Truman's second term. Truman (1949–52), 646 days; Eisenhower (1953–56), 518 days; Eisenhower (1957–60), 551 days; Kennedy/Johnson (1961–64), 698 days; Johnson (1965–68), 610 days; Nixon (1969–72), 732 days; Nixon/Ford (1973–76), 703 days; Carter (1977–80), 670 days; Reagan (1981–84), 593 days; Reagan (1985–88), 620 days; Bush I (1989–92), 561 days;

Clinton (1993–96), 634 days; Clinton (1997–2000), 599 days; and Bush II (2001–04), 622 days.

146   The four were John J. Parker, Abe Fortas the second time he was nominated, Clement Haynesworth, and Harrold Carswell. Not counted in this group is one nominee whose name was proposed for a seat that was expected to open up but did not. President Lyndon Johnson nominated Homer Thornberry for associate justice of the Supreme Court at the same time that he nominated Abe Fortas to be chief justice. Fortas at the time was an associate justice. Had he been confirmed as chief justice, his position would have been open and Thornberry's nomination would have been considered by the Senate. Although Thornberry may rightly be counted as someone nominated but not confirmed, counting the long process for consideration of Fortas's nomination as if it were also a long delay in considering Thornberry would be misleading.

147   Jerry Goldman, "Louis D. Brandeis," Oyez: U.S. Supreme Court Multimedia, http://www.oyez.org/oyez/resource/ legal_entity/67/biography.

148   Supreme Court Justice William O. Douglas described Brandeis as "a militant crusader for social justice whoever his opponent might be. He was dangerous not only because of his brilliance, his arithmetic, his courage. He was dangerous because he was incorruptible. . . [and] the fears of the Establishment were greater because Brandeis was the first Jew to be named to the Court." John Nichols, "The Nation: The New Justice," National Public Radio, August 7, 2009.

149   Michael Ariens, "Supreme Court Justices: Louis D. Brandeis (1856–1941)," in *Constitutional Law*, http:// www.michaelariens.com/ConLaw/justices/brandeis.htm; Reinhardt Krause, "Louis Brandeis Never Buckled; Acted with Courage: This Justice Was Determined to Take Reform to Highest Court," *Investor's Business Daily*, August 21, 2003.

150   Klebanow, Diana, and Jonas, Franklin L., *People's Lawyers: Crusaders for Justice in American History* (New York: M.E. Sharpe, 2003).

151   Neil A. Lewis, "Souter and Senate: How Far Should Questions Go?" *New York Times*, July 26, 1990.

152 *Brown v. Board of Education of Topeka.*

153 Scott E. Graves and Robert M. Howard, *Justice Takes a Recess: Judicial Recess Appointments from George Washington to George W. Bush* (Lexington Books: Lanham, MD, 2009).

154 Juan Williams, "Marshall's Law," *Washington Post*, January 7, 1990. Available online at http://www.thurgoodmarshall.com/speeches/tmlaw_article.htm.

155 Scott Johnson, "Saying Goodbye to a Great One," *The Weekly Standard*, May 31, 2005, 21.

156 *Philadelphia Inquirer*, "95 Years of the NAACP," July 7, 2004.

157 Obviously the confirmations during the Civil War period were also very contentious, but this helps prove the point that these battles are more difficult when there is more at stake.

158 *This Week with George Stephanopoulos*, ABC News, July 11, 2005.

159 Oona A. Hathaway, "The Politics of the Confirmation Process: The Selling of Supreme Court Nominees by John Anthony Maltese," *Yale Law Journal* 106, no. 1 (1996): 235–40.

160 Kermit Hall, ed., *The Oxford Companion to the Supreme Court* (New York: Oxford University Press, 1992).

161 "After confirmation, but before he took his seat on the Court, the news of Black's former membership in the KKK was made public. Black survived the furor, and remained on the Court for the remainder of his life." Michael Ariens, "Supreme Court Justices: Hugo Black (1886–1971)," in *Constitutional Law*, http://www.michaelariens.com/ConLaw/justices/black.htm.

162 American Bar Association, "Standing Committee on the Federal Judiciary: What It Is and How It Works," American Bar Association (2009): 3.

163 Senate Judiciary Committee, *American Bar Association Nomination Process*, 101st Cong., 2nd Sess., June 2, 1989. See also Eric Effron, "Judge Blasts ABA Panel," *Legal Times*, December 15, 1986. For a somewhat related discussion see also Christopher Drew, "Ginsburg Verdict Nominee's Past Indiscretions Give Senators Cause to Doubt His Judgment," *Chicago Tribune*, November 8, 1987.

164   Hearing of the Senate Judiciary Committee, "American Bar
       Association Nomination Process."

165   Ibid.

166   Tom Curry, "A Guide to the Supreme Court Nomination,"
       MSNBC, November 5, 2005, http://www.msnbc.msn.com/
       id/6694744/.

167   Kermit Hall, ed., *The Oxford Companion to the Supreme Court*
       (New York: Oxford University Press, 1992), 838–40.

168   Michael J. Gerhardt, "Toward a Comprehensive
       Understanding of the Federal Appointments Process,"
       Harvard Journal of Law and Public Policy 21, no. 2 (1998),
       467. See also http://partners.is.asu.edu/~george/vacancy/
       senate.html.

169   http://partners.is.asu.edu/~george/vacancy/senate.html

170   The Week, *National Review*, January 30, 2006.

171   Justin Wedeking and Dion Farganis, "Supreme Court
       Nominee Candor and Judiciary Committee Votes,"
       University of Kentucky Department of Political Science,
       August 25, 2010.

172   A joint hearing for Abe Fortas and Homer Thornberry in
       1968 took eleven days.

173   Dana Bash, interview with Senator Evan Bayh, *Inside
       Politics*, CNN, July 25, 2005. Transcript available online
       at http://transcripts.cnn.com/TRANSCRIPTS/0507/25/
       ip.01.html.

174   Charles E. Schumer, "Opening Statement of Senator
       Charles E. Schumer at Confirmation Hearing of Judge John
       G. Roberts, Jr.," September 12, 2005 (http://schumer.senate.
       gov/new_website/record.cfm?id=260413).

175   The most "no" votes anyone had previously received
       was twenty-six: Mahlon Pitney in 1912; Charles Evans
       Hughes in 1930; and Rehnquist in 1971, when he was first
       confirmed to the Court as associate justice. Hall, *Oxford
       Companion*: 965–71.

176   Linda Greenhouse, "Senate, 65 to 33, Votes to Confirm
       Rehnquist as 16th Chief Justice," *New York Times*,
       September 18, 1986.

177   Henry J. Reske, "Rehnquist Court Convenes Today."

178   *New York Times*, "Asst Atty Gen Rehnquist's Legal and Pol
       Career Detailed," October 28, 1971.

179 Greenhouse, "Senate, 65 to 33, Votes to Confirm Rehnquist."

180 *U.S. News and World Report*, "Belated Vote of Confidence for Rehnquist," September 29, 1986, 12.

181 Michael Kinsley, "The Cover-Up," *Washington Post*, August 6, 1986.

182 Editorial, "Northeast Journal," *New York Times*, November 16, 1986.

183 Editorial, "Valid Doubts About Justice Rehnquist," *New York Times*, September 11, 1986.

184 *Newsweek*, "Rehnquist and Scalia: Full Speed Ahead," August 18, 1996, 17.

185 LexisNexis searches were done to make this comparison. For Scalia, the search terms were (Scalia and confirmation and abortion and date bef September 17, 1986 and date aft June 23, 1986) and (Scalia and confirmation and (race or discrimination) and date bef September 17, 1986 and date aft June 23, 1986). For Rehnquist, the terms were (Rehnquist and confirmation and abortion and date bef September 17, 1986 and date aft June 19, 1986) and (Rehnquist and confirmation and (race or discrimination) and date bef September 17, 1986 and date aft June 19, 1986). For Scalia, the number of stories on abortion totaled 62, and the number on race or discrimination totaled 105. For Rehnquist, the number of stories on abortion totaled 71, and the number on race or discrimination totaled 202.

186 Hall, *Oxford Companion*: 527–28.

187 Reske, "Rehnquist Court Convenes Today."

188 See Andrea Neal, "Scalia Confirmation Seems Assured," United Press International, August 7, 1986.

189 Similarly, in 2005, John Roberts benefited from Rehnquist's death when Democrats decided to save their fire for this second slot.

190 For information on how conservative Scalia was perceived as being and additional information on his career prior to being on the Supreme Court, see Michael Ariens, "Supreme Court Justices: Antonin Scalia (1936–)," in *Constitutional Law*, http://www.michaelariens.com/ConLaw/justices/scalia.htm.

191 This perspective is based on a personal discussion with Peter Wallison of the American Enterprise Institute. Wallison worked on the nomination during the Reagan administration.

192 *Time*, "No Smoking Gun," August 18, 1986, 23.

193 William Schneider, "Spoiling for a Fight," *The Atlantic Online*, May 24, 2005, http://www.theatlantic.com/doc/prem/200505u/nj_schneider_2005-05-24.

194 Joseph Biden, interview by Bob Schieffer, *Face the Nation*, CBS, June 19, 2005.

195 Ibid.

196 Jacob V. Lamar Jr., "Gone with the Wind; Southern Senators May Doom the Bork Nomination," *Time*, October 12, 1987, 18.

197 Michael W. Lynch, "Covering the Spreads," *Reason* 30, no. 5 (1998): 23.

198 Stephen Advokat, "Publication of Bork's Video Rentals Raises Privacy Issue," *Chicago Tribune*, November 20, 1987.

199 Richardson gave Cox his promise of full and unquestioned authority "to call any witness, review any documents, see any evidence, investigate any suspect, and prosecute anyone involved in the Watergate case." (http://clinton5.nara.gov/textonly/Initiatives/Millennium/capsule/richardson.html). In addition, "During his confirmation hearings for the post of attorney general just five and a half months earlier, Richardson had promised the Senate Judiciary Committee that he would appoint a special prosecutor with broad powers to get to the bottom of the Watergate scandal. Richardson felt that he could not break this promise, and he told the president that firing Cox was not justified. In fact, the attorney general was prepared to resign rather than carry out the president's order." Thomas J. Vance, "The Saturday Night Massacre," in *Elliot Richardson and the Virtue of Politics: A Brief Biography* (Council for Excellence in Government: Washington, D.C., 2000).

200 Steven Greenhut, "Time to Stop 'Borking' Ashcroft," *Valdosta State University Spectator*, January 18, 2001.

201 United Press International, "Excerpts from Opening Statements," September 16, 1987.

202 For a general overview, see Douglas R. Cox, "Judge to Justice," *Policy Review* 97 (October 1, 1999), http://

www.policyreview.org/oct99/cox.html. For a discussion of how Bork's nomination compared with later ones on this dimension, see Barbara Bradley, "History of Cabinet Nominations and Confirmations," *Morning Edition*, National Public Radio, January 16, 2001, and Byron York, interview by Brit Hume, *Special Report with Brit Hume*, Fox News Channel, January 11, 2001.

203 A LexisNexis search for news articles during Judge Bork's confirmation hearings yielded 172 news articles using the word "extremist" within ten words of Bork's name.

204 Jacob V. Lamar Jr., "Advise and Dissent," *Time*, September 21, 1987, 12.

205 Abortion rights groups approached the confirmation process as if it were a political campaign and spent millions of dollars to defeat Bork. They created a new group, People for the American Way, to lead the campaign. They hired Gregory Peck as their public voice, ran advertisements against Bork, and lobbied senators to vote against him. Suzanne Garment, "The War against Robert H. Bork," *Commentary* 85, no. 1 (1988): 17-26, http://www. commentarymagazine.com/Summaries/V85I1P19-1.htm (accessed December 12, 2005).

206 Daniel Casey, executive director of the American Conservative Union, claimed that for Ginsburg, "It was the combination of the abortion and the drug thing; this guy was a '60s kind of guy. The '60s impression created so much concern—you weren't going to get any of the religious right groups geared up on this fight." Anne Kornhauser, "Right Licks Wounds, Readies for Kennedy Battle," *Legal Times*, November 16, 1987. The *Chicago Tribune* noted, "Despite Kennedy's more temperate tone, the women's lobby believes his decision in the Navy case raises questions about Kennedy's commitment to the court's 1973 ruling that barred states from prohibiting abortion." Joseph R. Tybor, "Judge Kennedy-Rulings with a Knack for Tact," *Chicago Tribune*, November 22, 1987.

207 Michael Kinsley, "Mr Justice Yuppie," *The Times* (London), November 7, 1987.

208 Frances Dinkelspiel, "Associates from Cornell Recall a Studious Suit-and-Tie Man," *The Post-Standard* (Syracuse, NY), November 7, 1987. For statements from classmates at

the University of Chicago Law School, see John M. Broder, "Collapse of the Ginsburg Nomination," *Los Angeles Times*, November 8, 1987.

209 Kenneth Karpay, "In Search of Judge Ginsburg," *Legal Times*, November 2, 1987.

210 Robert Reinhold, "Man in the News; Restrained Pragmatist Anthony M. Kennedy," *New York Times*, November 12, 1987.

211 Stuart Wavell, "Saturday People: Judgment Daze—Anthony McLeod Kennedy," *The Guardian* (London), November 14, 1987.

212 George Will, Commentary, *This Week with George Stephanopoulos*, ABC, May 15, 2005.

213 George W. Bush, *Decision Points*, (New York: Crown, 2010).

214 Jack Balkin, "The Miers Nomination," at Balkin.com, October 03, 2005 (http://balkin.blogspot.com/2005/10/miers-nomination.html).

215 The *Washington Post* article noted: "Supreme Court nominee Harriet Miers once pledged that she would "actively support" a constitutional amendment banning abortions except to save a mother's life, participate in antiabortion rallies, and try to block the flow of public money to clinics and organizations that help women obtain the procedure." Amy Goldstein and Charles Babington, "Miers Once Vowed to Support Ban on Abortion," *Washington Post*, October 19, 2005 (http://www.washingtonpost.com/wp-dyn/content/article/2005/10/18/AR2005101800715.html).

216 Laura Rozen, "Democrats, Rejoice: Right Says Wrong on Harriet Miers," National Public Radio, September 27, 2005 (http://www.villagevoice.com/2005-09-27/news/democrats-rejoice-right-says-wrong-on-harriet-miers/).

217 Focus on the Family founder and president Dr. James Dobson, a strong advocate of banning abortions, assured conservatives that Harriet Miers could be trusted on abortion and other issues. Dobson told his radio show listeners: "When you know some of the things that I know, that I probably shouldn't know, you will understand why I have said, with fear and trepidation, that I believe Harriet Miers will be a good justice." Advocates of abortion "accused [Dobson] of having some sort of inside information from

the Bush administration that led him to endorse Miers." Steven Ertelt, "Dobson Discusses Harriet Miers Supreme Court Pick, Abortion Views," LifeNews.com, October 12, 2005 (http://www.lifenews.com/2005/10/12/nat-1688/).

218 Jan Crawford Greenburg, *Supreme Conflict: The Inside Story of the Struggle for Control of the United States Supreme Court*, (New York: Penguin, 2007), 278-81.

219 Laura Rozen, "Democrats, Rejoice: Right Says Wrong on Harriet Miers," *The Village Voice*, September 27, 2005 (http://www.villagevoice.com/2005-09-27/news/democrats-rejoice-right-says-wrong-on-harriet-miers/).

220 Charlie Savage, "Miers foes see law questions as way to derail nomination: Groups aim to make her seem unqualified," *Boston Globe*, October 12, 2005 (http://www.boston.com/news/nation/washington/articles/2005/10/12/miers_foes_see_law_questions_as_way_to_derail_nomination/).

221 David D. Kirkpatrick, "GOP Aides Add Voices to Resistance to Miers," *New York Times*, October 12, 2005 (http://www.nytimes.com/2005/10/12/politics/politicsspecial1/12confirm.html).

222 Michael A. Fletcher and Charles Babington, "Miers, Under Fire from Right, Withdrawn as Court Nominee," *Washington Post*, October 28, 2005.

223 Armen A. Alchian, telephone interview by author, June 20, 2005.

224 Ibid.

225 Jeffrey Toobin, "Partners: Will Clarence and Virginia Thomas Succeed in Killing Obama's Health-Care Plan?" *The New Yorker*, August 29, 2011 (http://www.newyorker.com/reporting/2011/08/29/110829fa_fact_toobin).

226 Jan Crawford Greenburg, *Supreme Conflict: The Inside Story of the Struggle for Control of the United States Supreme Court*, (New York: Penguin, 2007), 278-81.

227 Alessandra Stanley, "Erotomania: A Rare Disorder Runs Riot—in Men's Minds," *New York Times*, November 10, 1991. Mark Levin, who served as chief of staff to Ed Meese while he was the U.S. attorney general, said on his national radio talk show on January 8, 2008 that Thomas was "one of the brightest justices in history."

228 Clarence Thomas and Thurgood Marshall couldn't have been much more different politically. Thomas opposed affirmative action laws, believing them counterproductive and patronizing to blacks. As a conservative, he placed more value on personal responsibility than on entitlements guaranteed by the state. Thomas had grown up poor; he was raised by his grandfather, who believed that helping oneself was the way to a better life. Thomas attended Catholic schools before going to Yale Law School, and some critics believed him to be highly skeptical of the Supreme Court's *Roe v. Wade* decision legalizing abortion. He also had served as chairman of the Equal Employment Opportunity Commission. Jonathan Ringel, "Bombshell in the Clarence Thomas Biography," August 5, 2004, http://www.law.com/jsp/article.jsp?id=1090180289132 (accessed December 12, 2005). Michael Ariens, "Supreme Court Justices: Clarence Thomas (1948–)," in *Constitutional Law*, http://www.michaelariens.com/ConLaw/justices/thomas.htm.

229 Wesley Pruden, "Democratic Magic on the Agenda," *Washington Times*, October 30, 1991.

230 Suzanne Moore, "Who's Afraid of Anita Hill?" *The Guardian* (London), May 21, 1993; Andrea Sachs, *Legal Times*, "The National Debate That Will Not End," *Legal Times,* December 26, 1994.

231 Pete Williams, "Letter to Obama: Sotomayor not that smart," October 28, 2010 (http://www.msnbc.msn.com/id/39899713/ns/politics-more_politics/t/letter-obama-sotomayor-not-smart/).

232 Benjamin Wittes, "Too Smart to Be a Judge," *Washington Post*, June 11, 2002.

233 Connectivity, "Judge Greene Made the Right Move," *PC Week*, March 15, 1988, C15.

234 U.S. Supreme Court, "The Justices' Caseload," http://www.supremecourtus.gov/about/justicecaseload.pdf; Pamela A. MacLean, "Bush's Nominees Likely to Put Stamp on Circuits; GOP Judges May Go from 60% to 85%," *National Law Journal* (March 28, 2005): 1.

235 Mark Ballard, "Bush-Senate Standoff Ending," *Texas Lawyer*, February 3, 1992.

236   Larry Margasak, "Reagan Nominee Hit for Placing Liens on Dying AIDS Victim's Property," Associated Press, June 14, 1988.

237   *The Bulletin's Frontrunner*, "Hatch Denies Racial Bias for Nominees," July 21, 2000.

238   Ibid.

239   Bob Dole, "Up, Down or Out." *New York Times*, April 27, 2005; U.S. Newswire, "RNC Chairman Ken Mehlman Remarks to RNC State Chairmen's Meeting," April 29, 2005.

240   Patrick Leahy, interview by Chris Wallace, *Fox News Sunday*, Fox News Channel, May 2, 2005. Transcript available online at http://www.foxnews.com/story/0,2933,155173,00.html.

241   Brian Beutler, "Schumer to GOP: We're Going to Rev Up Confirmation of Obama Judicial Nominees," The Talking Point Memo DC, April 13, 2010 (http://tpmdc.talkingpointsmemo.com/2010/04/schumer-to-gop-were-going-to-rev-up-confirmation-of-obama-judicial-nominees.php).

242   Editorial, "The Missing Judges," *New York Times*, January 3, 2011 (http://www.nytimes.com/2011/01/04/opinion/04tue1.html).

243   Lindgren (2001) examined just forty-nine nominations. My reference to this study being over six times larger than past work ignores my past work. Lott (2001) had a data set of eighty-nine nominations.

244   Editorial, *San Francisco Chronicle*, March 14, 2005.

245   The two sets of LexisNexis searches were: "(delays or length) W/3 confirmation and judges and date bef July 1, 2005 and date after June 30, 2004" and "confirmation rate and judges and date bef July 1, 2005 and date aft June 30, 2004."

246   Dirk Olin, "Can Mukasey Manage?" *Newsweek,* Web Exclusive, September 21, 2007 (http://www.newsweek.com/id/41163).

247   Dr. Cornel West, "Analysis: Colin Powell's Legacy as Secretary of State; Condoleezza Rice's Role as the New Secretary of State," *The Tavis Smiley Show*, NPR, November 17, 2004.

248 Executive Office of the President, "Budget of the U.S. Government," Fiscal Year 2011.

249 Executive Office of the President, "Budget of the U.S. Government," Fiscal Year 2011. In 2010, it is estimated that the Department of Education's budget was $56 billion, along with $51 billion from the American Recovery and Reinvestment Act. In 2011, the Department's budget was estimated to be $71 billion and the money from the ARRA was $23 billion.

250 Eric M. George and William H. Neukom, "The Judge Shortage," *Los Angeles Times*, December 3, 2010. Associated Press, "Clinton Blames Senate for Judicial 'Vacancy Crises,'" *Deseret News*, August 10, 1999. Associated Press, "Picking Judges Not an Easy Task," *The Madison Courier* (IN), February 15, 1995.

251 The two other Obama nominees who withdrew had significant problems. Senator Tom Daschle had a large tax problem, failing to pay $128,000 in back taxes, and withdrew from consideration to head Health and Human Services. Governor Bill Richardson withdrew from consideration to be Commerce Secretary over a grand jury investigation into corruption. Fox News, "Bill Richardson Withdraws Nomination as Commerce Secretary," Fox News, January 4, 2009 (http://www.foxnews.com/politics/2009/01/04/richardson-withdraws-nomination-commerce-secretary/) and Associated Press, "White House: Performance Czar Nancy Killefer Withdraws Candidacy," Fox News, February 3, 2009 (http://www.foxnews.com/politics/2009/02/03/white-house-performance-czar-nancy-killefer-withdraws-candidacy).

252 Sonya Ross, "Clinton Bypasses Congress, Appoints Civil Rights Chief," Associated Press, August 4, 2000; Jesse J. Holland, "Senate Approves Last Clinton Judges," Associated Press, October 4, 2000.

253 *The Bulletin's Frontrunner*, "Frist Participates in Religious Telecast on Judicial Nominations," April 25, 2005.

254 *The Hotline*, "Judges: Message Buster," April 29, 2005.

255 It could be that Paez faced a difficult confirmation because he was Mormon, but many other possible reasons exist. For example, he was being nominated to the controversial and

already left-leaning Ninth Circuit. With just one or even a few observations, it is simply impossible to tell what was happening.

256 There are a larger number of nominees for the more mainstream religions: Catholicism (thirty-nine nominees), Episcopalianism (eighteen), Judaism (fifteen), and Baptist (eleven).

257 Benjamin Wittes, "Too Smart to Be a Judge," *Washington Post*, June 11, 2002.

258 Denis Steven Rutkus, "Role of Home State Senators in the Selection of Lower Federal Court Judges," CRS Report for Congress, March 6, 2008 (http://www.fas.org/sgp/crs/misc/RL34405.pdf).

259 When Senator Orrin Hatch ran the judiciary committee during the Clinton administration, a vote would not occur "if either home-state senator objected to a nomination to the federal bench." This rule continued during George W. Bush's first term when the Democrats controlled the Senate. When the Republicans took over under Bush II, the rule was changed to only block votes when both of a home state's senators objected. George Curry, "GOP Ditching the Rules to Confirm Conservative Judges," *Capitol Outlook*, September 15, 2004.

260 William M. Landes, Lawrence Lessig, and Michael E. Solimine. "Judicial Influence: A Citation Analysis of Federal Courts of Appeals Judges," *Journal of Legal Studies* 27 (1998): 271-332 ; Stephen Choi and Mitu Gulati, Choosing the Next Supreme Court Justice: An Empirical Ranking of Judicial Performance (February 17, 2004), UC Berkeley Public Law Research Paper No. 141; Georgetown Public Law Research Paper No. 473281; Georgetown Law and Economics Research Paper No. 473281, http://ssrn.com/abstract=473281 (accessed December 12, 2005).

261 Philadelphia Bar Association, "Judicial Commission: Standards for Evaluation for Candidates," http://www.philadelphiabar.org/page/StandardsForEvaluatingCandidates.

262 Ibid. The Philadelphia Bar Association goes on to explain: "Among the qualities which comprise judicial temperament are patience, open-mindedness, courtesy, tact, firmness, understanding, compassion and humility. Because the judicial

function is essentially one of facilitating conflict resolution, judicial temperament requires an ability to deal with parties, counsel, jurors, and witnesses calmly and courteously, and the willingness to hear and consider the views of all sides. It requires the ability to be even-tempered, yet firm; open-minded, yet willing and able to reach a decision; confident, yet not egocentric. Because of the broad range of topics and issues with which a judge is typically required to deal, judicial temperament requires a willingness and ability to assimilate data outside the judge's own experience. Moreover, it requires an even disposition coupled with a keen sense of justice and a recognition that the administration of justice and the rights of the parties transcend the judge's personal feelings and desires. Judicial temperament implies, among other things, an absence of arrogance, impatience, and arbitrariness."

263 *Almanac of the Federal Judiciary* (New York: Aspen, 2004).

264 Frank Easterbrook, e-mail conversation with author, 2004.

265 The survey is asked of all lawyers who practiced before the judges, although not everyone answers this survey. No information is provided on the percent of lawyers who answer the questionnaire, but it could be determined if one was able to figure out how many lawyers had practiced before the judge. The newer judges have fewer quotes from lawyers and may have only a half dozen being reported. For older judges, not all lawyer statements are reported, but those that are were said to be representative of the different statements made by lawyers.

266 While there is no publicly available survey data on lawyers' views, there is a lot of evidence that the American Bar Association is extremely liberal. For example, the ABA actively takes liberal positions on the death penalty (http://www.deathpenaltyinfo.org/american-bar-association-resolution), abortion (http://connection. ebscohost.com/c/articles/4802400/aba-abortion-should-aba-rescind-resolution-106-c), and same sex marriage (http://gaymarriage.procon.org/view.source. php?sourceID=010634).

267 The search was done on September 5, 2011 at http:// fundrace.huffingtonpost.com/.

268   Paul L. Caron, "Law Prof Presidential Campaign
      Contributions: 95% to Obama, 5% to McCain," TaxProf
      Blog, September 10, 2008 (http://taxprof.typepad.com/
      taxprof_blog/2008/09/law-prof-presid.html).

269   Albert Diaz is the sole Obama nominee who went to
      both a top law school and was on the law review. Joseph
      Greenaway served on the Harvard Law School's Civil
      Rights and Civil Liberties Law Review, but that is not
      the prestigious Harvard Law Review. "Judge Joseph
      A. Greenaway: Nominee to the Third Circuit Court of
      Appeals," Alliance for Justice, undated (http://www.afj.
      org/assets/resources/nominees/afj-greenaway-report.
      pdf). Raymond Lohier was the editor in chief of the NYU
      Annual Survey of American Law, but again that is not the
      same thing as the NYU Law Review.

270   Landes, Lessig, and Solimine, "Judicial Influence"; Choi and
      Gulati, "Choosing the Next Supreme Court Justice."

271   Choi and Gulati, "Choosing the Next Supreme Court
      Justice," Appendix H.

272   Various factors can affect the number of decisions handed
      down by a judge, among them the types of cases that he is
      assigned. But since case assignment is random and we are
      talking about a fairly large number of judges being studied
      in each administration, there shouldn't be a systematic
      problem. Landes-Lessig-Solimine also use a regression
      approach that accounts for many different reasons for
      differences in judicial quality that are independent of the
      quality of the judge.

273   The regression approach used by Landes-Lessig-Solimine is
      largely responsible for some of the differences between their
      rating and the Choi-Gulati index. Most important, though,
      is that the two indexes both imply that higher-quality
      judges faced more difficulty being confirmed.

274   The Americans for Democratic Action voting scores are
      available online at http://www.adaction.org/. Since the
      estimates shown in the next sections for the length and
      rate of confirmations already account for the changes across
      administrations, they are already accounting for the changes
      over time in the ADA voting indexes, whether we measured
      the median or mean values of senators.

275 Negative binomial regressions were used because of the count nature of the data and because the mean and variance of the days-to-confirmation variable are not equal.

276 "Fixed effects" are what are used to account for average differences across geographic areas; in this case, states. They are dummy variables that equal one when a particular geographic area is being studied and the coefficient on that variable measures the average value for that area. The dummy variable for the top 10 law schools was also broken down into ten separate dummies for each school. Doing that showed that the top schools, Yale and Harvard, had the biggest impact, with the lower-level law schools in the top 10 having a smaller one.

277 I also examined separate estimates for confirmation length using the number of days between the initial nomination and the hearing date as well as between the hearing date and the confirmation date. These alternative measures produce similar results, although a noticeably longer delay exists for circuit court nominees after the hearing. From the Carter administration to the Bush II administration, the increase between the time from hearings to confirmation is about twice as long as the increase in the number of days between circuit court nomination and hearings. Just between the Clinton and Bush II administrations, the number of days between hearings and confirmation doubled for circuit court nominees. This evidence helps answer whether the increasing delays might arise simply because judges' records have become more complex over time and take longer to examine than in years past. Presumably, more complex records would require more time to review before the hearings. That hypothesis is not consistent with the evidence, however.

278 John R. Lott, Jr., "Pulling Rank," *New York Times*, January 25, 2006, p. 21.

279 These variables are not included in the general regressions shown in Figures 3-9A and 3-9B because so few of Bush II's nominees are covered by the *Almanac*'s survey. Including the variables does not produce any statistically significant results at the .10 level for a two-tailed t-test for whether a nominee was perceived as liberal, conservative, moderate, or Libertarian.

280   A variable was also used for whether the judge showed a Libertarian bias, but the number of judges in this category was very small and the effects were never statistically significant, so they are not reported.

281   The dummy variables for the different administrations are no longer included because of their collinearity with the Republican and Democratic dummies.

282   John Roberts, Antonin Scalia, Clarence Thomas, and Ruth Bader Ginsburg sat on the D.C. Circuit Court before being nominated to the U.S. Supreme Court. Robert Bork and Douglas Ginsburg were two other nominees who served on the D.C. Circuit Court before their unsuccessful nominations.

283   The results here are statistically significant at the 1 percent level.

284   A change of one standard deviation in the index equals almost exactly 1 (equaling 1.003). I regressed the Choi-Gulati index on the *Almanac*'s survey of judges' political beliefs and circuit court fixed effects and found no statistically significant relationship between political views and this measure of judicial quality. The only measure that came close to being statistically significant was whether the judge was Libertarian; the coefficient was negative (-2.1, $t = -1.50$). To put it another way, Libertarian nominees appear to be of lower quality, on average.

285   Robert Christensen and John Szmer, "Examining the Efficiency of the US Courts of Appeals: Pathologies and Prescriptions," IEL Paper in Comparative Analysis of Institutions, Economics and Law, May 2011.

286   To put this more formally, Easterbrook is 1.5 standard deviations above the third-ranked judge.

287   *Legal Affairs*, "Who Are the Top Twenty Legal Thinkers in America?" http://legalaffairs.org/poll/.

288   American Jewish Historical Society, "Justice Cardozo, Sephardic Jew," Chapters in American Jewish History, 1996. (http://www.ajhs.org/scholarship/chapters/chapter.cfm?documentID=261).

289   Kim Isaac Eisler, *A Justice for All: William J. Brennan, Jr., and the Decisions That Transformed America* (New York: Simon & Schuster, 1993), 40.

290 Thus, I tried a squared value for the Choi-Gulati total quality measure.

291 The coefficient on the squared term was statistically insignificant and empirically very small: the linear terms are between one and four percentage points larger than those shown in the table (18 percent, 36.5 percent, and 97.6 percent respectively).

292 For the specification corresponding to (1) in table 3, the coefficient on the Choi-Gulati composite ranking for judges increased slightly to 1.98 ($z = 7.65$) and the squared term is 0.971 ($z = -0.78$). I also tried seeing whether the coefficient values were different for values of the Choi-Gulati index above and below zero, but in none of the cases was the F test close to statistical significance.

293 As before, it is possible to examine whether the indexes have different correlations across different administrations. I therefore analyzed each quality measure for each administration. In obscure economics jargon, I "interacted each quality measure with the variable for each administration." The results consistently showed that for ten of the eleven quality measures, higher-quality judicial nominees were most likely to face long confirmation delays. President Reagan's nominees ranked first, facing longer delays for ten of the eleven quality measures. President Clinton's nominees ranked second on this dimension, facing longer delays for eight of the eleven measures.

294 Outside-circuit citations for total influence and inside-circuit citations for average influence are not statistically significant. Inside-circuit citations for total influence and outside-circuit citations for average influence are statistically significant.

295 This estimate is obtained by evaluating the linear estimates at the mean judicial quality.

296 David R. Jones, "Party Polarization and Legislative Gridlock," *Political Research Quarterly* 54 (2001): 125–41. Sean M. Theriault, "The Case of the Vanishing Moderates: Party Polarization in the Modern Congress" (working paper, Department of Government, University of Texas, Austin, 2004).

297 Theriault, "Vanishing Moderates," provides a detailed survey of these indexes.

298 Logit regressions were used to estimate these regressions. I also used Cox and Weibull hazard models; see my paper in the *Journal of Empirical Legal Studies*.

299 I used what is called an "exponential distribution survival time maximum-likelihood model" to estimate these results.

300 Law School Admission Council, http://www.lsac.org.

301 Unfortunately, the survey evidence cannot be used to analyze the length of the confirmation process because no judicial surveys focus on nominees who are defeated.

302 Keith Poole, "Voteview: NOMINATE Data," http://www.voteview.com/dwnl.htm. Another measure that I used was the DW-nominate voting indexes, which rank how politicians vote in terms of their support for more government, but I got similar results. The impact from changes in the DW-nominate index is even larger, with a one-percentage-point change in the index producing a 4 percent change in the length of confirmations for district court judges and a 9 to 10 percent change in the length for circuit court judges.

303 These results were all statistically significant at least at the 10 percent level for a two-tailed t-test.

304 The statistical significance for these two factors was only at the .15 level for a one-tailed t-test, with the $t \geq 1.1$.

305 To account for non-linear trends I used both time and time squared.

306 Using OLS for the data from 1946 to 2010, I got the following results (t-statistics in parentheses):

Journal Publications = .85694 Year - 0.01027 Year Squared - 11.7982 Republican Dummy + 3.953

    (2.06) (1.69) (2.88) (0.73)

Adjusted-R2= 0.2190, F-statistic = 3.71, Number of Observations

    = 30

Number of Books = .1911 Year - 0.0024 Year Squared - 1.7242

    Republican Dummy - 0.709

    (2.06) (1.69) (2.88) (0.73)

Adjusted-R2= 0.1398, F-statistic = 2.57, Number of Observations

    = 30

Op-eds or Popular pieces = .15926 Year - 0.00246 Year
Squared -

2.7063 Republican Dummy + 1.48675
(2.06) (1.69) (2.88) (0.73)
Adjusted-R2= 0.2190, F-statistic = 3.71, Number of
Observations
= 30

307 Conservative pundits were quite strong on the issue of whether Harriet Miers was competent enough to be on the Supreme Court. George F. Will, "Defending the Indefensible," *Washington Post*, October 23, 2005; Charles Krauthammer, "Miers: The Only Exit Strategy," *Washington Post*, October 21, 2005.

308 George W. Bush, *Decision Points*, 102.

309 People for the American Way, "The Record of Samuel Alito: A Preliminary Review," October 31, 2005 (http://media.pfaw.org/stc/AlitoPreliminary.pdf). Samuel A. Alito, Selected Resources in the Library of Congress Law Library Reading Room (http://www.loc.gov/law/find/alito.php).

310 For example, there is no equivalent of citations to judicial opinions for cabinet members. Also, while the quality of a cabinet nominee's education is available, additional information such as how well they did in school (the equivalent of being on law review) or the success of their careers immediately after school (the equivalent of clerking for an important court) is not immediately obvious.

311 Editorial, "Goodwin Liu's Precedents," *Wall Street Journal*, May 19, 2011 (http://online.wsj.com/article/SB10001424052748703730804576317564293961614.html?mod=WSJ_newsreel_opinion).

312 Nicholas D. Kristof, "Reagan Judiciary: Mostly White, Mostly Men," *Washington Post*, September 10, 1982.

313 Charles-Edward Anderson, "Screen Judges," *ABA Journal* 31 (1989). Marcia Coyle, "ABA Judges," *National Law Journal* (June 19, 1989).

314 Denis Steven Rutkus, "Role of Home State Senators in the Selection of Lower Federal Court Judges," CRS Report for Congress, March 6, 2008 (http://www.fas.org/sgp/crs/misc/RL34405.pdf).

315 Jacob V. Lamar Jr., "Advise and Dissent," *Time*, September 21, 1987, 12.

316 Ibid.

317 Michael Zahn, "The Lighter Side of the Seventh Circuit Court of Appeals," *Wisconsin Law Journal* 41 (2001).

318 William Grady, "After a Trial by Fire, Federal Judge Acquits Himself Well," *Chicago Tribune*, August 21, 1992.

319 Eric Herman, "Posner Pens the Most Opinions for Seventh U.S. Circuit Court," *Chicago Lawyer*, March 1996, 15.

320 "Conservative Stars," *The American Lawyer*, November 1991, 77. I must confess that I know both Easterbrook and Posner, and I have never known anyone to describe them any differently from these judges.

321 The University of Chicago Law School, "Richard A. Posner: Publications, Presentations, and Works in Progress," http://www.law.uchicago.edu/faculty/posner-r/ppw.html. Ironically, even the *ABA Journal* acknowledged, "Paper trails can be dangerous things, and Posner's makes Robert Bork's look skimpy by comparison." Alexander Wohl, "Paper Trailblazer," *ABA Journal* 39 (1997): 68–74.

322 Richard A. Posner, *Economic Analysis of Law*, 6th ed. (New York: Aspen, 2002).

323 The University of Chicago Law School, "Frank H. Easterbrook: Publications, Presentations, and Works in Progress (Books)," http://www.law.uchicago.edu/node/514/publications.

324 The LexisNexis search requests used were the following: "(Frank Easterbrook or Frank H. Easterbrook or Frank Hoover Easterbrook) and (court or judge) and (opposition or delay or ABA) and date bef October 1, 1985"; "(Richard Posner or Richard A. Posner or Richard Alan Posner) and (court or judge) and (Posner w/15 (opposition or delay or ABA)) and date bef January 1, 1982"; and "(James Wilkinson or James H. Wilkinson or James Harvie Wilkinson III) and (court or judge) and or delay or ABA) and date bef October 1, 1985."

325 U.S. Department of Justice, Office of the Solicitor General, "About the OSG: Functions of the Office of the Solicitor General," http://www.justice.gov/osg/about-osg.html.

326 Mark Asher, "1-A Delegates Oppose Playoff," *Washington Post*, June 30, 1984. Another case that Easterbrook litigated is discussed in David Ranii's "Third Circuit Softens Fee-Cut Decision," *National Law Journal* 27 (1985): 3.

327 Stephen M. Shapiro, Andrew L. Frey, and Kenneth S. Geller, "Frank Easterbrook: A Portrait of the Next Chief," The Circuit Rider, Mayer, Brown Rowe & Maw, 2006.

328 Herman Schwartz, "Reagan Packs the Federal Judiciary," *The Nation*, May 4, 1985, 513.

329 Collin Levey, "One Court-decided Election Is More Than Enough," *Seattle Times*, October 29, 2004.

330 Saundra Torry, "ABA's Judicial Panel Is a Favorite Bipartisan Target," *Washington Post*, April 29, 1996.

331 I know this from conversations with Posner while at the University of Chicago Law School during the 1990s.

332 Paula Zahn, "Benching the ABA," *The Edge With Paula Zahn*, Fox News Channel, March 29, 2001.

333 Richard Thornburgh, testimony before the Senate Judiciary Committee, "The Role of the ABA in the Judicial Selection Process," 104th Cong., 2nd sess., May 21, 1996.

334 David Reinhard, "ABA Adieu: Act of War or Self-Defense?" *The Oregonian*, March 29, 2001.

335 The following search terms were used in the initial LexisNexis search: "(American Bar Association or ABA) and Senate and (judge or judicial) and confirmation and date aft January 1, 2003." The articles were then read through by Brian Blase, research assistant to the author, to make sure that they were relevant.

336 Daniel E. Troy, testimony before the Senate Judiciary Committee, "The Role of the ABA in the Judicial Selection Process," 104th Cong., 2nd sess., May 21, 1996.

337 For example, the ABA opposed any federal restrictions on state's ability to define marriage as occurring between two partners of the same sex; opposes state or federal legislation which restricts the right of a woman to choose to terminate a pregnancy; supports increased funding for the Equal Employment Opportunity Commission; opposes states being able to restrict child custody rights based upon sexual orientation; and supports reauthorization of the National Endowment for the Arts with no restrictions on

the content, subject matter, idea, or message of what the Endowment may fund.

338   Associated Press, "ABA Keeps Its Role in Judge Selections," *Salt Lake City Desert News*, August 5, 2001.

339   John R. Lott Jr., "The American Bar Association, Judicial Ratings, and Political Bias," *The Journal of Law and Politics* 17 (2001): 41–62.

340   James Lindgren, "Examining the American Bar Association's Ratings of Nominees to the U.S. Courts of Appeals for Political Bias, 1989-2000," *The Journal of Law and Politics* 17 (2001): 1–40.

341   Lott, "The American Bar Association." My paper showed that very small changes in the specifications used by Lindgren completely altered the results. Lindgren, "Examining the ABA's Ratings," 1–40.

342   Because of the simple rank order of the ABA score on the arbitrary eleven-point scale, these regressions that use the ABA rating as the endogenous variable use ordered logit regressions.

343   The terms in the survey are left to those taking the survey to define. Survey takers are simply asked whether a judge is "neutral," "moderate," "conservative," etc.

344   The correlations are statistically insignificant and the coefficients are extremely small (often only about 1 percent of a one-level change in ABA ratings).

345   The one exception to this involves Federal judges who have been impeached, but that is exceedingly rare: Robert Wodrow Archbald, 1912 (removed from office by Senate); Samuel Chase, 1805 (acquitted by Senate); Harry E. Claiborne, 1986 (removed from office by Senate); Mark W. Delahay, 1873 (resigned); George W. English, 1926 (resigned); Alcee Hastings, 1989 (removed from office by Senate); West Hughes Humphreys, 1862 (removed from office by Senate); Samuel B. Kent, 2009 (removed from office by Senate); Harold Louderback, 1933 (acquitted by Senate); Walter Nixon, 1989 (removed from office by Senate); James H. Peck, 1830 (acquitted by Senate); John Pickering, 1804 (removed from office by Senate); Thomas Porteous, 2010 (removed from office by Senate); Halsted L. Ritter, 1936 (removed from office by Senate); and Charles Swayne, 1905 (Senate took no action).

346 Howard Fineman, "Torn Between Faith and Science," *Newsweek*, April 25, 2005, 26; Chuck Lindell, "Smith Echoes DeLay in Criticizing Judges," *Austin American-Statesman* (TX), April 8, 2005.

347 Steven G. Calabresi and James Lindgren, "Term Limits for the Supreme Court: Life Tenure Reconsidered," *Harvard Journal of Law & Public Policy* 26, no. 3 (Summer 2006).

348 Herman Schwartz, "Senate Filibusters Are the Sound of the Constitution at Work," *Legal Times*, March 7, 2005.

349 Steven G. Calabresi and James Lindgren, "Term Limits for the Supreme Court: Life Tenure Reconsidered," Northwestern University School of Law working paper, May 26, 2006, http://papers.ssrn.com/sol3/papers. cfm?abstract_id=701121. Steven G. Calabresi and James Lindgren, "Supreme Gerontocracy," *Wall Street Journal*, April 8, 2005.

350 Steven G. Calabresi and James Lindgren, "Supreme Gerontocracy," *Wall Street Journal*, April 8, 2005.

351 Interview of Senator Charles Schumer and Senator Lindsey Graham by Chris Wallace, Fox News Sunday, January 15, 2006 (http://www.foxnews.com/story/0,2933,181753,00.html).

352 Philadelphia Bar Association, "Judicial Commission," http://www.philadelphiabar.org/page/ StandardsForEvaluatingCandidates.

353 Choi and Gulati. "Choosing the Next Supreme Court Justice," 4, n. 6.

354 A well-known example supporting this hypothesis appears to have occurred recently when appointment of a conservative nominee to the U.S. Court of Appeals for the Sixth Circuit was delayed so as to affect the outcome of *Gratz v. Bollinger*, a high-profile case on the constitutionality of an affirmative action program at the University of Michigan. Alexander Bolton, "ACU Calls for Rehire of Miranda," *The Hill*, April 14, 2004.

355 Alec Gallup, *The Gallup Poll: Public Opinion 2005* (New York: Rowman & Littlefield, 2007), 190.

356 Lauren Cohen Bell, "Senatorial Discourtesy: The Senate's Use of Delay to Shape the Federal Judiciary," *Political Research Quarterly* 55 (2002): 589–607; Sarah A. Binder and Forrest Maltzman, "Senatorial Delay in Confirming Federal

Judges, 1947–1998," *American Journal of Political Science* 46 (2002): 190–9; D. C. Nixon and D. L. Goss, "Confirmation Delay for Vacancies on the Circuit Court of Appeals," *American Politics Quarterly* 29 (2001): 246–74.

357   There are some puzzles with the Nixon and Goss study. For example, while they claim to have examined all Federal Appeals Court vacancies from 1892 to 1996, there are only 395 replacement nominees in their sample. By contrast, this study has 297 appointments from 1977 through the end of 2004.

358   Ibid. Nixon and Goss do account for a D.C. Circuit dummy but do not do anything else.

359   Nolan McCarty and Rose Razaghian, "Advice and Consent: Senate Responses to Executive Branch Nominations 1885–1996," *American Journal of Political Science* 43 (1999): 1122–43.

360   R. E. Hartley and L. M. Holmes, "Increasing Senate Scrutiny of Lower Federal Court Nominees," *Political Science Quarterly* 117 (2002): 259–78.

361   Center on Democratic Performance, *Lower Federal Court Confirmation Database: 1977-2004*, http://cdp.binghamton. edu/lfccd.htm.

362   U.S. Department of Justice Office of Legal Policy, "Judicial Nominations—109th Congress." This information is no longer available from the Office of Legal Policy in the U.S. Department of Justice.

363   Federal Judicial Center, "Homepage," http://www.fjc.gov/.

364   American Bar Association, "ABA Standing Committee on Federal Judiciary," http://www.americanbar.org/ content/dam/aba/migrated/scfedjud/federal_judiciary09. authcheckdam.pdf.

365   The nominations clerk at the Senate Judiciary Committee who provided us access to the individual files was Swen Prior.

366   Clinton Presidential Materials Project, "White House Virtual Library," http://clinton6.nara.gov/.

367   Leonard Leo at the Federalist Society provided some data on about 20 percent of the Appeals Court judges studied here. The data from the Federalist Society is discussed in depth in my paper (Lott, "The American Bar Association").

368   George C. Edwards III, *Presidential Approval: A Sourcebook*,

with Alec M. Gallup (Baltimore: Johns Hopkins University Press, 1990). Edwards provided survey data up through 1988. Survey data after that date are provided from the subscriber portion of the Gallup website.

369   The clerk at the time of my research, Swen Prior, primarily provided answers to questions about ABA ratings, information later obtained from the ABA website after information was posted in mid-2004 for the 101st Congress to present.

SUPPLEMENT: FULL-PAGE GRAPHS

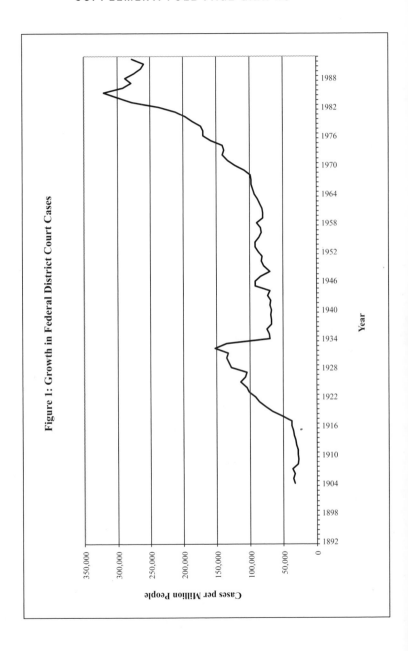

Figure 1: Growth in Federal District Court Cases

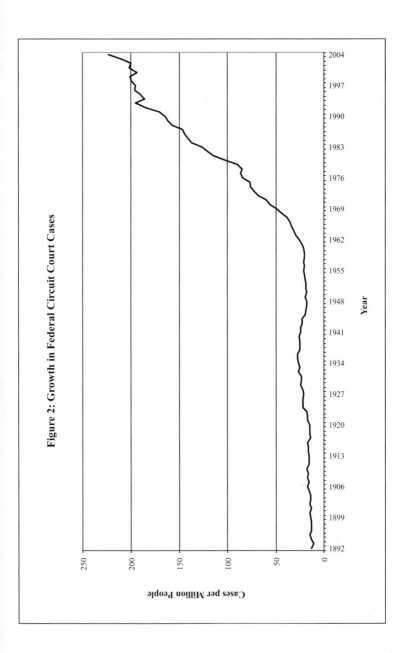

Figure 2: Growth in Federal Circuit Court Cases

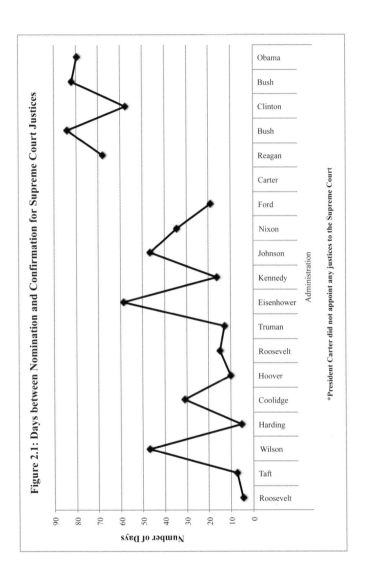

Figure 2.1: Days between Nomination and Confirmation for Supreme Court Justices

*President Carter did not appoint any justices to the Supreme Court

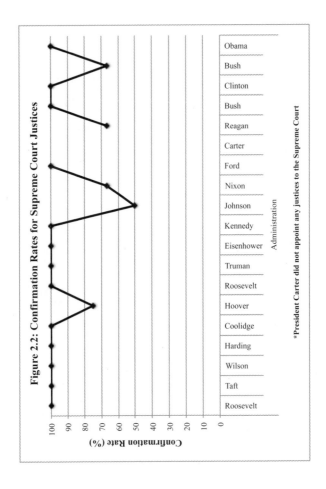

Figure 2.2: Confirmation Rates for Supreme Court Justices

*President Carter did not appoint any justices to the Supreme Court

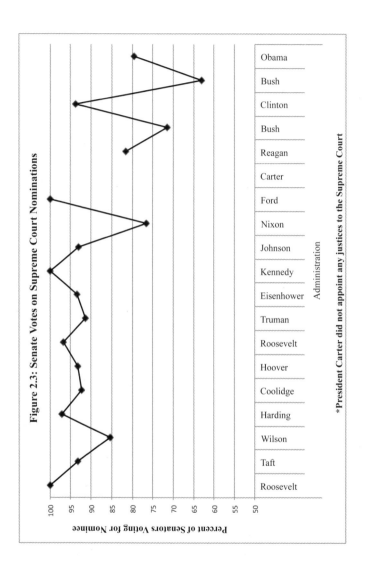

Figure 2.3: Senate Votes on Supreme Court Nominations

*President Carter did not appoint any justices to the Supreme Court

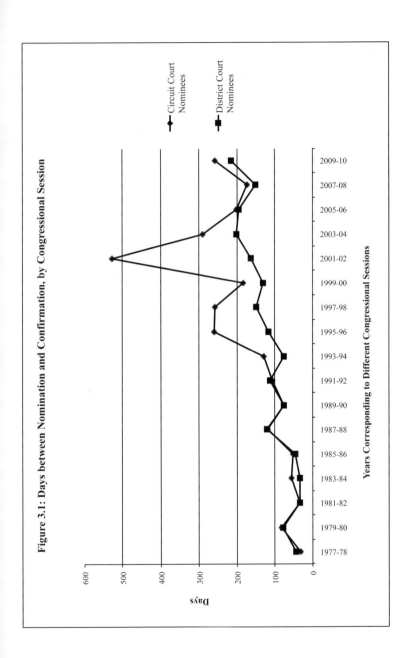

Figure 3.1: Days between Nomination and Confirmation, by Congressional Session

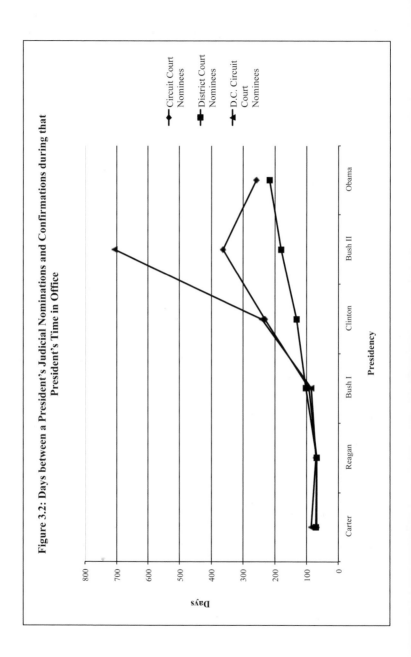

Figure 3.2: Days between a President's Judicial Nominations and Confirmations during that President's Time in Office

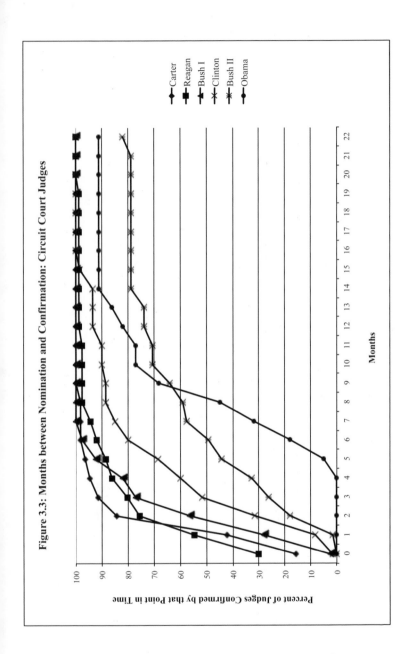

Figure 3.3: Months between Nomination and Confirmation: Circuit Court Judges

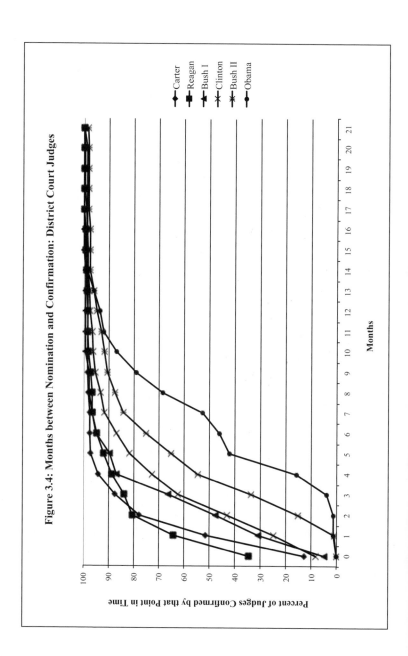

Figure 3.4: Months between Nomination and Confirmation: District Court Judges

Percent of Judges Confirmed by that Point in Time

Months

— Carter
— Reagan
— Bush I
— Clinton
— Bush II
— Obama

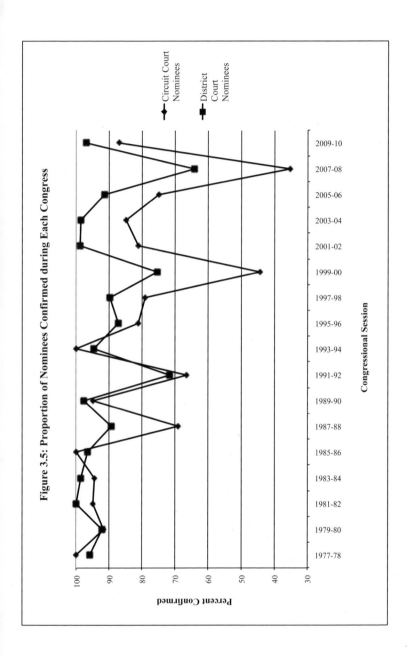

Figure 3.5: Proportion of Nominees Confirmed during Each Congress

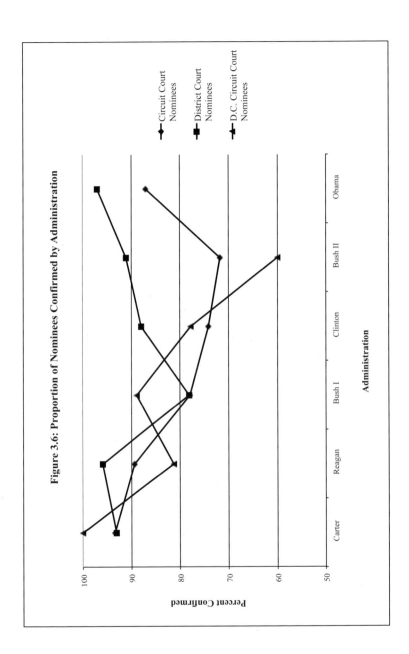

Figure 3.6: Proportion of Nominees Confirmed by Administration

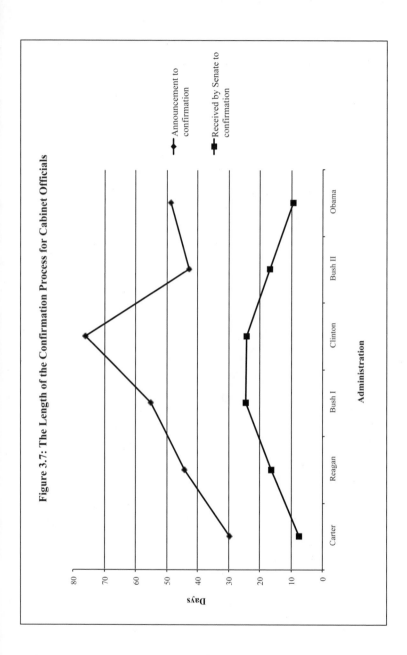

Figure 3.7: The Length of the Confirmation Process for Cabinet Officials

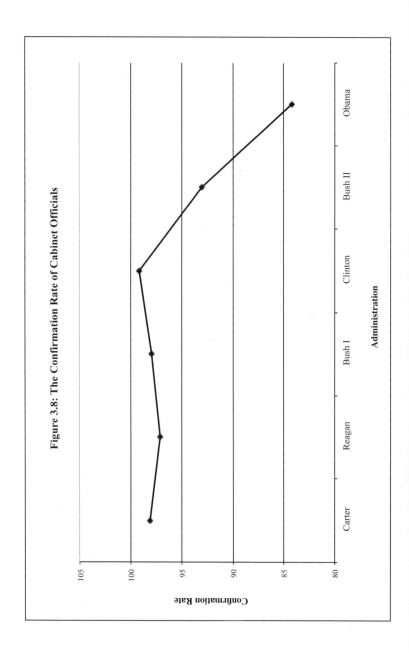

Figure 3.8: The Confirmation Rate of Cabinet Officials

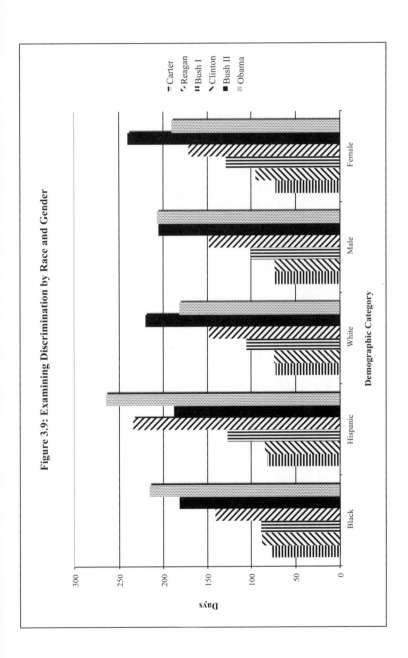

Figure 3.9: Examining Discrimination by Race and Gender

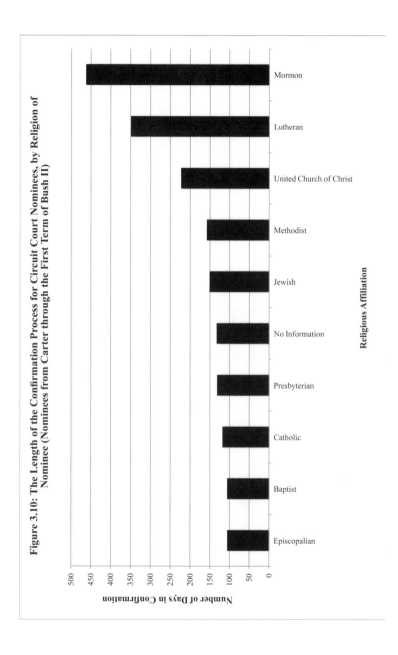

Figure 3.10: The Length of the Confirmation Process for Circuit Court Nominees, by Religion of Nominee (Nominees from Carter through the First Term of Bush II)

Figure 4.1A: Political Views of Circuit Court Judges as Indicated by Lawyers Surveyed by the *Almanac of the Federal Judiciary*

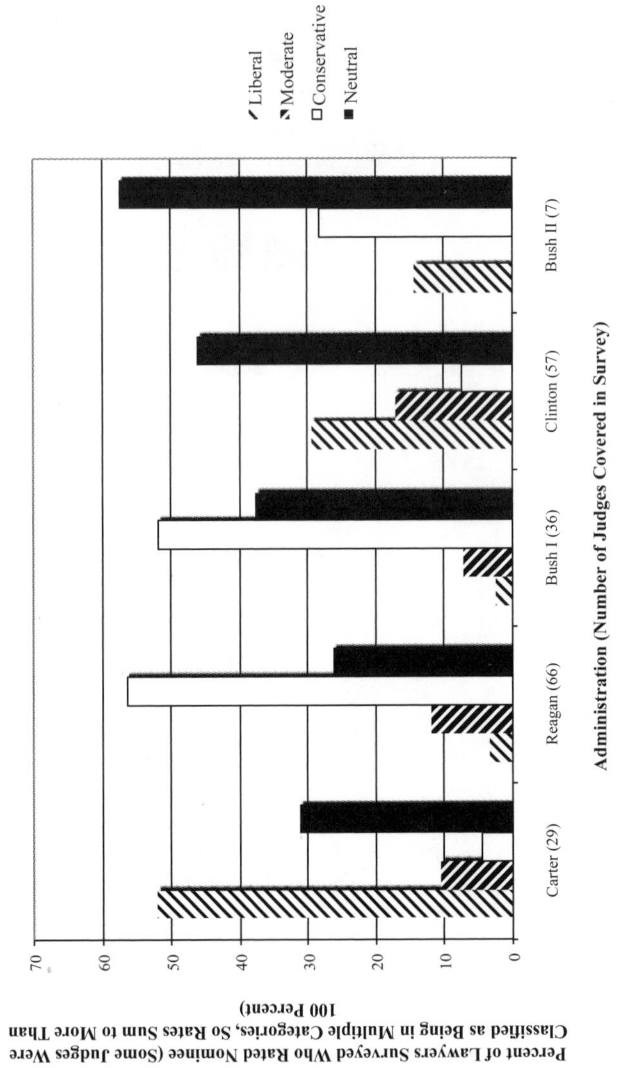

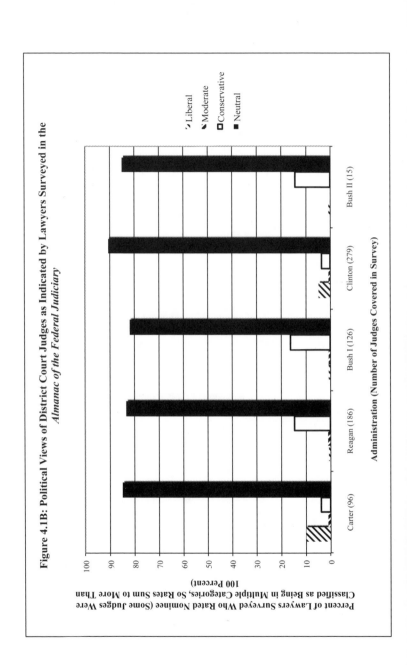

Figure 4.1B: Political Views of District Court Judges as Indicated by Lawyers Surveyed in the *Almanac of the Federal Judiciary*

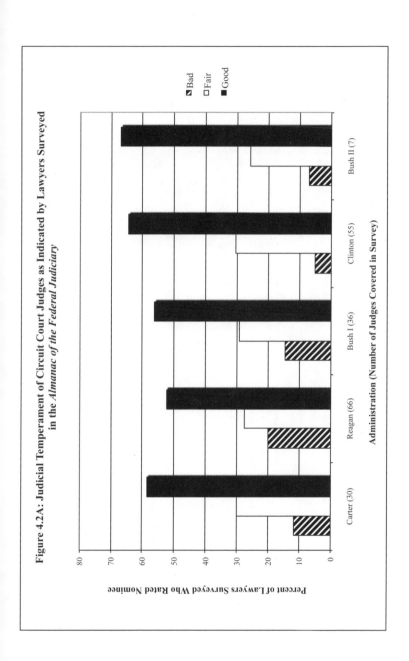

Figure 4.2A: Judicial Temperament of Circuit Court Judges as Indicated by Lawyers Surveyed in the *Almanac of the Federal Judiciary*

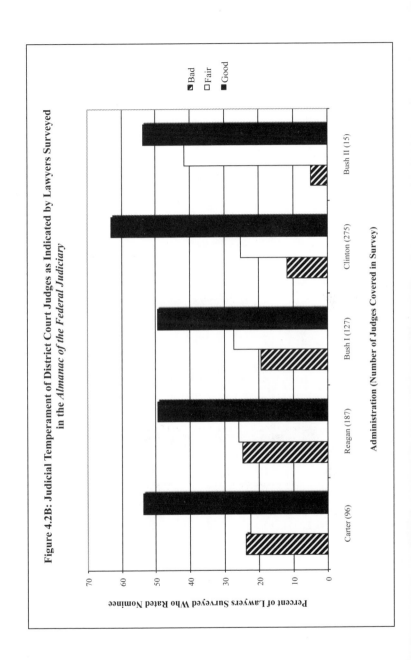

Figure 4.2B: Judicial Temperament of District Court Judges as Indicated by Lawyers Surveyed in the *Almanac of the Federal Judiciary*

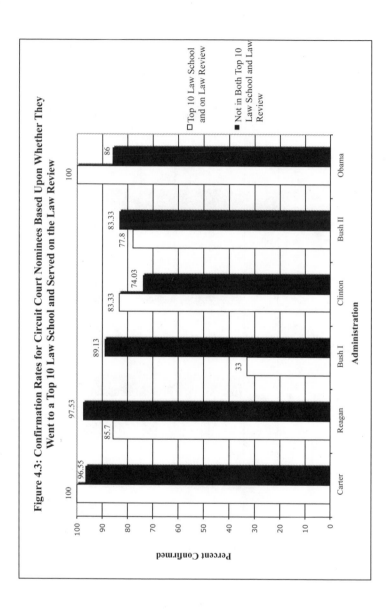

Figure 4.3: Confirmation Rates for Circuit Court Nominees Based Upon Whether They Went to a Top 10 Law School and Served on the Law Review

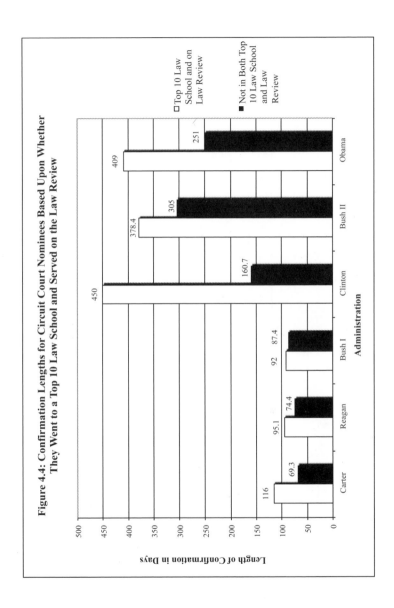

Figure 4.4: Confirmation Lengths for Circuit Court Nominees Based Upon Whether They Went to a Top 10 Law School and Served on the Law Review

□ Top 10 Law School and on Law Review

■ Not in Both Top 10 Law School and Law Review

Length of Confirmation in Days

Administration

Carter: 116, 69.3
Reagan: 95.1, 74.4
Bush I: 92, 87.4
Clinton: 450, 160.7
Bush II: 378.4, 305
Obama: 409, 251

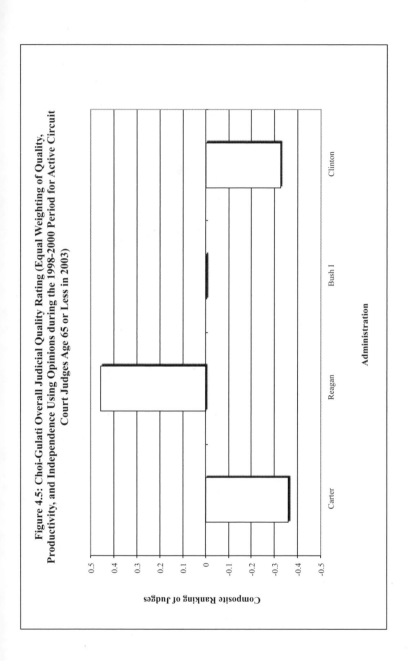

Figure 4.5: Choi-Gulati Overall Judicial Quality Rating (Equal Weighting of Quality, Productivity, and Independence Using Opinions during the 1998-2000 Period for Active Circuit Court Judges Age 65 or Less in 2003)

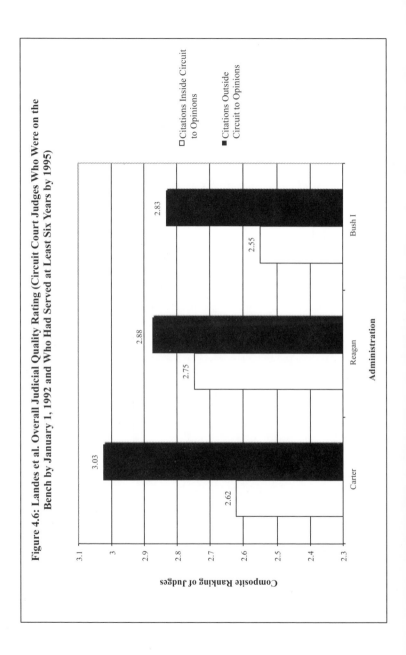

Figure 4.6: Landes et al. Overall Judicial Quality Rating (Circuit Court Judges Who Were on the Bench by January 1, 1992 and Who Had Served at Least Six Years by 1995)

□ Citations Inside Circuit to Opinions

■ Citations Outside Circuit to Opinions

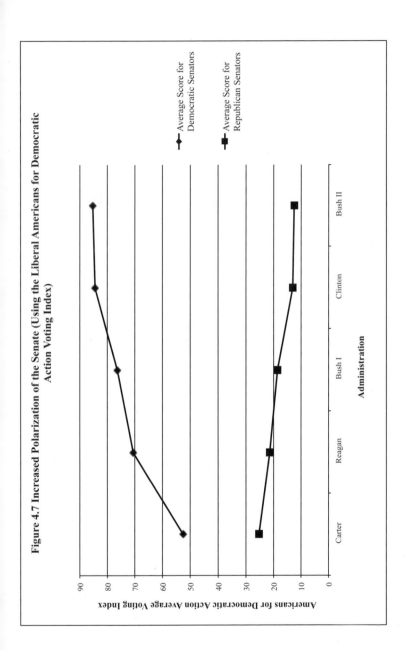

Figure 4.7 Increased Polarization of the Senate (Using the Liberal Americans for Democratic Action Voting Index)

◆ Average Score for Democratic Senators

■ Average Score for Republican Senators

y-axis: Americans for Democratic Action Average Voting Index

x-axis: Administration

Carter Reagan Bush I Bush II Clinton

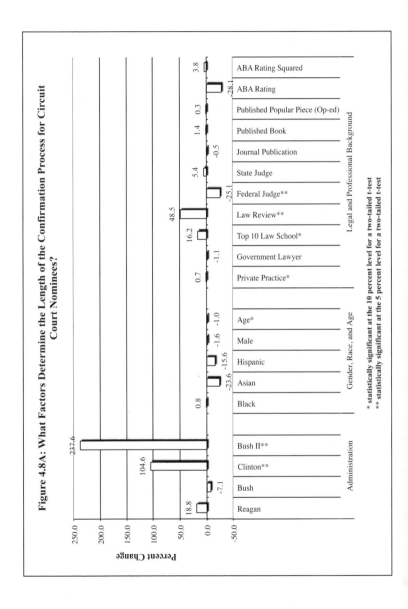

Figure 4.8A: What Factors Determine the Length of the Confirmation Process for Circuit Court Nominees?

* statistically significant at the 10 percent level for a two-tailed t-test
** statistically significant at the 5 percent level for a two-tailed t-test

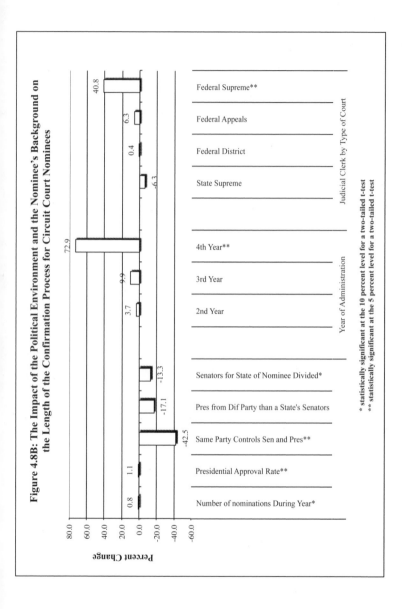

Figure 4.8B: The Impact of the Political Environment and the Nominee's Background on the Length of the Confirmation Process for Circuit Court Nominees

* statistically significant at the 10 percent level for a two-tailed t-test
** statistically significant at the 5 percent level for a two-tailed t-test

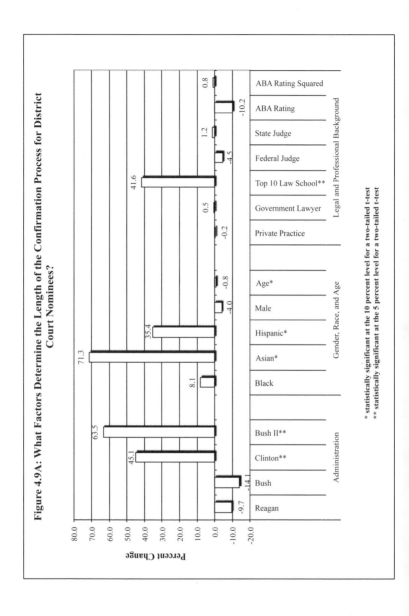

Figure 4.9A: What Factors Determine the Length of the Confirmation Process for District Court Nominees?

* statistically significant at the 10 percent level for a two-tailed t-test
** statistically significant at the 5 percent level for a two-tailed t-test

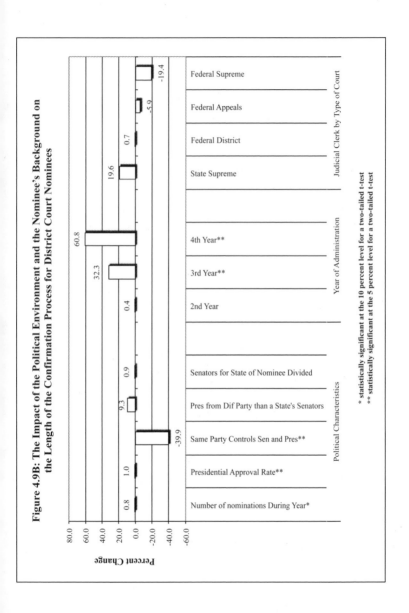

Figure 4.9B: The Impact of the Political Environment and the Nominee's Background on the Length of the Confirmation Process for District Court Nominees

Percent Change

80.0
60.0
40.0
20.0
0.0
-20.0
-40.0
-60.0

60.8

32.3

19.6

0.8 1.0 -39.9 9.3 0.9 0.4 0.7 19.6 -5.9 -19.4

Number of nominations During Year*
Presidential Approval Rate**
Same Party Controls Sen and Pres**
Pres from Dif Party than a State's Senators
Senators for State of Nominee Divided

Political Characteristics

2nd Year
3rd Year**
4th Year**

Year of Administration

State Supreme
Federal District
Federal Appeals
Federal Supreme

Judicial Clerk by Type of Court

* statistically significant at the 10 percent level for a two-tailed t-test
** statistically significant at the 5 percent level for a two-tailed t-test

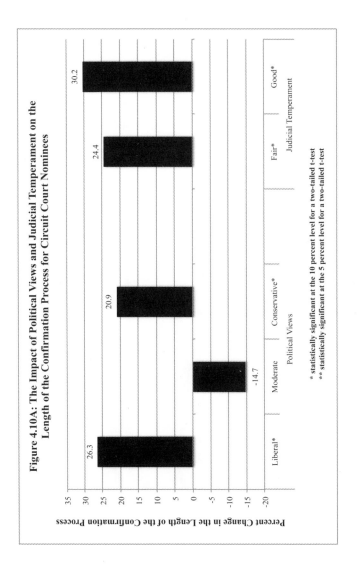

Figure 4.10A: The Impact of Political Views and Judicial Temperament on the Length of the Confirmation Process for Circuit Court Nominees

Chart showing Percent Change in the Length of the Confirmation Process:

- Liberal*: 26.3
- Moderate: -14.7
- Conservative*: 20.9
- Fair*: 24.4
- Good*: 30.2

Political Views: Liberal*, Moderate, Conservative*
Judicial Temperament: Fair*, Good*

* statistically significant at the 10 percent level for a two-tailed t-test
** statistically significant at the 5 percent level for a two-tailed t-test

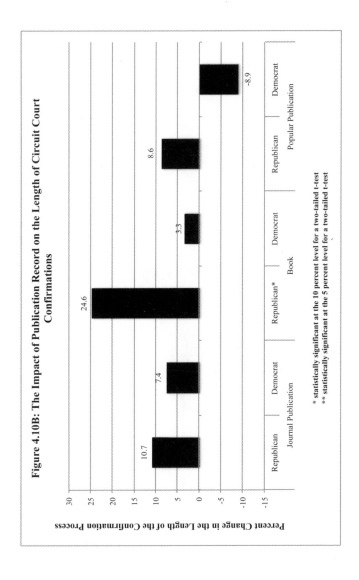

Figure 4.10B: The Impact of Publication Record on the Length of Circuit Court Confirmations

Percent Change in the Length of the Confirmation Process

* statistically significant at the 10 percent level for a two-tailed t-test
** statistically significant at the 5 percent level for a two-tailed t-test

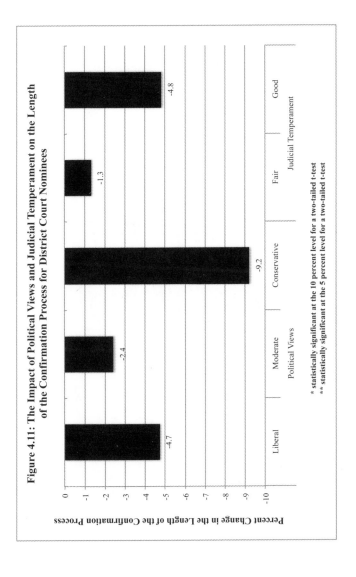

Figure 4.11: The Impact of Political Views and Judicial Temperament on the Length of the Confirmation Process for District Court Nominees

* statistically significant at the 10 percent level for a two-tailed t-test
** statistically significant at the 5 percent level for a two-tailed t-test

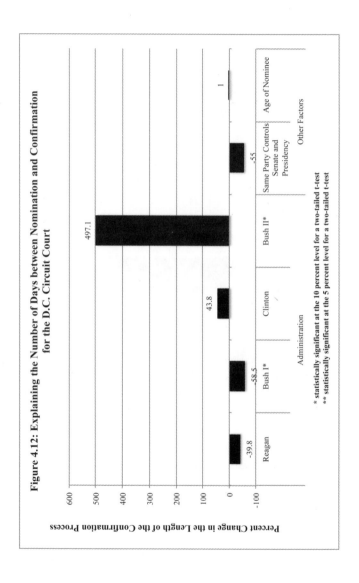

Figure 4.12: Explaining the Number of Days between Nomination and Confirmation for the D.C. Circuit Court

* statistically significant at the 10 percent level for a two-tailed t-test
** statistically significant at the 5 percent level for a two-tailed t-test

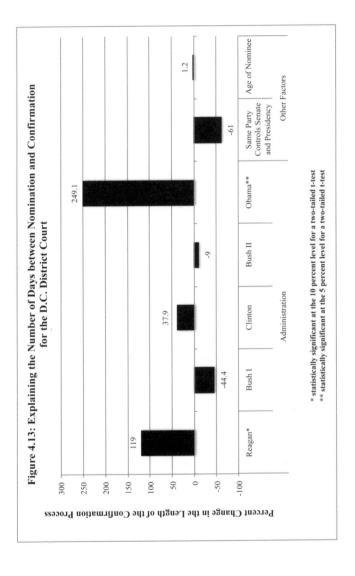

Figure 4.13: Explaining the Number of Days between Nomination and Confirmation for the D.C. District Court

* statistically significant at the 10 percent level for a two-tailed t-test
** statistically significant at the 5 percent level for a two-tailed t-test

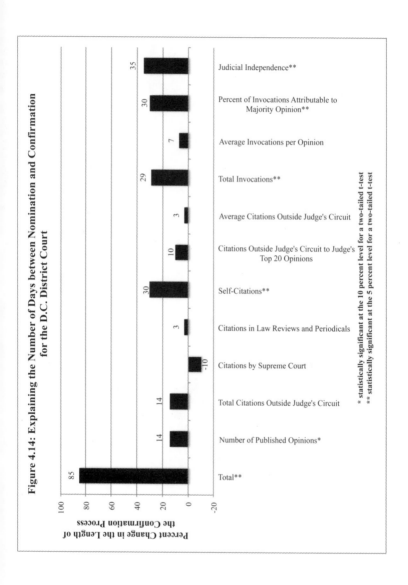

Figure 4.14: Explaining the Number of Days between Nomination and Confirmation for the D.C. District Court

* statistically significant at the 10 percent level for a two-tailed t-test
** statistically significant at the 5 percent level for a two-tailed t-test

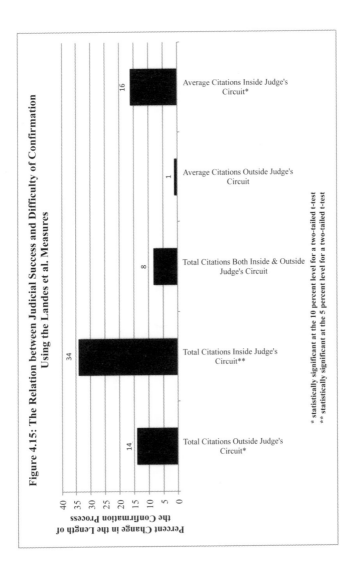

Figure 4.15: The Relation between Judicial Success and Difficulty of Confirmation Using the Landes et al. Measures

* statistically significant at the 10 percent level for a two-tailed t-test
** statistically significant at the 5 percent level for a two-tailed t-test

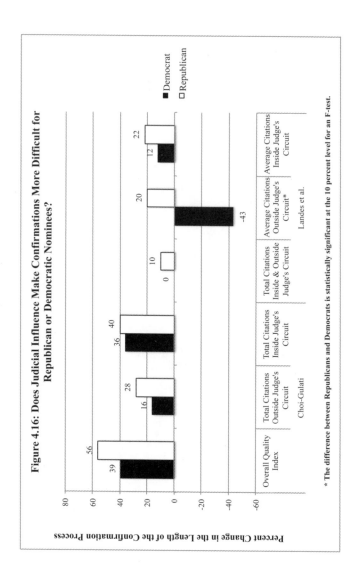

Figure 4.16: Does Judicial Influence Make Confirmations More Difficult for Republican or Democratic Nominees?

* The difference between Republicans and Democrats is statistically significant at the 10 percent level for an F-test.

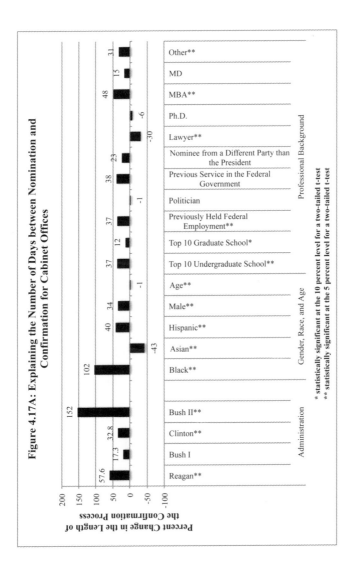

Figure 4.17A: Explaining the Number of Days between Nomination and Confirmation for Cabinet Offices

Percent Change in the Length of the Confirmation Process

* statistically significant at the 10 percent level for a two-tailed t-test
** statistically significant at the 5 percent level for a two-tailed t-test

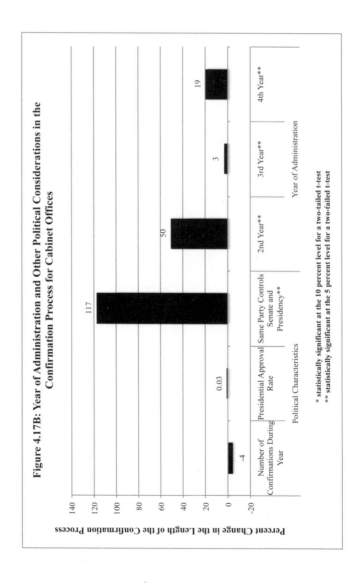

Figure 4.17B: Year of Administration and Other Political Considerations in the Confirmation Process for Cabinet Offices

* statistically significant at the 10 percent level for a two-tailed t-test
** statistically significant at the 5 percent level for a two-failed t-test

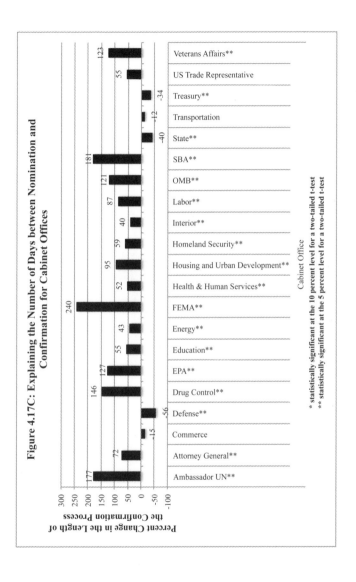

Figure 4.17C: Explaining the Number of Days between Nomination and Confirmation for Cabinet Offices

* statistically significant at the 10 percent level for a two-tailed t-test
** statistically significant at the 5 percent level for a two-tailed t-test

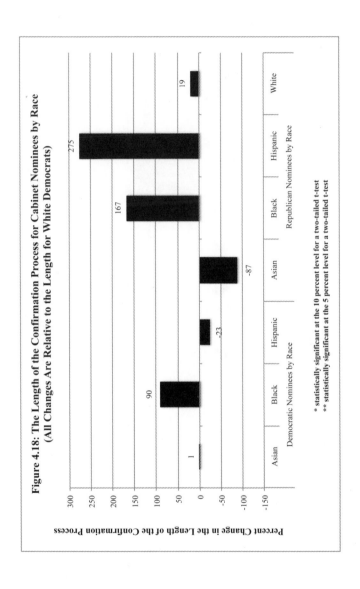

Figure 4.18: The Length of the Confirmation Process for Cabinet Nominees by Race (All Changes Are Relative to the Length for White Democrats)

* statistically significant at the 10 percent level for a two-tailed t-test
** statistically significant at the 5 percent level for a two-tailed t-test

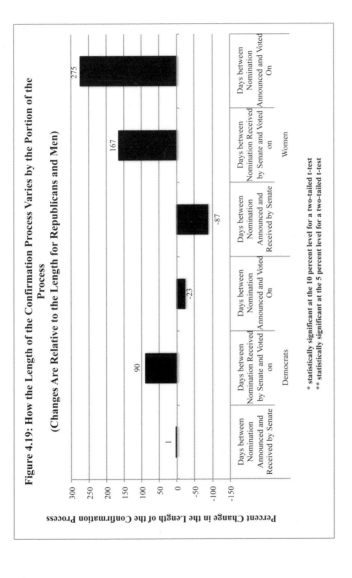

Figure 4.19: How the Length of the Confirmation Process Varies by the Portion of the Process

(Changes Are Relative to the Length for Republicans and Men)

* statistically significant at the 10 percent level for a two-tailed t-test
** statistically significant at the 5 percent level for a two-tailed t-test

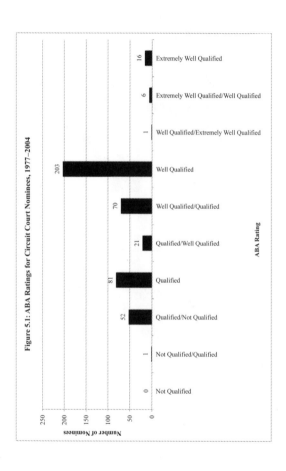

Figure 5.1: ABA Ratings for Circuit Court Nominees, 1977–2004

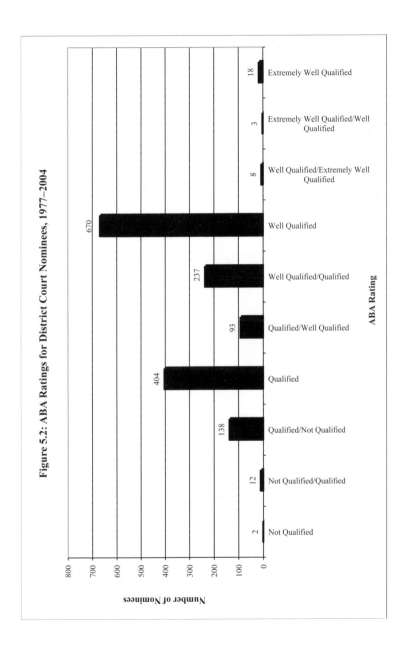

Figure 5.2: ABA Ratings for District Court Nominees, 1977–2004

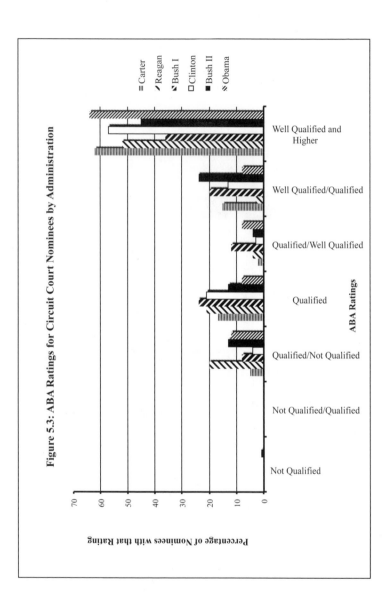

Figure 5.3: ABA Ratings for Circuit Court Nominees by Administration

314   JOHN R. LOTT, JR.

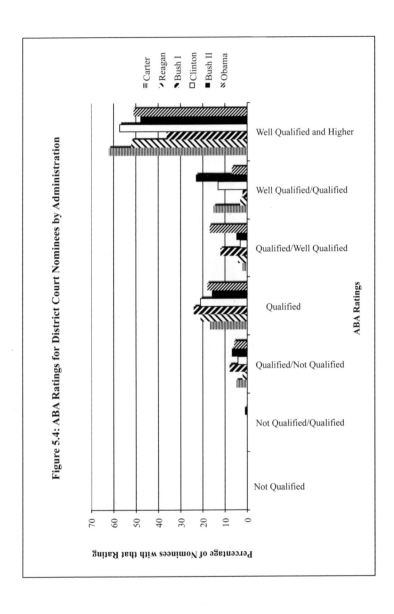

Figure 5.4: ABA Ratings for District Court Nominees by Administration

≡ Carter
↘ Reagan
↗ Bush I
□ Clinton
■ Bush II
↘ Obama

Well Qualified and Higher

Well Qualified/Qualified

Qualified/Well Qualified

Qualified

Qualified/Not Qualified

Not Qualified/Qualified

Not Qualified

ABA Ratings

Percentage of Nominees with that Rating

70   60   50   40   30   20   10   0

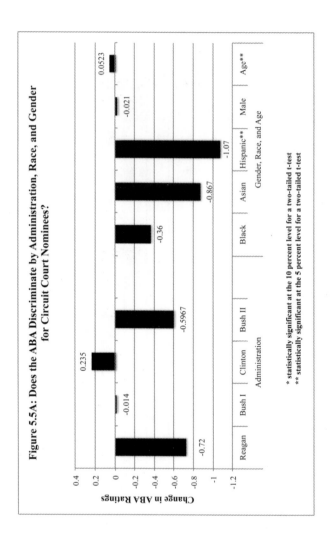

Figure 5.5A: Does the ABA Discriminate by Administration, Race, and Gender for Circuit Court Nominees?

* statistically significant at the 10 percent level for a two-tailed t-test
** statistically significant at the 5 percent level for a two-tailed t-test

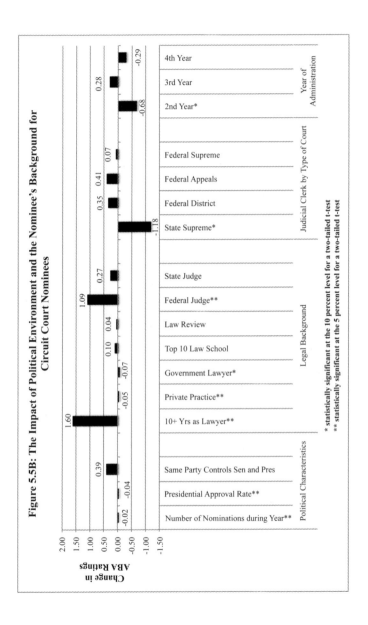

Figure 5.5B: The Impact of Political Environment and the Nominee's Background for Circuit Court Nominees

* statistically significant at the 10 percent level for a two-tailed t-test
** statistically significant at the 5 percent level for a two-tailed t-test

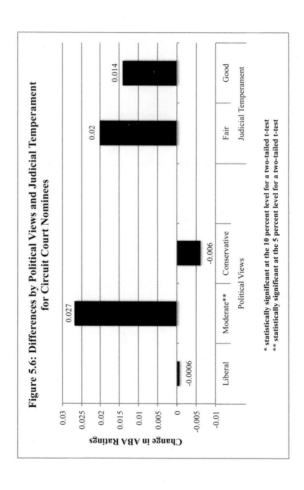

Figure 5.6: Differences by Political Views and Judicial Temperament for Circuit Court Nominees

* statistically significant at the 10 percent level for a two-tailed t-test
** statistically significant at the 5 percent level for a two-tailed t-test

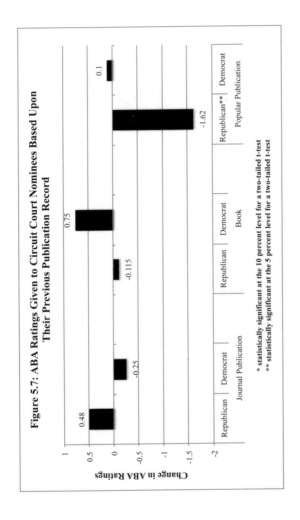

Figure 5.7: ABA Ratings Given to Circuit Court Nominees Based Upon Their Previous Publication Record

* statistically significant at the 10 percent level for a two-tailed t-test
** statistically significant at the 5 percent level for a two-tailed t-test

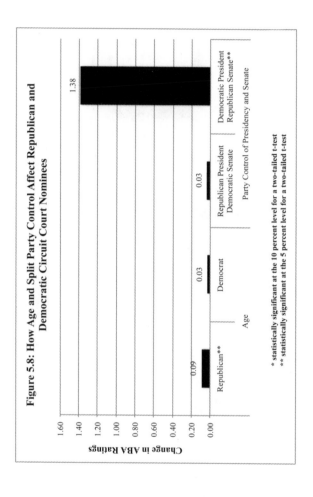

Figure 5.8: How Age and Split Party Control Affect Republican and Democratic Circuit Court Nominees

* statistically significant at the 10 percent level for a two-tailed t-test
** statistically significant at the 5 percent level for a two-tailed t-test

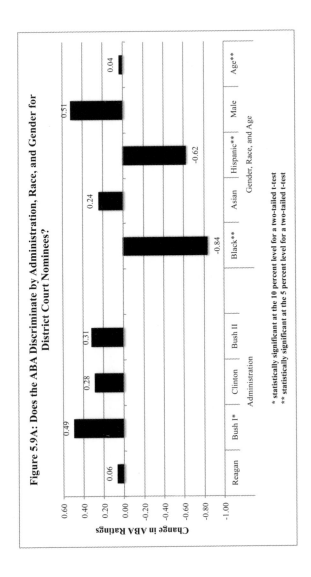

Figure 5.9A: Does the ABA Discriminate by Administration, Race, and Gender for District Court Nominees?

* statistically significant at the 10 percent level for a two-tailed t-test
** statistically significant at the 5 percent level for a two-tailed t-test

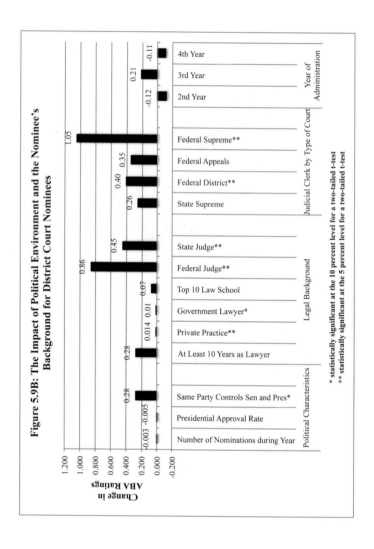

Figure 5.9B: The Impact of Political Environment and the Nominee's Background for District Court Nominees

* statistically significant at the 10 percent level for a two-tailed t-test
** statistically significant at the 5 percent level for a two-tailed t-test

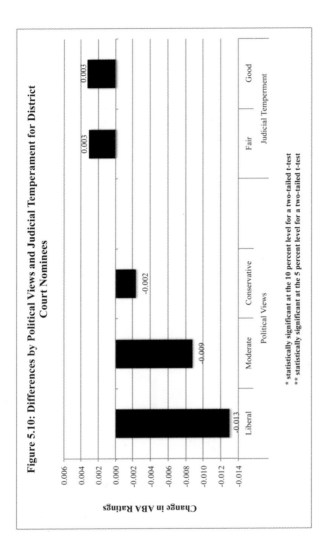

Figure 5.10: Differences by Political Views and Judicial Temperament for District Court Nominees

Change in ABA Ratings

Liberal -0.013
Moderate -0.009
Conservative -0.002
Political Views

Fair 0.003
Good 0.003
Judicial Temperment

* statistically significant at the 10 percent level for a two-tailed t-test
** statistically significant at the 5 percent level for a two-tailed t-test

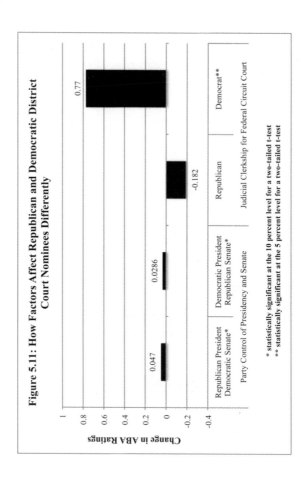

Figure 5.11: How Factors Affect Republican and Democratic District Court Nominees Differently

* statistically significant at the 10 percent level for a two-tailed t-test
** statistically significant at the 5 percent level for a two-tailed t-test

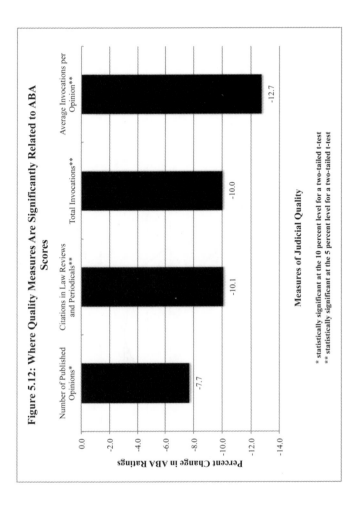

Figure 5.12: Where Quality Measures Are Significantly Related to ABA Scores

* statistically significant at the 10 percent level for a two-tailed t-test
** statistically significant at the 5 percent level for a two-tailed t-test

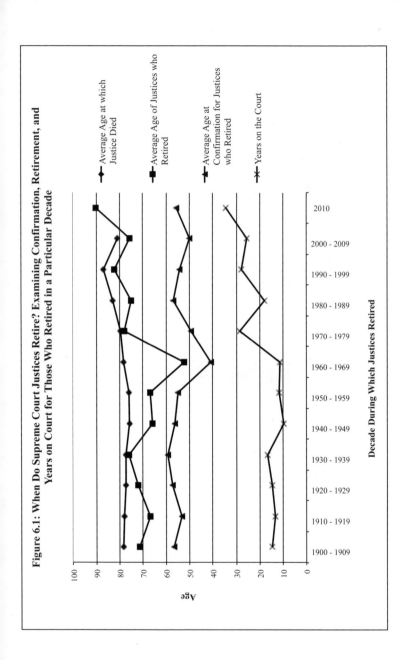

Figure 6.1: When Do Supreme Court Justices Retire? Examining Confirmation, Retirement, and Years on Court for Those Who Retired in a Particular Decade

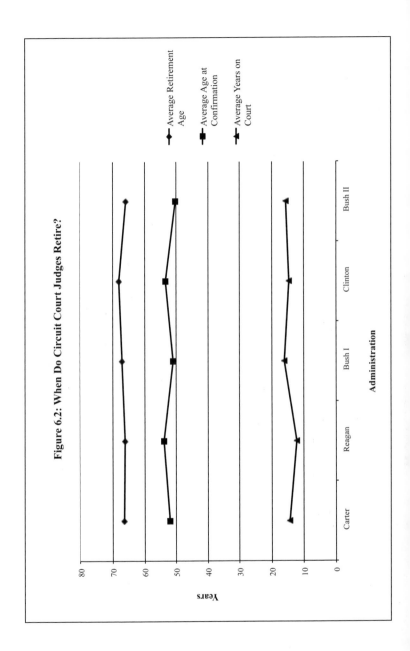

Figure 6.2: When Do Circuit Court Judges Retire?

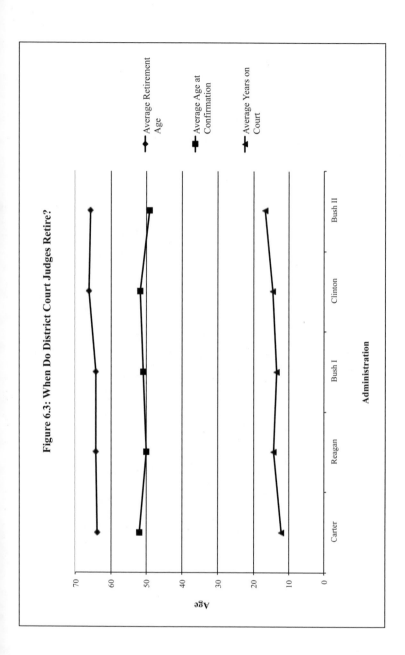

Figure 6.3: When Do District Court Judges Retire?

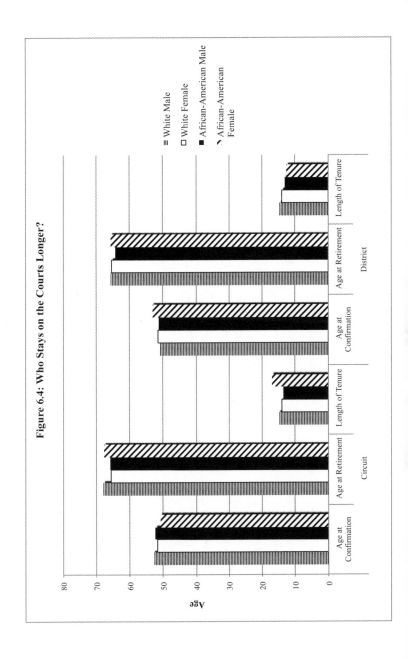

Figure 6.4: Who Stays on the Courts Longer?

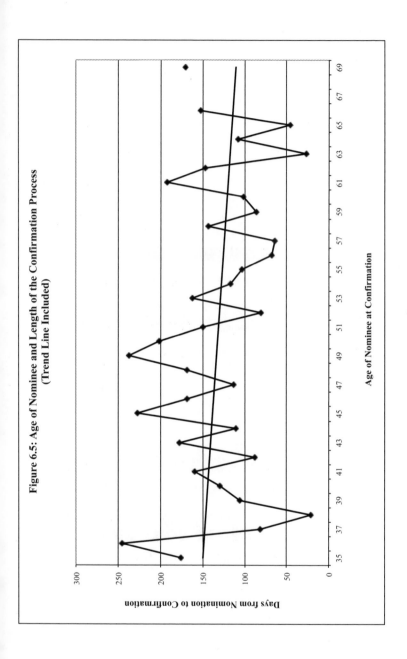

Figure 6.5: Age of Nominee and Length of the Confirmation Process
(Trend Line Included)

Days from Nomination to Confirmation

Age of Nominee at Confirmation

INDEX

Page numbers in **bold** indicate tables or graphs.

opposing parties controlling
presidency and
Senate, 90, 105–106
Owen, Priscilla, 77

P

Paez, Richard, 109
paperwork, 47, 49–50
Parker, John J., 60–61
partisanship, 84–87, 128–130,
129
personal characteristics that
are disadvantageous,
203
Pickering, Charles W., 39–40,
47–49
polarization, 128–130, **129,**
148–149, 151–152
political environment, **179**
political views. *See* ideology
Posner, Richard, 53, 76,
163–165, 167–171,
178, 235, 236, 244,
264, 265
Presbyterian nominees, **109**
president
approval ratings, 136–137
Senate controlled by
opposing party,
90, 105–106, **184,**
185–186
Senate controlled by same
party, 112, 134,
140–141, 185–186
year of term when
nominating, 106,
112, 135, 150, **159**

publication record
affect on ABA ratings,
183, 183–184,
190
decrease in, 154
impact on confirmation
time, **131, 138,**
140, 144, **144,**
147, 153–155
researching, 218

R

racial bias against nominees,
85, 106–**107,** 113–
114, **131, 132,** 136,
153, **158, 160,** 177,
178, 179, **187**
racial views of nominees, 56,
57, 69, 70
Randolph, A. Raymond,
117–118
Raymar, Robert, 45–46, 49
Razaghian, Rose, 210
Reagan, Ronald, 69, 213
recess appointments, 113–114
regulatory agencies, increase
in, 23–24
Rehnquist, William, 53, 59,
68–71, 196
Reid, Harry, 72, 78
religion, 56, 106, 107–110,
109, 146
Republicans
characteristics that affect
confirmation rate,
152
confirmation hearings,
views on, 32–36